Methodist Present Potential

Methodist Present Potential

And realistic hopes for the future

Edited by

Luke Curran and Angela Shier-Jones

✚ EPWORTH

Copyright © Luke Curran and Angela Shier-Jones 2009

The Editors have asserted their right under the Copyright,
Designs and Patents Act, 1988, to be identified as the Editors of
this Work

British Library Cataloguing in Publication data

A catalogue record for this book is available
from the British Library

978 0 7162 0651 4

First published in 2009 by
Epworth
Methodist Church House
25 Marylebone Road
London NW1 5JR

Typeset by Regent Typesetting, London
Printed and bound in Great Britain by
CPI Antony Rowe Chippenham SN14 6LH

Contents

The Contributors

Jane Craske   Revd Dr Jane Craske is a presbyter in the British Methodist Church, with experience in theological education, and currently is a superintendent minister. She is the author of a number of books, most recently *Being Human: In Conversation with Philip Pullman's* His Dark Materials (Inspire, 2007).

Luke Curran   Luke Curran is a lay theologian currently employed as Director of the Methodist Church in Wales Training Network and as an associate tutor in Cardiff University's School of Religious and Theological Studies. He has previously worked in the youth, communication and policy units of the British Methodist Church and currently convenes the theological education resource group of its Faith and Order Committee.

Jonathan Dean   Revd Dr Jonathan Dean is a presbyter in the British Methodist Church, currently serving the United Methodist Church in the Chicago area. He has acted as teacher and examiner for the University of Cambridge, Cliff College and Aurora University, Illinois, and as a chaplain in both prison and community project settings. He maintains research interests in Reformation history, sixteenth-century English mysticism and Wesleyan theology.

Rachel Deigh   Revd Rachel Deigh is a presbyter in the British Methodist Church. She is currently stationed in the Croydon circuit of the London District and is involved in developing an ecumenical fresh expression of church aimed at reaching those with no church background.

Dion Forster Revd Dr Dion Angus Forster is a presbyter of the Methodist Church of Southern Africa. He is the former Dean of John Wesley College, the seminary of the Methodist Church of Southern Africa, and a lecturer in Systematic Theology and Ethics at the University of South Africa. He is a research associate in the Department of New Testament Studies at the University of Pretoria. Among his publications are three books on Southern African Methodism and a number of scholarly articles on Methodism and Wesleyan theology.

Richard Heitzenrater Dr Richard P. Heitzenrater is an elder in the United Methodist Church, and William Kellon Quick Professor of Church History and Wesley Studies at the Divinity School, Duke University. He presently co-chairs the Wesleyan Studies Group of the Oxford Institute of Methodist Theological Studies, is a member of the World Methodist Council Executive Committee, and is General Editor of the Wesley Works Editorial Project. He has published several works on Methodism, including *Wesley and the People Called Methodists* (Abingdon Press, 1995), which has been translated into six languages.

Karen Jobson Revd Karen Jobson is a presbyter in the British Methodist Church. She is a member of the World Methodist Council Executive and is a representative on the International Bilateral Dialogue with The Salvation Army. Research interests include ecumenism, mission and urban theology.

Clive Marsh Dr Clive Marsh is a local preacher and has been involved in theological education for 20 years. He was, for seven years, Secretary of the Faith and Order Committee of the Methodist Church in Great Britain and is now Director of Learning and Teaching at the Institute of Lifelong Learning in the University of Leicester. His books include *Christ in Focus* (SCM Press, 2005), *Christ in Practice* (Darton, Longman & Todd, 2006) and *Theology Goes to the Movies* (Routledge, 2007).

Martin Ramsden   Revd Dr Martin Ramsden is a presbyter in the British Methodist Church, currently stationed in Middlesbrough as a Circuit Superintendent. He is a member of the Faith and Order Network and has published on Methodist sacramentology in *The Epworth Review*.

Angela Shier-Jones   Revd Dr Angela Shier-Jones is a presbyter in the British Methodist Church. She is a member of the World Methodist Council Executive and a co-Chair of the Oxford Institute of Theological Studies. She has written and co-edited several works on Methodism and Wesleyan Theology including *A Work in Progress* (Epworth, 2005) and *Unmasking Methodist Theology* (Continuum, 2004)

Shirlyn Toppin   Revd Shirlyn Toppin is a presbyter in the British Methodist Church. She is a member of the Oxford Institute of Theological Studies and the Pastoral Issues resource group of the Faith and Order Network. She has published articles in *Black Theology: An International Journal*.

Introduction

LUKE CURRAN AND
ANGELA SHIER-JONES

It is a time-honoured religious practice to reflect on the past and to prophesy concerning the future and the relationship between God and the people of God. While few Methodists would want to make any exclusive claims to being the people of God, they do count themselves among that number, and some are even bold enough to claim the denomination was raised up as 'a work of God'. It is now ten years since a number of those in the so-called 'missing generation' engaged in this practice and reflected publicly on the British Methodist tradition and on the question 'What keeps people in church?' through the publication of *Methodism and the Future*.[1] The subtitle of that volume, *Facing the Challenge*, has in a very real sense provided the motivation for this volume: ten years on, what present potential does Methodism possess to enable it to face and rise to the challenge of the future?

In the course of the last decade, the British Methodist Church has undergone a significant process of reshaping and refocusing through the *Our Calling* consultation process and the adoption of *The Priorities for the Methodist Church*.[2] These two issues are referred to explicitly by most of the British contributors to this volume. In many ways, this book is a continuation of that process, as it offers some of the first feedback on where the Church is now. The overriding impression seems to be that we are still 'pilgrims on a journey' although the destination is not yet clear.

As with the original volume, none of the contributors would want to claim that they are either individually or collectively representative of the whole of the Methodist tradition. Each has written from their own perspective, and so speaks with their own voice from within, and directed toward, their specific part of the tradition. No bold claims are made for all of Christianity or even for the denomination as a whole, but the contributors do dare to suggest some things which, in their opinion, might be done to release the potential which they believe to be present in Methodism today.

Perhaps not surprisingly, given the increasing trend towards globalization and the ever present plurality of the postmodern world, the issue of diversity within Methodism is a common, if not dominant, theme. Diversity of membership, practice, theology, and understanding are all explored, as is the constant danger of losing them. But running in parallel to these discussions on the values and advantages of diversity, is the more pressing underlying theme of identity. The same questions repeatedly surface: 'How do we become Methodists?' and 'How do we learn what it means to be Methodist?' If the contributors are to be believed, the cry of *Methodism and the Future* is still the same: there is a fundamental need for re-engagement with the Methodist tradition to enable Methodism to face the future. While British Methodism in particular continues to underplay its important theological emphases of grace and Christian perfection, there is nonetheless a strong conviction that the worth of the individual soul and personal responsibility, key emphases of the tradition, are just as important today as they were in Wesley's time.

Although no common vision for the future emerges out of the chapters, there is a repeated call for the Church to be more proactive rather than reactive in all that it does. This is based on a fairly optimistic belief that the tradition still holds in trust certain positive elements which the Church catholic needs to retain. It is surprising therefore to find that there is some suspicion of 'fresh expressions of Church' within the volume. Clearly for some, it is not the panacea that many seem to think it is. In true Wesleyan spirit however, the Church is nonetheless called to engage with the movement, keeping its eyes open both to its possibilities and its dangers especially vis-à-vis the targeting of specific groups and the creation of niche churches. How, it is asked, can such 'churches' truly express kingdom values of inclusivity? In this and many other ways, the dynamic between the needs of individual Christians and those of an institutional Church engaged in mission and not just maintenance are explored in most chapters.

The book is written in two parts. In the first part, seven younger Methodist scholars were asked to reflect on their understanding of some of the key aspects of Methodist identity: Evangelism, Scripture, Sacraments, Diversity and Inclusivity, Connexionalism, Ecumenism and the World Church. Other subjects could of course have been chosen, and it would have been easier in many respects to frame a volume written around the so-called Wesleyan Quadrilateral. However, the areas were chosen to reflect those dimensions of Church life which had, in the opinion of the editors, been most significantly critiqued over the last decade. Taken as a whole, they provide an insight into the umbra and penumbra of Methodist preoccupation with itself, its engagement with the wider world and its calling in the light of God and in the shadow of the cross.

In the first chapter, 'An Evangelistic Faith', Rachel Deigh argues for a renewed hope in evangelism as a whole-church activity, rather than a specialist activity. She usefully explores the definition 'making known the good news of what God has done and persuading people to believe it in faith' and differentiates it from the more common understanding of mission. The rediscovery of Wesley's model of evangelism leads her to urge the adoption of a broad approach to proclaiming the gospel. In particular, she stresses that evangelism should be motivated by compassion for those who do not yet know God, rather than any other motive, regardless of how 'fresh' or 'traditional' it might seem to be. Above all, she stresses the need for evangelism to be an activity of the whole Church rather than of a few specialists.

In 'A Biblical Faith', Jonathan Dean invites the reader to reengage with the biblical text as a living document which he is convinced still has relevance for our contemporary society. He argues that the interpretive tools necessary to engage with, for example, popular period drama, can also be applied to Scripture. To justify this, he explores John Wesley's understanding of Enlightenment dualism and identifies the value of his integrative approach to Scripture. He argues likewise that our hymns can also provide an important interpretive tool and urges that their value should be rediscovered for a new generation. Methodists, he suggests 'are going to need to be poets again. If the Bible is to speak in new, creative and transforming ways, it must be cherished as poetry, as an expression of faith which will always elude us, often surprise us, frequently exasperate us, but unfailingly inspire us.'

The importance and relevance of the sacraments to contemporary Methodists is explored by Martin Ramsden in Chapter 3. In keeping with the main thrust of the book, Ramsden argues for a greater focus on the missiological potential of the sacraments, particularly that of baptism. He argues his case carefully, placing current practice within the context of Wesley's thought, particularly with regard to grace. It is this which he believes enables the sacraments to be recognized and celebrated as converting, conforming, and nurturing ordinances.

Perhaps the hardest chapter for British Methodists to read is that written by Shirlyn Toppin, which explores the diverse faith of the Church. Her chapter offers an uncompromising critique of the current state of race relations within contemporary British Methodism from the perspective of a young black female presbyter. In so doing, Toppin challenges us to consider what it actually means to be an inclusive church, not just in words but also thought and action. Toleration, as she so effectively points out, cannot be equated with inclusion and she pleads for better education throughout the Church. The chapter is, above all, a call for the proper celebration of diversity, rather than conformity.

In Chapter 5, 'A Shared Faith', Luke Curran expressed the worry that contemporary patterns of belonging work against Methodism continuing to be a broad church in terms of the types of believer. It did not do enough he claims, to keep 'Thatcher's children', despite a strong historical emphasis on grace, individual accountability and Christian perfection which combined could have formed a persuasive message for this emerging postmodern generation. He suggests Methodism in the future will survive but that it will be much poorer for having failed this particular missiological challenge.

At a time when many are speaking of an ecumenical desert, Karen Jobson remains optimistic about the future of ecumenism. In Chapter 6, 'An Ecumenical Faith', she argues that ecumenism still has relevance for contemporary Methodism. She does however qualify her conviction and suggests that its relevance will lie not so much in its existence as a movement towards visible union such as dominated much of the twentieth-century debates, but rather as a process for enabling Christians to use their various traditions to the benefit of the churches' mission. Complementarity rather than uniformity is the emergent model for this generation's engagement with others.

The final chapter in Part One, 'A World Faith', written by Dion Forster, a member of the Methodist Church in Southern Africa, introduces a world perspective on what could otherwise be seen as rather local concerns. He considers how the struggle in the apartheid years shaped the identity of contemporary Methodism in South Africa, transforming it from a Western European missionary Church into a genuinely African Church with its own voice and place in God's mission. This was achieved, he insists, without losing a Methodist identity, by building on the strengths and insights gained by holding firm to the doctrine of Christian perfection. The transformation has not been easy, neither is it complete as yet, but already it is bearing significant fruit. From that experience and reflection, Forster suggests that, as a worldwide Church, Methodism needs to understand the dynamics between a central identity that we all share and the need for particular cultural expressions of that identity for specific contexts.

The second part of the book offers an initial response to the earlier chapters, not as a critique, but as a means of opening up the dialogue between the generations. Chapter 8, written by Richard Heizenrater, one of Methodism's most noted historical theological scholars, effectively highlights both the challenge and the choices facing this generation. The ease with which Heizenrater draws on the tradition to reflect on its current state unwittingly emphasizes the great void of knowledge in British Methodism concerning its own roots. He is nevertheless encouraging and positive about most of the steps that are being suggested by the contributors as being in keeping with the Spirit of Wesley. Angela Shier-Jones explores whether or not the contributions in Part One are merely a denial of the reality of a dying Church given the all too obvious decline in Church membership. Each of the earlier chapters is examined for evidence that Methodism has not become what Wesley feared it might – a dead sect. The final words however, belong to Jane Craske and Clive Marsh, the co-editors of *Methodism and the Future: Facing the Challenge*. Their note of caution is, as they point out, an echo of the criticism of their own volume a decade ago, which still bears hearing. They rightly call for a greater level of critical engagement in order for the potential identified to be recognized by those who are perhaps outside the tradition, and who need more than preaching or rhetoric to convince them. It is nonetheless the nature of youth to be bold as well as passionate in the claims which they make in the pursuit of what inspires and motivates them. In the end, the book offers as one of the most hopeful signs of the present potential for Methodism the fact that there was no difficulty in finding seven such enthusiastic and engaged younger scholars committed to play a part in the future of Methodism.

Notes

1 Jane Craske and Clive Marsh, *Methodism and the Future: Facing the Challenge*, London, Cassell, 1999.

2 See Appendices 1 and 2.

Part One

I

An Evangelistic Faith

RACHEL DEIGH

Throughout Lent a Methodist circuit undertook a 'listening exercise' during Sunday worship by asking those present in its seven congregations the following four questions:

- What is the mission of this church?
- What do you enjoy most about belonging to this church?
- What are the key activities that take place here?
- What impact does this church have on the local community and wider world?

Gathering together all the responses and reflecting on the results, one thing stood out very clearly: the significant number of responses to the first question which expressed each church's mission in terms which could be called 'evangelism' but without using that word. These included expressions such as: 'to save souls', 'to preach the gospel', 'to share or spread the good news', 'to reach out into the community', 'to make Christians', 'to bring the gospel to the community'. Good news, it seemed: evangelism is alive and well in the circuit!

However, when this information was put alongside the responses to the third and fourth questions, although all the churches had in varying degrees said that 'evangelism' (however expressed) was the mission of their church, it was not explicitly mentioned in the same way as a key activity or one through which their church has an impact on the local community or wider world. The findings didn't match up. Not so good news!

Something more hopeful emerged when each congregation was then put into small groups and asked to consider 'What would you like to see happening at this church during the next twelve months?' This produced some desire for growth, both numerically and spiritually, though again not expressed by the word 'evangelism' itself. This is not a criticism of the faithfulness of the members of those congregations, but it reveals the challenge before us in terms of the evangelistic task of the church if the Methodist Church (I do not believe that this circuit is unique) is going to recover, or perhaps discover, its evangelistic potential.

What is going on here? Is it simply a question of education – do we just need to teach church members better and train them in the task of evangelism? Is it the case that somewhere in the church's psyche there is a residual belief that evangelism is something that the church ought to be doing? Is it a searching for a distant memory? Or is it a growing hope and longing for the church to truly be the church it is called to be? Why the reluctance (conscious or otherwise) to use the word 'evangelism'?

Let's Stay with the Word Itself for a Moment: Evangelism

What comes to mind when you hear that word? What emotions does it evoke in you? Whenever I have asked groups in local churches these questions they usually evoke negative images and emotions, and particular stereotypes. Billy Graham. Street preachers telling us to 'Repent for the end is nigh'. Cold calling, talking to strangers, knocking on doors like the Jehovah's Witnesses. Tele-evangelists whose lives don't always match their message. And emotions? Fear is usually near the top of the list, closely followed by feelings echoing a lack of confidence and bemoaning how society has changed. As a result, either intentionally or otherwise, evangelism is left to certain individuals or sections of the church. It is something we expect of our trained preachers, those whom we regard as evangelists, or of the various para-church organizations and missionary societies established for that task – so we leave it up to them. If we are good Methodist people we may think of people like the late Rob Frost, those who have been on a Share Jesus Mission or to Easter People.[1] We may be aware of the work of Cliff College or have hosted a Cliff College mission.[2] Or we may be in a Methodist District which has a District Evangelism Enabler. However, if we are formal members of the Methodist Church we may notice that there is now mention of evangelism on our annual membership tickets reminding us that evangelism is also for people like us – whatever we may think or feel about it.

In 2000 the Methodist Church adopted *Our Calling* as a shared vision of what the Church is for embracing worship, learning and caring, service and evangelism. A summary of *Our Calling* is printed on the annual Methodist membership tickets and, in reminding us of the place of evangelism in the life of the whole Church, it would seem that the Methodist Church has begun to discover a renewed interest in evangelism. In his Presidential Address to the 2003 Conference, the Revd Dr Neil Richardson spoke of the need for 'God-centred evangelism', and a succession of presidents have continued to challenge the Methodist Church with regard to evangelism. A year later the Methodist Conference adopted the *Priorities for the Methodist Church* which include: 'Developing confidence in evangelism and in the capacity to speak of God and faith in ways that make sense to all involved' and 'encouraging fresh ways of being Church'[3] and since September 2004 the Methodist Church has been a partner with the Church of England in 'Fresh Expressions'.[4]

But how much of our feelings towards evangelism is a question of the language we use and a misunderstanding of what evangelism is? In reality we don't seem to be able to agree as to what it actually is or isn't. In order to unlock the potential of evangelism for the (Methodist) Church today we need to regain a breadth and depth to our understanding which, hopefully, will move us beyond the fear that many feel to an excitement and joy which is truly good news, and therefore to an evangelism which can be embraced and owned by the whole Church.

Language – defining Evangelism

Called to Love and Praise, the 1999 Methodist Conference statement on the nature of the Church, reminds us that the mission of
God to the world is two-fold: it is God's 'outgoing, all-embracing
love for his creation';[5] and it is also the bringing about of the
Kingdom of God as we pray 'on earth as in heaven'.[6] The Kingdom of God is 'not only announced, but represented, even lived'
by Jesus[7] – both strands are brought to completion in his death
and resurrection. The Church's calling remains the same as for the
first Christians – 'to participate in God's mission and to proclaim
God's reign as Jesus had done. The worship of God through,
and because of, the risen Jesus, characterized and created such
a mission.'[8] The Nicene Creed describes the Church as 'one holy
catholic and apostolic'. The apostolic nature of the Church is a
reminder that the Church is sent into the world to call others to
share the life of the Kingdom, as Jesus himself was sent into the
world through his incarnation and as Jesus then sent the apostles
to preach and live the gospel message.[9]

Mission and evangelism are often confused as interchangeable
words meaning the same thing. The Church's mission, as we see
from the above, is understood in the broad sense of the mission
of God which is all God is and does, the sharing of that same
all-embracing love for his creation and the bringing about of the
Kingdom of God. This broad mission includes the specific task of
evangelism.

Evangelism is not easy to define. *Our Calling* suggests that it is
simply and broadly 'making followers of Jesus Christ'[10] – telling us
very little about what evangelism actually is and telling us nothing
about why most of us struggle with it. Another definition suggests
that evangelism is 'making known the good news of what God has
done and persuading people to believe it in faith'.[11] This is not an
uncommon definition of evangelism (it bears similarities to many
of the responses of the circuit listening exercise) and there is nothing wrong with this definition in itself. I use it to help us to think
through why we may feel the way we do about evangelism today.

First, we have tended to interpret 'making known the good news' in a narrow way through examples which lead to the stereotypes and emotions mentioned above, and without realizing it evangelism becomes synonymous with a very narrow kind of preaching where confidence can sometimes be misunderstood as arrogance. If this is our only experience of evangelism then it is a reasonable conclusion to draw, so although we accept evangelism as part of the church's activity we decide that it is not for us and evangelism becomes an individualistic activity as opposed to a corporate activity undertaken and 'owned' by the whole Church. We accept that there is only one way to do evangelism, rather than ask ourselves 'How can I use the gifts God has given me to make known the good news of what God has done?' Hope will come when we realize that we have more than one tool in our evangelism toolkit.

Second, we don't sit comfortably with the word 'persuading'. If we live in the West, we live in a culture where truth has become relative. It may be your truth, but it may not be my truth. And if it's true for you, why do you need me to be persuaded otherwise, as long as it doesn't affect me and we can live together in peace and harmony? To speak of God's truth is therefore particularly difficult and so we avoid it if we can or leave it to the 'experts' (whoever they may be). This has left the Church in a difficult, and often defensive, place – in danger of throwing the 'baby' of God's mission out with the 'bathwater' of how that mission is to be expressed because we don't want to offend others. We go out to look for other ways of cleaning the baby, only to discover that we've lost the baby along the way. As evangelism moves more centrally on the Church's agenda we need to look again at our motivation for evangelism – is it 'church-centred' or is it 'God-centred', beginning 'in a passion for the gospel and in a compassion for people'?[12] If it begins here then it will be God who does the persuading as his grace goes before us. Hope will come as we rely on the Holy Spirit to prompt and guide us, and from a compassion for all people as we begin to see them through God's eyes.

Third, what is the 'it' we hope to persuade people to believe? Not only have our methods of evangelism become individualistic but so has the message of good news which is at the heart of evangelism. The 'good news of what God has done' is reduced to the realms of personal salvation and a profession of personal faith. What I believe is more important than how it affects the way I live and my relationships with others; it is first and foremost about my own personal relationship with God. While this is of course important, it is only one aspect of that good news. In remembering that God's mission is also about his Kingdom, we cannot talk about God's Kingdom to the exclusion of its communal aspect. A kingdom is about a people over whom someone reigns and with whom they therefore have much in common. Therefore God's Kingdom is about how we live with those with whom we are 'one in Christ' if God reigns over us. The church should be a community of God's Kingdom, a sign of it or the doorway into it rather than an end in itself. Hope will come in a (re)discovery of the place of the church in the good news we proclaim and what it means to be 'Kingdom people'. Are our communal gatherings truly good news? Do they reveal the life of God's Kingdom, offering society an alternative community? This aspect is also a particular weakness of the brevity of the *Our Calling* definition of evangelism. However, it is timely that much thinking is now being given to ecclesiology (the nature of the church) not in isolation from evangelism but alongside it, especially through the growing interest in fresh expressions of church and 'emerging church'.

And, last, we tend to neglect the 'and'. In my experience of the Methodist Church, we have tended to think that we are reasonably good at the first half of the definition, 'making known the good news of what God has done'. For example, some of the churches I have been involved in over the years have run holiday clubs for primary-age children, typically for a week each year. Without exception each club has attracted significant numbers of children who throughout the rest of the year normally have little or no contact with that church, and with whom after the holiday club week the church continues to have little or no contact. The church concludes that it has 'done' evangelism and fulfilled its commitment to it. We have made known 'the good news of what God has done' and sown some seeds of the gospel. We have loved those children with God's love while they have been with us. And so nothing then happens until the following year and the cycle continues until the children are too old to come to the holiday club. The 'and' of the definition reminds the church that it is not 'doing' evangelism without also doing the second part of the definition, 'persuading people to believe it in faith.' Evangelism does include the sowing of seeds, but if that is all that the church does at what point do those seeds germinate and begin to grow? It is God who provides the harvest[13] but the work of evangelism and the task of the church are not over with the planting of the seed. Hope will come when the church begins to take risks and challenge people to respond to the good news and grow. The church needs to embrace evangelism as a part of its whole life throughout the year rather than simply as one-off events here and there which are unrelated to the rest of what the church is and does.

In recovering our hope in evangelism we will begin to discover something of what it means for the church to be an agent of evangelism. According to Methodist theologian William Abraham there are four agents in the process of evangelism: the primary agent is God, the second agent is the church – 'which is called to embody the rule of God in its worship, life and ministries', the third agent is the evangelist and the fourth agent is the person or persons evangelized.[14] If the church takes the view that evangelism is someone else's responsibility, it will rely on the first agent (God) with an attitude that says 'God will bring people in so we don't need to worry or do anything' or on the third agent (the evangelist) with the attitude that 'leaves it up to them' and that often means that the evangelist has to go out on a limb or go it alone, leading, if one is not careful, to a separation between the work of the evangelist and the church.

Perhaps evangelism is becoming more acceptable in the church because the church is beginning to wake up to the predicament of declining numbers and influence. However, Neil Richardson contrasts 'God-centred evangelism' with 'church-centred evangelism' which he suggests is of the 'evangelize or perish' kind and takes as its starting point an anxiety for the future of the church and a drive to recruit new members.[15] This is not the same as the church being an agent of evangelism. The issue is one of motivation: what are we aiming at? Put crudely, do we aim at preserving the church or at embodying and celebrating the life of the Kingdom of God? Each will lead to different expressions of what it means to be the church and different outcomes and attitudes within it. Hope for realizing our potential for evangelism lies in the church discovering a holistic approach for evangelism which goes right across the life of the church, in everything we are, everything we do and at the heart of every decision we make. It is a church that truly sees the four agents of evangelism working together, whatever it may cost, for the sake of God's Kingdom rather than for the sake of the church.

Another symptom of an individualistic approach to evangelism is that it becomes 'compartmentalized rather than functioning as the central core of the church's identity'.[16] While *Our Calling* has put evangelism more firmly onto the church's agenda, in some ways it has also reinforced an individualistic approach and continues to compartmentalize it. *Our Calling* has been presented in a way that presents the four areas as separate and distinct from one another. We can 'tick off' what we have done or how we have measured up in each area as we are encouraged to review the life of the church in each area. It does not encourage a holistic or whole-church approach to evangelism. If it did, we would be asking questions such as: In what ways is our learning/caring/service/worship drawing people into a fuller awareness of and involvement in God's Kingdom? Or how, through our learning/caring/service/worship, are we making more followers of Jesus Christ? We are not actively encouraged to look at how these areas of the church's life interweave. Do they all carry equal weight or priority? If we were to ask these kinds of questions, evangelism would begin to become a whole church activity at the heart of all that the church is and does which, according to our understanding of God's mission and the nature of the Church, evangelism should be.

Perhaps it is time for a different definition of evangelism. William Abraham offers his definition of evangelism as 'that set of intentional activities which is governed by the goal of initiating people into the Kingdom of God for the first time'.[17] While there are limits to every definition this one, with its clearly stated goal, places the activity of evangelism within the communal aspect of

God's Kingdom. The key word here is 'initiating'. As Abraham goes on to point out, that initiation comes through many different and varied activities:

> Evangelism will involve such acts as proclamation, basic instruction, prayer, and ensuring that those who respond are brought to baptism or confirmation. It may require acts of mercy, patient conversations, stern rebuke, or the organization of mass meetings. It may depend on the sharing of one's personal spiritual pilgrimage, or on an act of calculated silence, or on the ministering of a special rite of exorcism, or on the provision of catechesis, or on the laying on of hands, or on widespread use of the mass media, or on the development of small groups. No rule exists for the setting or limiting the boundaries of action that the responsible evangelist may have to perform in order to carry out fitting and appropriate acts of evangelism.[18]

What matters is that as a result of whatever activity we engage in and through using whatever gifts we have been given, people are being initiated into the Kingdom of God and we seek to do this intentionally. In reminding us that the Kingdom is our starting point, not the church, Abraham helps us to realize that there are indeed many tools in the evangelism tool box, and to see evangelism as a process, a journey. Initiation implies movement: an entering into something in order to progress further. The Engel Scale is a tool devised to show the number of steps people may take between first hearing the gospel and becoming a Christian and then some of the steps that may be taken in moving towards maturity as a disciple of Christ. It helps us to keep this perspective of movement in mind by breaking down what seems like the enormous task of evangelism into 'bite-sized' pieces or manageable steps.[19] Whatever our gifts, we may just take someone one step closer to becoming initiated into the Kingdom of God and at some point someone else, we hope, may challenge them to take that step which enables them to cross the line, which becomes the next step on the journey of discipleship. This is the whole Church's evangelistic task and thus becomes within the reach of us all.

Searching for a Distant Memory – A Brief Methodist Checklist

This is all very well but is it 'Methodist'? If by this we seek an understanding of evangelism discerned by those who are Methodists, one of the difficulties is that there is little, besides Conference reports, written about evangelism by Methodists worldwide. In his introduction to *Theology and Evangelism in the Wesleyan Heritage*, James C. Logan talks of a 'great divorce' between theology and evangelism.[20] This collection of essays included the major presentations from a symposium held in Atlanta USA by the United Methodist Church to address this concern with a focus on 'our Wesleyan roots'. Looking for a British Methodist understanding of evangelism proves even more difficult.[21]

The next step therefore must be to combine what little there is with our Methodist tradition and heritage, seeking to discern any underlying reasons why evangelism is or should be significant to the people called Methodists in the twenty-first century. Can we truthfully say that we have an 'evangelistic faith'? We do this recognizing that we are in a different time and culture to what has gone before, and recognizing that talking of John Wesley and the early Methodist Societies is very different to talking of the denomination that is the Methodist Church today.

However, from John Wesley's ministry we can discern certain distinctive features of his model of evangelism. First, it seems that Wesley had a broad approach to evangelism. This can be interpreted in several ways.

His evangelism took more than one form, using different tools from the evangelism toolbox. While Wesley may be best known for his preaching ministry, it was often in the small groups he called 'classes' that people received Christ. These classes were open to any who wished 'to flee from the wrath to come' – these were people who had been spiritually awakened, or reawakened, by the preaching of Wesley or other Methodist preachers. Conversation, what Wesley sometimes called 'close discourse', was another tool that Wesley encouraged to be used in the task of evangelism. He 'observed that, without conversation, people can hear sermons for years and still not get it'.[22]

His evangelistic approach reflected his social concerns, including prison visiting, building orphanages, medicine, education and encouraging Wilberforce in his work to abolish the slave trade. According to Albert Outler, writing from an American perspective in 1971, it would probably be the 'polarities between evangelism, Christian nurture, missions and social action' that Wesley would least approve of today.[23] Bearing in mind our consideration of *Our Calling* above, perhaps the same could be said in regard to the British Methodist Church today. And if Outler is right, given Wesley's belief that he had no other business than to 'save souls' in the broadest possible parish, the whole world, would Wesley have seen the four aspects of *Our Calling* as carrying equal weight, or would he have given a higher priority to the task of evangelism, encompassing the rest?

His evangelism embraced what Wesley knew as the Catholic Spirit, 'an openness of heart and mind that cherishes diversity within the larger unity of essential faith and commitment'.[24] Perhaps it is in the understanding of evangelism that theological divisions within the Church have been most clearly evident. We often regard certain activities as belonging to particular schools of thought or theology rather than as belonging to the whole Church. Is this not a time when we need to embrace more fully Wesley's Catholic Spirit and put such distinctions aside for the sake of the gospel, learn from each other and 'reclaim' the task of evangelism for the whole Church?

His evangelism was also broad in terms of the outcomes that he sought. He was not just concerned that individuals made a profession of faith, what might be called conversion, but rather his 'preaching Christ' was aimed at 'fullness of faith and the endless maturing of life in grace' and this was seen as a lifelong process.[25] The significance of this broad emphasis and in particular the organization of people into classes is seen most clearly when we compare Wesley's legacy with that of his contemporary George Whitefield. Whitefield is often regarded as being the more able preacher of the two yet he neglected the fruit of his preaching: he writes towards the end of his life 'My brother Wesley acted wisely. The souls that were awakened under his ministry he joined in class, and thus preserved the fruit of his labours. This I neglected and my people are a rope of sand.'[26] Although Whitefield seems to understand the purpose of the classes as being to nurture the Methodists in their new-found faith, it was in the classes that the work of God in evangelism, beyond the initial proclamation of the gospel, also took place. Evangelism interpreted in this way is seen as a process – something people are initiated into.

Second, Wesley's evangelism was motivated by his compassion for people. Outler pinpoints the turning point in Wesley's ministry as being when 'his passion for truth had been transformed into compassion for persons'.[27] This compassion included a concern for the transformation not just of hearts but also of lives, and not just individuals but also the transformation of the church and society. The essence of his message was love of God, love of humanity and the reality of God's grace for all, with a preference for the poor and the marginalized within society. Wesley told his people: 'You have nothing to do but to save souls. Therefore spend and be spent in this work. And go always, not only to those who want you but to those who want you most.'[28] Again Outler reminds us that 'The difference between healthy and unhealthy evangelism has less to do with the fervor of a man's faith or the pure truth of his doctrine than with the quality of his love for others.'[29] This transformation was essentially the transformation made possible and brought about through emphasis on the Kingdom of God, and holding in tension the in-breaking of the Kingdom in our lifetime, transforming life here and now (echoed in Charles Wesley's hymn 'O for a thousand tongues to sing' where we find the line 'Anticipate your heaven below'[30]) with the eschatological aspect of the Kingdom – of its fulfilment yet to be and our striving for more (expressed in, for example, Charles Wesley's hymn 'Love Divine' and in particular the verse which says 'Changed from glory into glory, till in heaven we take our place'[31]).

Third, as the Methodist societies became evangelistic in their own right[32] evangelism became what we would now be calling a whole-church activity. The task was not dependent on Wesley alone but on the many who ministered in and through the societies and classes – whether class leaders, preachers, visitors of the sick or some other role. Everyone who ministered also evangelized through sharing Wesley's primary objective to 'save souls'.[33] This was about, as Wesley instructed his helpers, bringing 'as many sinners as you possibly can to repentance; and, with all your power, to build them up in that holiness without which they cannot see the Lord'.[34] Evangelism was not the sole task of those who could be labelled 'specialists' or of a particular section of a Methodist society or of ordained ministers. Methodism was after all essentially a movement of lay people, and it reminds us that evangelism is the '"normal" work of the whole Church all the time – unless she has ceased, in truth and indeed, to be the Church of Christ'[35] – something of which John Wesley and his Methodist societies sought to remind the established church in their day, showing how the church can truly be good news and find its place as an agent in the process of evangelism.

So, in answer to the question 'is it Methodist?' it seems that we can answer 'yes', for not only is evangelism part of the DNA of the Church, but it appears to be a particularly dominant gene in the DNA of the Methodist Church in terms of who, how and why the people called Methodists were raised up. Evangelism is 'in our blood'.[36] However, looking around the Church at present we would be hard pressed not to conclude that if this is true then we must be suffering from a serious blood disorder. While we may recognize that 'evangelism' is the calling of the Church (both through something like the circuit listening exercise and through official Conference reports) and while we may sing about it in our hymns and affirm it in our statements of faith, the evidence of what we are doing in terms of evangelism and the fruit of it seems to paint a different picture. Whether we recover from this disorder or whether it proves to be fatal for the Methodist Church will depend on the next steps that the Church takes and whether we are able to fulfil our potential.

Future Potential

Much of the present potential for evangelism within the Methodist Church is being invested in 'fresh expressions of church'. While initially an Anglican initiative arising from the *Mission-Shaped Church* report,[37] the concept has been embraced by the British Methodist Church and work in this area has developed through the joint Fresh Expressions initiative.[38] A fresh expression is 'a form of church for our changing culture established primarily for the benefit of people who are not yet members of any church'.[39] If the Church finds authentic fresh expressions of church then we could well realize many of the hopes expressed above and remain faithful to our Methodist heritage and evangelistic faith. After all, it could be said that the Methodist Church began as a 'fresh expression' within the Church of England.

Fresh expressions could help us discover that we have more than one tool in our evangelism toolkit. For too long, the Methodist Church has had a 'one-size-fits-all' expression of Church. If you belong to a Methodist church and visit or worship in another Methodist church anywhere in the country the chances are that, even allowing for slight regional variations, it will have a familiar feel to it. Through the development of fresh expressions of church this is being challenged as every local church is encouraged to give serious consideration to the nature of the community to which it belongs, how it engages with that community and how that community is enabled to engage with the things of God. As this begins to happen everywhere we will begin to see a wider variety of ways of being church appropriate to the people each church finds itself among and therefore help the Church be more appropriately evangelistic.

Alongside this 'one-size-fits-all' expression of church, the Methodist Church has also developed over the years a 'one-size-fits-all' model of ministry which has enabled its ordained presbyters to move very easily between appointments anywhere in the connexion – the model of church being so similar everywhere, the nature of presbyteral ministry needed is therefore necessarily similar to all. The expectation therefore of that ministry is that it will have an inward-looking, church-centred, static focus rather than the outward-looking ministry of the travelling evangelist which the early Methodist itinerant preachers once were because such a church does not engage effectively with its community. As George

Hunter puts it, we have moved from '"the world is my parish" to "my parish is my world!" The "fishers of men and women" have become "keepers of the aquarium," the hired private chaplains of groups of organized Christians.'[40] In a 'one-size-fits-all' model of church a 'one-size-fits-all' model of ministry is a reasonable response. But as expressions of church change and vary in response to the changing world in which we live, the 'one-size-fits-all' form of ministry is no longer an adequate response. As we recognize our need to be, once again, a missionary movement within our society we urgently need church leaders, both lay and ordained, who are trained in evangelism and have a fresh vision of the Church and Kingdom.

There seems to be a growing need for broadly speaking three kinds of church leader: first, for specialists and pioneers who can lead the way in evangelism, who can by listening to the prompting of the Holy Spirit and through reading the signs of the times enable the church to fulfil its apostolic and evangelistic calling. Second, there is a need for good general practitioners who can celebrate all that is good within the church as it is, offer good palliative care to churches where it is necessary and generally encourage the church to be faithful to the God who called it into being. And, third, there is a need for church leaders who can somehow stand in the gap between the other two, especially through this time of change. Those who have the gifts necessary on the one hand to encourage, enable, release and hold to account those who would be pioneers and hold them within the ministry of the whole Church, and who can, on the other hand, also offer a much needed prophetic voice to those in the inherited/traditional forms of church, strategic leaders who can enable resources to be released strategically. Developing this variety of ministry begins to move us away from a 'one-size-fits-all' model of ministry and begins to release the many and varied gifts already present within the Church for the sake of the task of evangelism. It takes seriously people as individuals with different gifts, experiences, and callings. It will need a variety of appropriate models of discernment and training, and it will require that we value the ministry of each other as it will need all to work together collaboratively. I have deliberately used 'church leader' here instead of 'minister' or 'presbyter'. If we are to experience renewal in the Church we need to rediscover the meaning and reality of the ministry of the whole people of God. Martyn Atkins reminds us that 'a recurring theme in almost every renewal of the Church in Christian history is a rediscovery of the ministry of the laity as the quintessential Christian "ministry".'[41] If ministry is simply to be about being 'keepers of the aquarium' we can continue as we are in an aging church until all the fish have gone. However, if we are truly to be 'fishers of men and women' we need to engage with evangelism and discover a different model of ministry.

Fresh expressions could also help the church (re)discover its place in the good news it proclaims. But in doing so, we do need to be careful not to make the Church and the Kingdom one and the same. In his theological response to the *Mission-Shaped Church* report, the British theologian John Hull raises concerns about the weakness of the original report in this regard.[42] My hope is that we will rediscover the church as an expression of the life of the Kingdom. Sadly, in many places, the church has already become anything but this. It is more of a social club than a community of people who live according to the values of the Kingdom of God, where the Church is preached rather than Christ and the Kingdom. However hard it is to face, this kind of expression of church must be allowed to die in order for something new to take root in and among us.

Taking an appropriate concern for the nature of church, and holding it together with a renewed expression of evangelism is a huge task of which fresh expressions of church are only the beginning and only a part of a much bigger whole. The discovery of the church as an agent of evangelism, an agent chosen by God to work with him in the work of his Kingdom, would be an exciting church to belong to. Kester Brewin, in a book commissioned by SPCK about networking and emergent church, compares the purpose of fresh expressions to punk in the late 1970s, which he suggests only really existed for about eight months in its purest form. He quotes Johnny Rotten from an interview in 1976 who reportedly said 'I want people to see us and start something' and goes on to suggest that even though 18 months later punk was no more, 'punk had done its work. It had had a hugely cathartic effect on the music industry and by tearing down these structures the way had been cleared for major new directions to be explored by those who came after it.'[43] If he is right about his comparison with the role of fresh expressions it could be an exciting place to be, maybe not for us but for those who will come after us as the church seeks to be good news.

If I have a fear for fresh expressions of church it is that, if we are not careful, we may lose the Methodist emphasis 'for all', which has given a distinctive shape to Methodist theology and evangelism. We risk losing it if we get confused between the nature and methods of evangelism and the nature of the church. These are separate but related concerns, as we have seen. Many fresh expressions of church are being created to reach out to particular groups of people, or to subcultures within our communities. Reaching out to specific groups of people with particular methods of evangelism is one thing; whether we can truly call it 'church' as an expression of the Kingdom is another matter. As we develop fresh expressions of church for particular groups of people we are in danger of creating potentially exclusive communities of faith. What will it mean for such churches to be agents of evangelism?

How and why do we 'choose' to evangelize the people we do? For example we may choose to reach out to the young. This has a particular attraction, especially in a church with an aging membership. But why? Is it truly for their own sake, to seek to initiate them into the Kingdom, or is it in order to have those we can train to continue 'our' church once we are no longer able? Do we have the same enthusiasm for evangelism among the elderly? Who will go to them? They are in need of being initiated into the Kingdom of God as much as the young are, as are all ages in-between. And what about the most vulnerable members in our society? Let us be honest about our motives. Are we driven by the church's own needs or the needs of those we seek to reach out to?

We may 'choose' to reach out to 'people like us'. Is this because that is where God sends us or because we find it easier – because

we feel it is the road of least resistance, of minimal risk, less fearful? The church sometimes seems to 'buy into', without consciously fully thinking through all the implications, the teaching
of the Church Growth Movement where strategy replaces prayer
and guidance as our starting point for evangelism, and numbers
become more important that individual human needs. What is
strategic for the growth of the Church as a human institution may
not be strategic in terms of the economy of the Kingdom of God.
We are told that 'men and women like to become Christians without crossing racial, linguistic or class barriers'[44] and this may be
an observable reality in some contexts, as Donald McGavran observed as a missionary in India. But if the Church applies this to
every context and adapts it so that people can become Christians
without crossing any kind of barriers at all, they may not experience fully the transforming nature of the Kingdom of God both
now and to come. The Church needs to recognize which barriers
need to be crossed and which do not because they are cultural
expressions of the Church in that place. We must discover what
it means to be truly an 'alternative' society bearing witness of a
greater reality to the world in which we live. Otherwise we will
continue to play it safe, we won't take risks and we will stick with
those we know and what we know. Jesus did not promise that
becoming his disciples would be easy – if anything, his teaching
reveals the opposite. It will be hard. But it will be worth it. In the
Incarnation we discover a God who crosses every possible barrier in order that we might discover the Kingdom of God. And
he calls his followers to do the same. If we prioritize evangelism
to those who are 'like us', however we interpret that, then what
about those whom the church will never reach because there are
no people 'like them' in the church? What about God's preference
for the poor and the marginalized? What about the imperative to
go to those most in need? Do we hear the Spirit asking 'Whom
shall I send, and who will go for us?'[45] or have we already decided
where we will go? The Church needs to keep asking: Who are the
people who need us most? How do we celebrate God's grace for
all? Where is God sending us? We will not find answers to these
questions easily, but I am convinced that as we prayerfully wrestle

with them God will reveal the way of his Kingdom for us and we will be faithful to our Methodist heritage.

If we bear this in mind, fresh expressions could help the Church (re)discover a genuine compassion for people – especially those who have not yet heard or been persuaded of the good news of the Kingdom of God, who are not yet Christian. Reading again the various reports that the Methodist Church has produced over the last 20 years or so, from *Sharing in God's Mission*[46] in 1985 through to *Changing Church for a Changing World*[47] in 2007, I do feel a sadness that nothing much seems to have changed. *Sharing in God's Mission* could have been written for the Church today. So will fresh expressions of church really make a difference and change anything or simply be the next big thing? If there is a glimmer of hope I believe that it will be in whether the Church really discovers a compassion for all people and whether this is seen in our intention to be Church 'for the benefit of those not yet members of the Church', whoever they may be. This will require of us a difference in terms of our intention for all we do and in what is our overriding motivation, putting the Kingdom before 'our' (or 'the') Church, the needs of others before our own personal preferences, God's mission before our mission. It is a question of integrity, of being true to ourselves in terms of what we profess and believe the Church to be.

I have heard it argued that God will not leave the world without a witness; therefore the Church will always be with us so we don't need to worry about its future. Of course God can, and will, raise up witnesses (from stones if necessary[48]) but it will not necessarily be the church as we recognize it today. It will be found in new, perhaps surprising, places, and in new and exciting forms. It may even be found without us, a warning we all need to hear and heed, which will probably either scare us, driving us to despair or further into denial, or it will excite us and give us renewed hope for the future and for the evangelistic task before us.

In writing this chapter I have felt very much how I imagine King Josiah might have felt when he discovered the book of the Law which had been lost and which led to the renewal of the Covenant.[49] My hope is that the Methodist Church will rediscover the evangelistic impetus and imperative which was at the heart of John Wesley's ministry and reinterpret it for the present age and in every community. As we (re)discover this – we must repent that it has been hidden (if not lost) for so long – we must rejoice in and give thanks for those faithful saints who have kept this tradition alive so that it can be (re)discovered, and we must renew our covenant as the people of God called Methodists and live out our evangelistic faith wherever he places us in the world as we look to the future.

In order to realize its present potential, the Methodist Church will need to:

- discover a genuine compassion for all people, especially those who are not yet Christian – which motivates all that the Church does;
- seek first the Kingdom of God rather than the future of the Church;
- rediscover the place of the Church in the good news it proclaims;
- embrace evangelism across the whole of the life of the Church, at the heart of all that the Church is and does, learning what it means for the church to be an agent of evangelism;
- discover that it has more than one tool in its evangelism toolkit and therefore develop a broad approach to evangelism which sees it as a process and not a one-off event or activity.

Notes

1 www.sharejesusinternational.com

2 www.cliffcollege.ac.uk

3 www.methodist.org.uk/index.cfm?fuseaction=opentogod.content& cmid=559

4 www.freshexpressions.org.uk

5 *Called to Love and Praise*, Peterborough: Methodist Publishing House, 1999, p. 9, paragraph 2.1.2.

6 The Lord's Prayer.

7 *Called to Love and Praise*, p. 9, paragraph 2.1.3.

8 *Called to Love and Praise*, p. 10, paragraph 2.1.7.

9 *Called to Love and Praise*, p. 20, paragraph 2.4.5 .

10 http://www.methodist.org.uk/index.cfm?fuseaction=opentogod. content&cmid=11

11 Jeffrey W. Harris, *Can British Methodism Grow Again?*, London: Methodist Church Home Mission Division, 1981, p. 10.

12 Revd Dr Neil Richardson, Presidential address 2003, http://www. methodist.org.uk/index.cfm?fuseaction=opentogod.content&cmid=609.

13 *Sharing in God's Mission*, London: Methodist Church Home Mission Division, 1985, p. 33.

14 William Abraham, *The Logic of Evangelism*, Grand Rapids: Eerdmans, 1994, pp. 103–4.

15 Revd Dr Neil Richardson, Presidential address 2003.

16 James C. Logan, *Theology and Evangelism in Wesleyan Heritage*, Nashville: Kingswood Books, 1994, p. 11.

17 William Abraham, *The Logic of Evangelism*, p. 95.

18 William Abraham, *The Logic of Evangelism*, p. 104.

19 Rob Frost, *Sharing Jesus*, Bletchley: Scripture Union, 2008, pp. 132–3 for a simplified version of the Engel Scale.

20 James C. Logan, *Theology and Evangelism in the Wesleyan Heritage*, p. 12.

21 For example: Rob Frost and Martyn Atkins, and David Wilkinson more specifically in the area of apologetics. Howard Mellor was a representative at the symposium and contributed a chapter to the book. In the USA we can look particularly to William Abraham (an Irish Methodist) and to George Hunter III who has written widely particularly on church growth.

22 George Hunter III, *Radical Outreach*, Nashville: Abingdon Press, 2003, p. 194.

23 Albert Outler, *Evangelism in the Wesleyan Spirit*, Nashville, Tidings, 1971, p. 55.

24 Albert Outler, *Evangelism in the Wesleyan Spirit*, p. 36.

25 Albert Outler, *Evangelism in the Wesleyan Spirit*, p. 23.

26 Quoted in Stephen Tompkins, *John Wesley – A Biography*, Grand Rapids: Eerdmans, 2003, p. 128.

27 Albert Outler, *Evangelism in the Wesleyan Spirit*, p. 20.

28 'The Twelve Rules of a Helper 1753' in *The Constitutional Practice and Discipline of the Methodist Church volume 1*, Peterborough: Methodist Publishing House, 1988, p. 77.

29 Albert Outler, *Evangelism in the Wesleyan Spirit*, p. 36.

30 *Hymns and Psalms*, Peterborough: Methodist Publishing House, 1983, Hymn no. 744.

31 *Hymns and Psalms*, Hymn no. 267.

32 Albert Outler, *Evangelism in the Wesleyan Spirit*, p. 28.

33 George G. Hunter III, 'The apostolic identity of the Church and Wesleyan Christianity' in James Logan, *Theology and Evangelism in the Wesleyan Heritage*, p. 165.

34 'The Twelve Rules of a Helper 1753' in *The Constitutional Practice and Discipline of the Methodist Church volume 1*, p. 78.

35 Franz Hildebrandt, *Christianity According to the Wesleys,* Grand Rapids: Baker Books, 1996, p. 49.

36 Revd Dr Martyn Atkins, Presidential address 2007, http://www.methodist.org.uk/index.cfm?fuseaction=opentogod.newsDetail&newsid=217

Also the Revd Dr Neil Richardson in his Presidential address of 2003 suggested that 'God-centred evangelism' is the 'lifeblood of the church'.

37 *Mission-Shaped Church*, London: Church House Publishing, 2004.

38 www.freshexpressions.org.uk

39 Pete Pillinger and Andrew Roberts, *Changing Church for a Changing World*, Peterborough: Methodist Publishing House, 2007, p.17.

40 George G. Hunter III, 'The Apostolic Identity of the Church and Wesleyan Christianity', in James Logan, *Theology and Evangelism in the Wesleyan Heritage*, p. 167.

41 Martyn Atkins *Resourcing Renewal*, Peterborough: Inspire, 2007, p. 191.

42 John Hull, *Mission-Shaped Church: a Theological response*, London: SCM Press, 2006. See also John Hull, 'Mission-shaped and kingdom focus?' in Steven Croft (ed.), *Mission-shaped Questions*, London: Church House Publishing, 2008.

43 Kester Brewin, *The Complex Christ*, London: SPCK, 2004, pp. 71–2.

44 Donald McGavran, *Understanding Church Growth*, revised edition, Grand Rapids: Eerdmans, 1980, p. 62, also p. 223 and developed in the following pages.

45 Isaiah 6.8.

46 *Sharing in God's Mission*, London: Methodist Church Home Mission Division, 1985.

47 Pete Pillinger and Andrew Roberts, *Changing Church for a Changing World*.

48 Luke 3.8 and 19.39–40.

49 2 Kings 22 and 23.

2

A Biblical Faith

JONATHAN DEAN

Period Pieces

Ann, a colleague and dear friend, understands the principles of biblical interpretation better than almost anyone I know. She does so, not because she teaches in theological college or because she has spent more time studying the Bible than anyone else. Though she is an excellent minister and has a sharp intellect, it is not because she spends more time in her study or has a larger book budget than her colleagues in ministry. Her deep and intuitive sympathy for the task of enabling a text to speak from one generation to another comes because of what she does in her spare time.

Ann is an author. To be precise, she writes period romances and to date she has had 13 accepted for publication. Her dramas encompass a range of protagonists, from young girls embarking on the European Grand Tour to caddish rakes exploiting the world and everyone around them, apparently irredeemably selfish. They all centre on the world of the eighteenth century and are enormously popular with her devoted readers. This is because she tells a good story well and loves language, but also because she does her preparation carefully before she ever sets a word on the page. She reads and researches and buries herself in the world and culture against the backdrop of which her stories play out. Consequently, she is able to explore with great insight the drama of the human condition, our fears and hopes and loves and losses, and speak to her readers despite the historical dissonances between her stories' settings and those of her public. In other words, her books have historical authenticity while still managing to convey something timeless and profoundly true.

So it is, also, that Ann can so well understand how to interpret the Bible Sunday by Sunday: she is able to draw out of cultural dissimilarity something of eternal human truth. The need to peel away the layers of what is unfamiliar and difficult in order to reach the level at which connections can be made between an ancient text and modernity is fundamental for her. Further, she is reflecting the fact that, with a little encouragement, the rest of us know how to interpret a historical text for the present, too. We also know how to enjoy it, and even be consumed by it. Ann's choice of subject matter reflects a heightened interest among British television viewers and cinema-goers in all things eighteenth century, most especially the works of Jane Austen. Austen's perceptiveness and flawless insights into human nature and character have had us all entranced for many years, long before Mr Darcy, on primetime TV, took off his riding jacket and plunged himself into the cooling waters of the lake at Pemberley. Few of us could imagine wearing breeches or being thrown by a wealthy sister out of our home or experiencing the shame that a silly sister's elopement brings on the whole family but we have effortlessly learned how to overcome those obstacles of unfamiliarity and understand the story's meaning and message. If only we could apply those insights to our reading of the Bible, we might be better at hermeneutics – and find it much more fun – than we ever imagined.

The Old Testament scholar Walter Brueggemann in one of his heartfelt prayers expresses well the difficulty and the hope involved in reading Scripture:

Our eyes are scaled
and our ears are uncircumcised
and we are children of another world.

We pray for the gift of perception.
We pray for energy and courage,
that we may not leave the text
until we wrench your blessing from it.[1]

Perception, energy and courage can be quickly depleted when Christians try to understand, and agree on, the message of Scripture. Beneath the superficial level of our difference of views about how – and indeed, whether – it should be interpreted for the contexts and circumstances of our contemporary lives, lurk more serious and threatening concerns. Once we concede that some form of interpretation is necessary, that the Holy Spirit's word for us in this place and time will not always simply leap from the page into our waiting hearts, a range of secondary skills is required. Like Ann, we are going to have to do our work before getting to grips with the text. We may come to different conclusions and insights by a range of different means; how, then, are we going to reconcile our varied viewpoints? More likely, the fear is that we simply lack the wherewithal to start the project at all. In what follows, I shall hope to survey the causes and effects of these kinds of fears, which Methodist Christians share with their sisters and brothers in other churches, and to offer some thoughts on how Methodists have traditionally approached the challenge that contemporary exigencies have brought to the reading of Scripture. We are not alone, and in each generation Christians of all hues have had to rediscover the poetic power of sacred texts to open them up to divine transformation. In our turn we need to do so too. We might even find ourselves enjoying it.[2]

Modern Methodists and the Bible

In the days when I was a circuit tutor for Local Preacher training, I always dreaded Unit Four of the *Faith and Worship* course.[3] That was the unit in which students were asked to get to grips, fairly quickly and at a reasonably sophisticated level, with notions of biblical authority. I dreaded it because to many of them it came as an 'academic' bolt from the blue. They were still too nervous about ever being competent to interpret the Bible for the worshipping community. The assignment involved asking them to offer an assessment of their own attitude to Scripture, and their understanding of its weight and authority within the Church's life. To help them, they were shown the seven-point spectrum of beliefs contained within the Methodist Church's statement on the Bible.[4] On the one end was fundamentalism, and the language of 'inerrancy'; on the other, a mild liberal view that the Bible contained some wisdom but was not to be regarded as primary or even authoritative. Students were always able to find things in each statement that attracted them, but often found the tiny shades of nuance and shift between the statements somewhat unclear. Few of them had ever had to place their own beliefs on such a scale before. While it was an important stepping-off point for learning how to handle Scripture and preach from it, their marks usually reflected their sense that they were a little at sea. Coming so early in their study, when they most needed confidence, it could be a tough month to navigate with them.

Asked to identify their own understanding of biblical authority, Methodists would undoubtedly plot their answers on as wide a map as any other branch of the Christian faith. Many of them would express the same difficulties in giving an answer as the trainee preachers. Perhaps more so, given that candidates for preacher training often represent the more biblically literate members of churches. Methodism certainly has its share of fundamentalists, who reject the need for interpretation at all, preferring to claim that the direct word of Scripture does indeed speak directly without need of any mediation. It is easy to dismiss such people, but worth remembering the tendency in all of us to slide into such behaviour when we 'proof text',[5] or offer easy answers to complex questions without acknowledging the ways in which Scripture speaks to Scripture and the range of voices it contains.

More commonly, it is the range of obstacles thrown up by the modern world to a clear understanding of the authority and place of Scripture that leads to a heightened uncertainty about it in our churches. Methodists, reasonable and open people that they are, are affected deeply by questions of science, knowledge, and reason. They are also often duped by the idea that human progress has always been for the good. In common with all Christians, therefore, they experience a set of questions and difficulties in knowing exactly how to receive and appropriate the Bible in their own, modern, contexts. At the top of the list of these questions is the very cultural dissimilarity already described. The places and times against which the biblical narrative takes place are often just too different from our own; the people involved just too unlike us. It can seem profoundly troubling, for instance, to see what we have to do with Joshua, Deborah and Gideon or how the God who commands the sacrifice of Isaac could be our God. As L. P. Hartley wrote, 'the past is a foreign country: they do things differently there'.[6] When the events of the past are also, literally, taking place in a foreign country, the interpretive challenges are even greater. Added to that is the bewildering range of genres and styles in which the Bible is written, and the myriad human responses, passions, and dispositions which those genres represent. The American Presbyterian writer Frederick Buechner describes the problem well:

> One way to describe the Bible ... would be to say that it is a disorderly collection of sixty-odd books which are often tedious, barbaric, obscure, and teem with contradictions and inconsistencies. It is a swarming compost of a book, an Irish stew of poetry and propaganda, law and legalism, myth and murk, history and hysteria...let him who tries to start out at Genesis and work his way through conscientiously to Revelation beware.[7]

The challenge of this historical problem, the sheer difference between biblical and modern cultures, gives rise to a series of critiques of the Bible on the basis of proper intellectual conduct and behaviour. It simply isn't reasonable, the argument goes, to base one's values and beliefs on such stories. The nature of much of the subject matter, particularly of the Old Testament, has already been alluded to. Such criticism, and the mindset which accepts it, is based on the (false) assumption that human societies and sensibilities have progressed far beyond the cruel and primitive standard of ancient Israel, or even early Christianity. Buechner again summarizes these complaints, that the Bible contains much which affronts modern ears, both sociological and theological:

> The barbarities, for instance. The often fanatical nationalism. The passages where the God of Israel is depicted as interested

in other nations only to the degree that he can use them to whip Israel into line. God hardening Pharaoh's heart and then clobbering him for hardheartedness. The self-righteousness and self-pity of many of the Psalms, plus their frequent vindictiveness. The way the sublime and the unspeakable are always jostling each other.[8]

How do modern people make any sense of such things, still less treat them as sacred? In this land of dissimilarity, very often our first response is to lose ourselves in the confusion of trying to make any sense of it. It can be tempting to give up altogether, before understanding anything that is timeless in the Bible's story of human cruelty and divine presence, and of the use the one often tries to make of the other.

In our own day, science has proved a particularly combative dialogue partner, and scientific progress has often thrown up a range of new challenges to biblical understanding. Through the mouths of some of its more strident practitioners, science has also been presented as the antidote to a belief in biblical 'mythology' and supernaturalism of all kinds. Richard Dawkins, the Professor of the Public Understanding of Science at Oxford University, expresses the point of view succinctly in his book *The God Delusion*:

By contrast, what I, as a scientist, believe ... I believe not because of reading a holy book but because I have studied the evidence. It really is a very different matter. Books about evolution are believed not because they are holy. They are believed because they present overwhelming quantities of mutually buttressed evidence. In principle, any reader can go and check that evidence. When a science book is wrong, somebody eventually discovers the mistake and it is corrected in subsequent books. That conspicuously doesn't happen with holy books.[9]

This has been a seductive viewpoint for many twenty-first century people, even within the Church. Consequently, the doubt many feel about how exactly the Bible is to be read and understood has only increased. However broad the diversity of views about religion is within the scientific community, polemical and publicity-loving figures like Dawkins will always amplify the common understanding that an acceptance of scientific methods and knowledge and a biblically based Christian faith are incompatible.

The shrinking of the world, too, and the exposure of Christians to people of many different faiths and cultures, can throw up further difficulties in understanding the revelation contained in the Bible as authoritative. As Christians begin to discover that their neighbours of other religious practices and systems have truth of their own to live by, which illumines and enlivens them, they often return to their own texts and traditions with chastened hearts, but also less certain in their fundamental outlook. Is the Bible still of primary authority in forming and growing faith? Or is it simply one text among many which claims to speak of God and as such should be treated with greater caution and be subjected to greater scrutiny by the others? Christians of all kinds have wrestled with these questions, and some have come to the conclusion that the Bible has no particular right to be the only read text in services. I have been in circuit staff meetings in Britain in which a lay worker insisted that she wanted Hindu scriptures read in public worship, and have attended a Congregationalist church in the USA in which the pastor regularly places extracts of the Tao Te Ching alongside Matthew's Gospel or Paul's letter to the Romans. What does it mean, in a religiously plural age, still to insist upon the primacy of the Bible without rejecting either the integrity or the faith of our neighbours?

Even within the Church, movements and schools of thought of all kinds exist which have comprehensively challenged and utterly redrawn traditional understandings of and approaches to the Bible. The more radical of these base their own methods upon the kinds of scientific rationalism already described. To take one well known example, the North American 'Jesus Seminar' has profoundly affected the attitudes of Christians on both sides of the Atlantic. For some, the work of the Seminar's scholars represents water in a dry land of traditional Christian piety; for others, it is a dangerous subversion of time-honoured truth. The basis of the Seminar's work has been to re-examine the Gospel texts with attention to the discomfort modern believers feel around the historical and cultural differences between their time and ours. The individual members each cast votes about the sayings of Jesus, based on their own perceptions of the likelihood that he actually said them. The result has been a biblical text shorn of much that rubs against modern sensibilities: claims to divinity, supernatural intervention, and apocalyptic imagery.

The Jesus Seminar embodies several of these modern objections to the biblical text, and has taken action in an attempt to 'rescue' a faith that sits more easily with the contemporary world and its would-be believers. There seems to be an essential arrogance, it must be said, which denies Jesus the mindset and outlook of his own time on the basis that it does not fit with our own, and thereby silences him on matters which seem to have been central to him. For all that, the work of the Seminar has brought new energy to many less conservative Christians, just as it lays bare their very modern preoccupations, and the divisions between them and their more traditional companions. In the large suburban church I currently serve, the Jesus Seminar-inspired Sunday class meets at the opposite end of the hallway from one whose members adopt a much more orthodox and 'unacademic' method for studying Scripture together. The latter occasionally mutter about the former's 'heresy', while the former sit at the feet of the founders of the Jesus Seminar, Robert Funk and John Dominic Crossan, with only a rare hint of their frustration with the credulity of their friends a few yards down the corridor. The modern world indeed forces Christians who would study the Bible into perplexing, disturbing, and difficult terrain.

For the most part, of course, the questions asked of Christians by modernity, and the challenges with which it confronts them, are felt more vaguely by those in the pew, as a general discomfort, or as a mild loss of the old certainties and their characteristic nerve. More vaguely, the so-called 'postmodern' discomfort with religious narratives and timeless truths has also weakened our confidence. Time and again, in small Bible study groups in local churches, lay leaders and ministers experience the raft of niggling questions which bedevil such an enterprise for those who refuse simply to retreat into cloistered piety. The world we live in leaves our religious identity confused and in danger of collapse. How are we to navigate the Bible? How can we agree, when there is so much division between us, and do we need to? If something doesn't speak our language, how shall we interpret it? How shall we resist the rush to overlay an ancient text with an easy interpretation that lies close at hand, even if doing so denies the text its original power? Leading Advent studies on Isaiah, and trying to place the messianic promises of chapters 7, 9 and 11 in an original, eighth-century BC context, our desperate rush to get to the Christmas interpretation always reminded me of the old story about a preacher who went into Sunday School. 'What is grey, with a bushy tail, and jumps through the trees?' he asked the children. To which one replied: 'Well, it sounds like a squirrel, but I know that the answer to the questions here is always Jesus.'

Methodists are no more or less affected by these questions than any other Christians. They may find, however, that they are not as unique or new as sometimes imagined. There exist, both in the story of Methodism's birth and in its essential character, some compelling parallels concerning the reading and understanding of Scripture which may offer guidance and comfort. Before examining those in more detail, it is worth being reminded more generally of what our forebears in faith have often understood: that any interpretation of the Bible is necessarily hesitant and humbly offered. We are always on holy ground, and treading carefully is wise. So is a refusal to place too much store by human reasoning and intellect alone. The words of Thomas Traherne, the seventeenth-century poet and mystic, remain a firm foundation for any interpretative exercise:

When thou dost take this sacred book into thy hand
think not that thou the included sense dost understand.

It is a sign thou wantest sound intelligence
If that thou think thyself to understand the sense.

Be not deceived thou then on it in vain mayst gaze;
The way is intricate that leads into a maze.

Here's naught but what's mysterious to an understanding eye;
Where reverence alone stands ope, and sense stands by.

'A Man of One Book'? Early Methodism and Scripture

The early Methodists found themselves shaping their distinctive responses to faith in a whirlwind of cultural, intellectual, and scientific turmoil which even the early twenty-first century would be hard pressed to rival. Methodism grew from an Evangelical Revival whose reliance and emphasis upon the primary authority of Scripture still accurately echoed the preoccupations of Martin Luther, John Calvin, and the Reformation which had swept through Europe two centuries earlier. Nevertheless, its engagement with the Bible was also formed uniquely by its own context. It is, indeed, fascinating to see the extent to which the secular mindset of eighteenth-century Europe and North America, where Methodism had its being, mirrors that already described as belonging to modernity. Equally, in attempting to articulate a vision of religious faith which took contemporary discoveries and challenges seriously while faithfully honouring its inherited Christian tradition, Methodism placed itself creatively and openly between colliding worlds, offering something to members of each.

That background, of course, was predominantly that of the Enlightenment. So much was encompassed by the thinkers and writers of the Enlightenment movement that generalizations are difficult and perhaps unwise. But, by the mid eighteenth century, the work of pioneers such as Descartes and John Locke had spawned a whole generation of disciples, those who emphasized the importance of evidence and proof, who relied upon scientific method and the principles of 'empiricism' for the foundation of any truth claim, and who were swift, in their reliance on human powers of reason and thought, to call into question anything that spoke of the metaphysical or supernatural. Religion, naturally, was high on that list, despite the fact that several key Enlightenment figures, including Locke, retained a belief and even argued for its coherence.[10] Across the ocean in America, President Thomas Jefferson, that political embodiment of Enlightenment idealism and Deist faith, would later, while in the White House, excise from his New Testament the passages his empiricist mind could not tolerate, a full two centuries before the Jesus Seminar.

In the mid eighteenth century, when Methodism was consolidating its extraordinary growth in Britain and America, the leading Enlightenment mind in Europe, Voltaire, published his *Philosophical Dictionary*. It is worth pausing to take note of its content and of the kinds of arguments he deploys against Christianity, Judaism, and religion in general, which, but for their greater elegance and more subtly nuanced character, would look and feel at home in one of Richard Dawkins' polemics. Describing the Old Testament books of Kings and Chronicles, for instance, Voltaire noted that, besides their internal disagreements:

> If the style of the history of the Kings and of the Chronicles is divine, it may nevertheless be true that the actions recorded in these histories are not divine. David murders Uriah; Ishbosheth and Mephibosheth are murdered; Absalom murders Ammon; Joab murders Absalom; Solomon murders his brother Adonijah ... We pass over in silence many other minor murders. It must be acknowledged that, if the Holy Spirit did write this history, He did not choose a subject particularly edifying.[11]

Turning to the New Testament, Voltaire ridiculed the claims around Jesus' divinity, tore into ridiculous notions about the performance of miracles, subjected many historical claims of the Gospels and Acts to rigorous analysis, dwelt lovingly upon further examples of dissonance between different passages, and, in all this, repeatedly charged Christian believers with a dereliction of their duty to be sensible. The question of Saul's conversion is a case in point:

> Which is the most probable – humanly speaking – that St Paul became a Christian as a result of being thrown from a horse by

the appearance of a great light at noon day, and that a celestial voice cried out to him ... or that Paul was irritated against the Pharisees, either by the refusal of Gamaliel to give him his daughter or by some other cause?[12]

While it is small wonder that the book was banned and hated by the Church, it represented an elegant, caustically witty expression of the essential ideals of the Enlightenment applied to religious revelation. Leaders of eighteenth-century religious movements had to be up to the challenge.

John Wesley himself, however, was in some senses a child of Enlightenment thinking. Arriving at Oxford not long after Locke's death and into the whole intellectual arena of the new philosophical approaches, he drank deeply as student and scholar at the wells of scientific and empiricist thought. Those who examine Wesley's own thought have described how he embraced Locke's essential belief, that knowledge is the product of the human senses acting upon human reason and intellect, while modifying Locke's thesis somewhat to allow for a *spiritual* sense and to realize the *transformative* nature of what we undergo. The historical theologian George Croft Cell went so far as to talk of Wesley's 'theological empiricism'.[13] Wesley himself was clear that the two worlds, of revelation and intellect, could and should be held together. 'Knowing religion', he observed, 'was not designed to destroy any part of our natural faculties, but to exalt and improve them, our reason in particular'.[14]

This sense of the need for the spiritual sense to be active and engaged in order for belief to be formed was expressed nowhere more than in relation to the Bible. Reminding the Methodists to be cautious about interpreting the Bible, and thus claiming private revelation, without proper safeguards, Charles Wesley simultaneously threw back at sceptical empiricists their inability to appreciate its more hidden qualities:

Whether the Word be preached or read,
no saving benefit I gain
from empty sounds or letters dead;

unprofitable all and vain,
unless by faith thy word I hear
and see its heavenly character.

If God enlighten through his Word,
I shall my kind Enlightener bless;
but void and naked of my Lord,
what are all verbal promises?
Nothing to me, till faith divine
inspire, inspeak, and make them mine.[15]

In stealing their own language, of 'Enlightenment', he was, perhaps, making a wry critique of their endeavours: in matters of eternal consequence, they were in danger of seeing some trees but missing the forest.

John Wesley similarly understood the difficulty of biblical interpretation, and the need for help, divine and human, in doing its work. Thus, while he proudly declared in his preface to the 1746 collection of his sermons that he desired to be 'a man of one book', he conceded in the same breath that this was a hazardous occupation. Reading and correctly interpreting the Bible, he acknowledged, required thought and prayer, a deep knowledge of the whole of Scripture and not just isolated passages, the company of other believers and the legacy of the past, in testimony and reflection and learning. Thus, while he expresses the unadorned battle cry of the Reformation: 'Scripture alone!', he willingly admits, as the Reformers had done less graciously, the irresponsibility and impossibility of attempting to interpret the Bible without the help of the community of faith, both present and past.[16] So it was, influenced by the philosophy of his day and believing in its imperative optimism concerning human possibility and progress, that he rejected what he saw as Calvinist pessimism because it was an unreasonable view of both God and humanity, whatever isolated scriptural texts could be summoned in its favour. He also refused to conclude from the clear scriptural acceptance of slavery that his own fierce opposition to the slave trade was wrong.

Wesley further answered the charges of the Enlightenment against evangelical Christianity by cleverly deploying the Bible as a prime check on the worst excesses of the 'enthusiasm' which was so abhorrent to many leading thinkers and writers of the day, inside and outside the established churches. The Bible, he suggested, actually contained and constrained individual experience of the divine that might otherwise issue in the kinds of emotional behaviour that Enlightenment intellectuals found so vulgar and repulsive. 'What is most rarely to be met with', Voltaire had sneered, 'is the combination of reason with enthusiasm. Enthusiasm is precisely like wine: it has the power to excite such ferment in the blood vessels, and such strong vibrations in the nerves, that reason is completely destroyed by it ... Reasonable enthusiasm is the patrimony of great poets.'[17] Ever a soul imbued with poetry of several sorts, as well as a deep love of order and dignity, Wesley used the Bible to fend off the worst excesses of what he called 'religious madness, fancied inspiration', and to correct and hold in due measure the kinds of religious experience which characterized his movement but also, in excess, endangered its credibility on several fronts.

With Locke, but with quite different emphases, he argued that the Bible, far from encouraging religious hysteria and gullibility about the impossible, actually fostered 'reasonable' Christianity.[18] It also engendered, or should do, the kind of tolerance of diverse views which was so espoused by Enlightenment thought. In his frequent appeals for respect for divergent 'opinions', Wesley was showing his intellectual debts, but also giving them a scriptural basis.[19]

In other senses too, the Wesleys bore out Voltaire's observation about 'reasonable enthusiasm'. Poetry was at the heart of early Methodism's best use of Scripture. It was through poetry that the religion of the Wesleys, and its scriptural heritage, was given best and most extraordinary expression. Arguing both against fundamentalist readings of Scripture and against modern scientific understandings that rejected its value altogether, Wesley's sermons took for granted its primacy whilst employing its verses as 'poetic' springboards to further instruction. Sometimes, he did this in ways quite far removed from the plain meaning of the text; for instance in his sermons *The Almost Christian, The Nature of*

Enthusiasm and *A Caution against Bigotry*.[20] Perhaps even more remarkably, however, the Methodists were primarily moulded, instructed, and helped to interpret and apply Scripture in their own lives through the hymns of Charles, which remain a body of popular religious poetry almost without equal.

Charles Wesley's hymns are absolutely saturated in allusions and references to, and direct quotation of, the Bible. Indeed, they have been described as 'Scripture in solution'. One commentator claimed to find over 60 biblical references in one hymn.[21] As such they not only conveyed to illiterate and unlearned Methodists the stories and images of the Bible, important work though that was; they also interpreted and applied those stories and verses in creative and quite beautiful ways. They turned a scriptural story around so that it spoke to the believer's own experience and connected her to the tradition and its insights. They retold the Gospel reading so as to involve the singer in the action in a direct, almost Ignatian way. They took complex passages of biblical theology and turned them into simple yet profound reflections upon everyday Christian hope and experience. As the historian and theologian David Hempton comments, though they rarely directly articulated doctrine, they emphasized the Christian life as pilgrimage, in a myriad of scripturally based ways. Complex ideas were expressed in accessible language; the will and emotions were engaged but also tempered by scriptural order; the surrounding culture was referenced and the reality of life acknowledged, as we have seen already; community was built. Above all, the verses of Charles Wesley were more easily memorized than the Bible, and thus his hymns were able to 'redact the gospel narrative and draw the believer into that narrative' in ways of which sermons, class groups, and classroom instruction could not boast.[22]

In his hymnody, Charles Wesley could make a silk purse from the most unpromising sow's ear, and apply to the hearts and minds of his congregations the least accessible passage. Take, for instance, Leviticus 6.13, part of the instructions concerning sacrifices in the Mosaic Law: 'a perpetual fire shall be kept burning on the altar; it shall not go out'. From this inauspicious beginning, he penned one of his finest creations, a soaring prayer for commitment and inspiration in the Christian life, still sung at every ordination in the British Methodist Church:

> O Thou who camest from above,
> the pure celestial fire to impart,
> kindle a flame of sacred love
> on the mean altar of my heart.
>
> There let it for thy glory burn
> with inextinguishable blaze ...[23]

The Bible's great adventure stories were, in Wesley's hands, directly applicable to the eighteenth century individual too. The dramatic episode of Peter's release from jail in Acts 12 he retuned into an arresting, utterly memorable description of conversion:

> Long my imprisoned spirit lay
> Fast bound in sin and Nature's night;
> Thine eye diffused a quickening ray –
> I woke; the dungeon flamed with light.
> My chains fell off, my heart was free,
> I rose, went forth, and followed thee.[24]

Above all things, the Wesleys wanted their followers to draw from their reading of and meditation upon Scripture a clear idea about the character of the God they worshipped. Their own theology, as has been said, was clearly indebted to Enlightenment optimism and reason, and they were unapologetic and unremitting in their efforts to communicate their message. The task led Charles to his finest use of Scripture, re-presenting and reimagining passages from across the Bible to convey his passionate faith in a benevolent, gracious Creator whose action in Christ was for the whole world. Supremely and sublimely, he found in Jacob's strange nocturnal wrestling at Peniel, in Genesis 32, the opportunity to present this insight. The hymn reflects so many of the concerns and attitudes of the day: intellectual striving and relentless enquiry to uncover the truth; a determination to discover things of eternal value; a refusal to be easily deterred from the pursuit of genuine Christianity. The resulting intellectual and theological triumph is described in poetry of great poise and accomplishment:

> My prayer has power with God; the grace
> Unspeakable I now receive;
> Through faith I see thee face to face,
> I see thee face to face, and live!
> In vain I have not wept and strove:
> Thy nature and thy name is Love.[25]

As the American Methodist theologian S. T. Kimbrough Jr comments, it is through passages like this that 'the dramatic mythology of the Bible comes alive'.[26] Resisting literalism and inflexibility, allowing his poetic imagination to inhabit the text and draw it into the contemporary world and the believer's own experience, Charles Wesley imbued the reading of Scripture with new beauty, fresh possibilities, and unlimited transformative potential.

The Freedom of the Poetic Word

Methodism's own tradition may help us rediscover some confidence and wisdom about our use of Scripture today; but a cautionary note is as necessary with interpretations of history. as of Scripture itself. Others will engage with the formation of Methodist Christianity and come to different conclusions; these are offered, as Traherne advises, humbly and with due respect for that which refuses to be tamed or contained by any of us, or even all of us. There seems to be, however, some value in returning to current insecurities around the Bible and seeing how our tradition helps us to address them.

Nothing, of course, replaces the need simply to work hard at appropriating Scripture for our own times and places. Some of that will be necessarily exegetical: understanding better what scholars call the 'life situation' of the passages we read. John Wesley published the *Explanatory Notes* to be a digest of his own learning and scholarship for those without much education but a deep desire to understand Scripture better and apply it to their own lives. It will always be important that theological educators, ministers, lay preachers, and small-group leaders apply themselves to the same task of sharing knowledge. Such basic knowledge remains a vital foundation for biblical interpretation of all kinds; we should not lose our nerve about being a movement which educates as it inspires.

That should not, however, place any limits on the places to which interpretation takes us. The second piece of 'work' that will always remain necessary in our scriptural interpretation is the work of community. Conference itself offers an important model here, in its methods of thinking and speaking for the whole Church. In our local churches, lectionary groups, class meetings, home fellowship gatherings, and *lectio divina* cells[27] all provide space for the word to be shared and meditated upon and for new understandings to emerge. In an increasingly disparate, individualized, fragmented world, such groups will always offer the hope of community and the energy of life shared around an openness to inspiration. They also preserve what has been an important feature of Methodism specifically and Protestantism generally: what the Brazilian theologian Rubem Alves calls the rediscovery and democratization of 'the magical-poetic power of the Word'. Methodism, perhaps above all, has the ability in re-learning its own tradition of faith to resist the tendency of institutions to restrict interpretation and stifle creativity. As Alves contends, the transformative power of Scripture is not unleashed as long as we insist on turning images into dogmas and 'metaphors into doctrines'.[28] Christian history itself, in fact, contains many occasions on which old beliefs changed as faithfulness to interpreting Scripture for the present context demanded. It will always be crucial, too, to remember John Wesley's extraordinary latitude in his tolerance of a variety of theological interpretations, while never doubting his own!

As Wesley was open to the thought-worlds of his day, learned from them, and critiqued them too, so surely must we. There is a secondary series of communities with whom modern Christians need to be in dialogue as they interpret the Scriptures, among them the communities of science, global diversity, intellectual enquiry, and secular humanism. We are often in danger of losing our nerve in this regard, of believing too quickly and too much the lazy challenges of those who denounce the value of holy texts and books and of religion in general. Too often, we retreat into our quiet corners of piety, because we are afraid to engage with the world around us and its new questions and challenges. And, just as nothing circumvents the hard work of our own engagement with Scripture, so too nothing gets us off the hook of engaging with the world as well, and finding the points at which 'deep speaks to deep', the places where our scriptural faith suddenly takes new flight. Such dialogue should indeed remind everyone involved that we all 'stand on the shoulders of giants', reliant on the past, in forming our beliefs, opinions, and outlooks. If the Bible is no longer to be useful in forming a faith response, then Galileo, Newton, and Darwin are of no further use to scientists, and Jane Austen is well past her sell-by date for students of literature and the human condition. When imbued with the confidence of our founders, modern Methodists can accept difference, embrace diversity, and be open to new insights from wherever they come, because they believe that God's eternal word can be trusted to take flesh in new ways in each generation.

Above all, Methodists are going to need to be poets again. If the Bible is to speak in new, creative, and transforming ways, it must be cherished as poetry, as an expression of faith which will always elude us, often surprise us, frequently exasperate us, but unfailingly inspire us. The hymnody of Charles Wesley especially offers a model of how a poetic imagination enables biblical interpretation to come alive. As Susan White contends, rediscovering this aspect of our heritage of faith will help us not to be 'mired in the prosaic and the mundane', but it will also 'provide potent and engaging alternatives to the increasingly influential forms of literalistic interpretations of texts, interpretations which are fuelling so much of the tension and terror around the globe'.[29] John Wesley's stance on slavery, and his ability to bring Scripture into dialogue with itself and with tradition, reason, and experience to produce something new and yet faithful, is a case in point. Our biblical debates about homosexuality and abortion could often use a measure of the same poetic humanity, as they also should seek to move on towards other pressing matters in which the Word must be heard: climate change, genetic manipulation, global poverty and international relations.

By engaging in the necessary work of education and Christian community, by being open to difference and accepting of diversity, by thoughtful dialogue with all our various partners in other disciples and endeavours, by becoming expectant of surprise and content with mystery, we leave ourselves the possibility that once again we might inhabit stories of cultural and historical dissimilarity with new insight and power. Further, if we also regain our poetic vocation, opening ourselves to being drawn afresh into biblical narratives in ways which engage heart, mind, and soul and so rebuild community both globally and locally, we shall experience the Word taking flesh in our own lives and actions. We shall discover grace and truth. The potentials for goodness and growth in this are limitless, as are the opportunities to plant justice, peace, and joy as the people of God in a wounded and divided world.

A poet should have the last word. R. S. Thomas, standing on one of his beloved Welsh mountains, saw beneath him the endless human activity of the world around. He saw too the churches whose members had allowed them to become empty, an irrelevant monument to an outdated way of life which opted for disengagement while modernity carried on oblivious to it. For all that, the empty churches contained within them, unknown perhaps even to those who occasionally frequented them, the resources necessary for revolution and renewal:

Ah, Jerusalem, Jerusalem!
Is it for nothing our chapels were christened
with Hebrew names? The Book rusts
in the empty pulpits above empty
pews, but the Word ticks inside
remorselessly as the bomb that is timed soon to go off.[30]

In order to realize its present potential, the Methodist Church will need to:

- realize that the way we've looked at things before can inform our current identity, and need not be an embarrassment, a straitjacket or an irrelevance;
- allow such a historical perspective to re-engender confidence and creativity as we seek to commend a sacred text and a living faith to a sceptical, postmodern age;
- work hard and afresh to engage passionately in that apologetic task, and refuse to retreat from dialogue, especially with the communities, social, industrial, philosophical, politic, and scientific beyond the church;
- rediscover the value of hymnody in enabling Scripture to come alive for the believer and allow this to inform what music we choose for public worship;
- encourage and equip its people to become poets as they read, ponder, pray over, and interpret the Bible.

Notes

1 W. Brueggemann, *Awed to Heaven: Rooted in Earth*, Minneapolis: Fortress Press, 2003, p. 81.

2 Ann writes as Ann Barker, and her books are published by Robert Hale.

3 This is a reference to the training material used by the British Methodist Church for the initial training of local preachers. *Faith and Worship*, Peterborough: Methodist Publishing House, 1991.

4 *A Lamp to my Feet and a Light to my Path*, Peterborough: Methodist Publishing House, 1998.

5 The practice of arguing a point based on the use of a single short text from Scripture to the exclusion of other passages.

6 L. P. Hartley, *The Go-between*, London: Hamish Hamilton, 1953.

7 F. Buechner, *Wishful Thinking: A Theological ABC*, New York: Harper & Row, 1973, pp. 8–9.

8 Buechner, *Wishful Thinking*, p. 8.

9 R. Dawkins, *The God Delusion*, New York: Mariner Books, 2008, p. 319.

10 In Locke's case, *The Reasonableness of Christianity* (1695), which took a scriptural, but characteristically Enlightenment, view of the faith.

11 Voltaire (ed. John Iverson), *Philosophical Dictionary*, New York: Barnes and Noble, 2006, p. 233.

12 Voltaire (ed. Iverson), *Philosophical Dictionary*, p. 335.

13 See, among others, Theodore Runyon, *The New Creation*, Nashville: Abingdon Press, 1998, pp. 70–81; David Hempton, *Methodism: Empire of the Spirit*, New Haven and London: Yale University Press, 2005, p. 50; Henry Rack, *Reasonable Enthusiast*, London: Epworth Press, 1992, pp. 383–5.

14 John Wesley, *Explanatory Notes upon the New Testament*, London: Wesleyan Methodist Book Room, referring to 1 Corinthians 14.20.

15 *United Methodist Hymnal*, 595.

16 *The Standard Sermons of John Wesley, Vol. I*, London: Epworth Press, 1955, p. 32.

17 Voltaire (ed. Iverson), *Philosophical Dictionary*, pp. 182–3.

18 D. Hempton, *Methodism: Empire of the Spirit*, pp. 36–7.

19 So, for instance, his most famous plea, the sermon on *The Catholic Spirit*, which he based on the story in 2 Kings 10 of Jehu and Jehonadab.

20 See *The Standard Sermons of John Wesley* numbers 2, 37 and 38.

21 Comments made by Revd Dr John Newton in a public lecture at Aurora University, Illinois, 16 April 2008: 'Methodist Spirituality in the hymns of Charles Wesley'.

22 D. Hempton, *Methodism: Empire of the Spirit*, pp. 71–3.

23 *Hymns and Psalms* 745; again, I am indebted to Dr Newton for this reference.

24 *Hymns and Psalms*, 216.

25 *Hymns and Psalms*, 434.

26 Quoted by Susan White in 'Charles Wesley and Contemporary Theology', in K. G. C. Newport and T. A. Campbell, *Charles Wesley: Life, Literature & Legacy*, Peterborough: Epworth Press, 2007, p. 525.

27 *Lectio divina* (Latin for 'divine reading') is a traditional method of praying with Scripture aimed at gaining insight into the text.

28 Rubem Alves, *The Poet, The Warrior, The Prophet*, London: SCM Press, 2002, pp. 102–3.

29 White, in Newport and Campbell (eds), *Charles Wesley*, p. 527.

30 'Waiting', in R. S. Thomas, *Collected Poems 1945–1990*, London: Phoenix, 2000, p. 468.

3

A Sacramental Faith

MARTIN RAMSDEN

The Methodist Church recognizes two sacraments namely baptism and the Lord's Supper as of divine appointment and of perpetual obligation of which it is the privilege and duty of members of the Methodist Church to avail themselves.[1]

Reflecting on Experience: The Missiological Power of the Sacraments

I was baptized at Portobello Street Methodist Church in Hull on 26 February 1973. I was three months old. I don't remember it. My family then attended church until I was four years old before drifting away. It wasn't until I was 14 that I started going back to church again. In the intervening years I had never once thought about the significance of my baptism. I had looked back at the photographs but it didn't strike me as particularly meaningful. At the age of 16 I was confirmed and during the preparation my minister asked me if I had been baptized. When I said yes there was a sigh of relief because, it was explained, I needed to be baptized before I could be confirmed. But the reason for this wasn't made clear and I still didn't think about the significance of my baptism, I just pressed on, was confirmed and received into the membership of the Methodist Church. When I was 19 I experienced a sense of calling to be a Methodist minister. This became clear to me as a sense of calling to baptize people. As I worked through this, with the guidance of the church, I finally started to understand that the baptism I had received in infancy had continuing relevance for my life in Christ.

As a 15-year-old worshipping at Hull Methodist Central Hall I received Holy Communion for the first time and I remember it vividly. In receiving Communion I felt that I had taken a significant step in my faith which I would not be able, nor did I want, to step back from. For me this sharing in communion was in some sense a converting ordinance and, in every sense, a confirming ordinance, terms I will explain later. I have never looked back. From that time on, the Lord's Supper has been precious. I remember the sense of gravitas that accompanied the words, 'Please stand and turn to page B12', the page on which the communion service started in the 1974 *Methodist Service Book*.[2] Today, usually as celebrant, I value greatly the regular participation in the Lord's Supper facilitated by the various seasonally appropriate liturgies of the current *Methodist Worship Book*.

In reflecting on these experiences I ask myself some questions:

- Why did Holy Communion become so special to me so quickly? What is its power?
- Why, for so many years, did I not regard my baptism as significant for my life as a disciple of Jesus? Would I have been helped if I had?
- What is the importance of baptism and Holy Communion for Christian discipleship?

Reflecting on these questions I have become more aware of the missiological potential of the sacraments. The mission of God, and our role within that mission, can be communicated to us in the sacraments and the sacraments play an important role in the formation of the Church as God's missionary people in the world.

In recent times there have been some significant developments in thinking about mission within British Methodism. In 2000 the Methodist Conference approved the document *Our Calling*, which defined the calling of the Methodist Church under four headings:

- *Worship*
- *Learning and Caring*

- *Service*
- *Evangelism.*[3]

A subsequent Conference considered it appropriate, within the parameters of *Our Calling*, to establish *Priorities* in order to focus 'prayers, resources, imagination and commitments'. In doing so it set the overriding priority for the British Methodist Church as:

To proclaim and affirm its conviction of God's love in Christ, for us and for all the world; and renew confidence in God's presence and action in the world and in the church.

In order to realize this priority the Church committed itself to address five particularly pressing mission-driven concerns. Among these concerns are the need to underpin everything we do with God-centred worship and prayer and to develop our capacity to speak of God and faith in ways that make sense to all involved. The sacraments of baptism and the Lord's Supper are crucially important here: they have the potential to keep our worship and prayers God-centred, and they enable us to speak richly about God and faith in ways that make sense. So in this chapter I am seeking to encourage a mission-shaped sacramental understanding within Methodism which may well lead us to imagine fresh expressions of the sacraments appropriate to the present age.

Sacraments in Methodist Tradition

An emphasis on the sacraments of baptism and the Lord's Supper is consistently applied throughout Methodist documents on Faith and Order. The 1999 Methodist Conference report on ecclesiology, *Called to Love and Praise*, affirms 'the centrality of the sacraments of Baptism and Eucharist' as characteristics which are essential to the church.[4] John Wesley understood the term 'sacrament' as referring to 'an outward sign of inward grace, and a means whereby we receive the same'.[5] He spoke of them as 'ordinary channels whereby He [God] might convey to men[6] preventing, justifying, or sanctifying grace'.[7] Or put another way, the sacraments work to convey to humanity the mysterious love of God which is:

- demonstrated in the life, death and resurrection of Jesus Christ before humanity is itself able to respond (preventing or prevenient grace);[8]
- received through repentant faith, setting humans free from the guilt of sin as they experience God's forgiveness (justifying grace);[9]
- continuously poured out, leading a disciple to grow in grace and holiness towards 'the measure of the stature of the fullness of Christ' (sanctifying grace).[10]

Yet Wesley did not view the grace signified in the sacraments to be automatically applied to humanity independent of faith. On the contrary, Wesley cautioned against a reliance on the mere 'form of godliness, without the power'.[11] Indeed, Wesley counsels:

In using all means, seek God alone. In and through every outward thing, look singly to the power of His Spirit, and the *merits* of His Son. Beware you do not stick in the *work* itself; if you do, it is all lost labour ... Remember also, to use all means *as means*; as ordained, not for their own sake, but in order to the renewal of your soul in righteousness and true holiness. If, therefore, they actually tend to this, well; but, if not, they are dung and dross.[12]

Wesley was at pains to demonstrate that the outward and visible sacramental sign pointed to, but did not in itself achieve, the inward and spiritual grace that it signified. This reasoning is especially clear in his thinking about the sign of baptism which he seeks to distinguish from the new birth which it signifies. The reason for this is that he wanted to convince his hearers that they should not think of themselves as justified in the sight of God and born again, simply because they had been baptized. He argued that it was possible to deny one's baptism by choosing to live in a manner inconsistent with and rebellious to the inward and spiritual grace of God which it signified.[13] All of this points to an important emphasis in Wesley's theology of the need to be seeking after God:

> Settle this in your heart, that the *opus operatum*, the mere *work done*, profiteth nothing; that there is no *power* to save but in the Spirit of God, no *merit*, but in the blood of Christ; that, consequently, even what God ordains conveys no grace to the soul, if you trust not in Him alone. On the other hand, he that does truly trust in Him cannot fall short of the grace of God, even though he were cut off from every outward ordinance, though he were shut up in the centre of the earth.[14]

So for Wesley, God is not restricted only to minister grace to human hearts by virtue of outward signs, nor is God constrained to minister grace to human hearts through mere outward signs practised as mechanical ritual without a desire to seek after God, but when these outward signs are celebrated in the context of being truly open to and seeking after God, then we can know them to be 'ordinary channels of conveying His grace into the souls of men'.[15]

Let us now consider how the sacraments of baptism and the Lord's Supper might be understood today as conveying God's grace to human beings.

How Might Sacraments Convey Grace?

In right relationship with the word

Presbyters are ordained to a ministry of word and sacrament. These two elements are most helpfully understood as being inter-related. The word is to be proclaimed and taught in a manner which gives the sacraments their proper context in the church's self-understanding. Sacraments should be practised in such a way that they amplify the word, declaring through visible and tangible sign what is proclaimed and taught in the life of the community. This is a very important consideration in understanding how a sacrament is able to convey grace. This is because a sacrament, like any sign, derives its meaning from the cultural-linguistic context in which it is set.[16] As Kevin Vanhoozer, the American systematic theologian, has argued, 'Language creates a "world," that is, a cultural framework in which we live and move and process our experience.'[17] What we understand by a visible and tangible sign is dependent upon the interpretative context in which the sign is used. For instance, a red light at a junction on a road can be understood to mean 'stop' because of its context in a set of ideas about safe road use. Without the ideas the red light would just be a red light. Therefore without the careful establishment of widely known and accepted ideas signs cannot effectively signify meaning.

Sacraments are understood to convey the grace of God to human hearts. This is most effective when the human context of ideas in which they are practised is properly established and carefully maintained. The sacraments, therefore, can be understood as means of grace as they are celebrated in right relationship to the proclamation and teaching of the gospel.

As enactments of the Gospel

This is closely related to and develops the notion that word and sacrament belong together. It is clear, however, that sacraments are intended to be more than visual aids for the proclaimed word, they are themselves dramatic presentations of the Gospel and its benefits. This principle is explored, in connection with baptism, by the German Lutheran theologian Edmund Schlink, who wrote:

> There is a flatly mechanical way of baptizing which is satisfied with the barest essentials even when there is no emergency ... While the validity of such baptisms cannot be questioned, the perfunctory manner of their administration permits neither the baptized nor the congregation to recognize the riches of what God is here doing for them.[18]

This is not an argument for a heavily ritualized sacramental performance. Sometimes the over-elaboration of sacramental ritual can be just as effective at obscuring the drama of salvation as the overly-minimalist celebration. But it does suggest that the manner in which a sacrament is performed is important and deserves critical attention. This is because the sacraments are dramatic re-presentations of the gospel of God's grace and this is one way in which they are able to convey grace to our souls.

As invitations to participate in the drama of salvation

If sacraments are to be thought of as dramatic re-presentations of the gospel of God's grace then it needs to be acknowledged that the spectacle is not just for watching. Rather the sacraments present the drama of salvation in a way that invites participation. The baptismal liturgy in the *United Methodist Book of Worship* expresses this well when it declares 'Brothers and sisters in Christ: Through the Sacrament of Baptism ... we are incorporated in God's mighty acts of salvation.'[19] This articulates well the sense of the baptismal command of Christ as found in Matthew 28.19. As Matthew presents the narrative of God's mighty acts of salvation in Jesus Christ so, at the Gospel's conclusion, the setting of the drama is extended both in terms of geography and time. As the eleven, gathered on the Galilean mountain, are directed to go out into all the world and make disciples through baptizing and teaching, the reader understands that by also having received the message and the sign they too have been caught up in the story. In baptism, as a sign of discipleship, the Christian is incorporated in God's mighty acts of salvation and by obeying everything that Christ commanded, the Christian is compelled to continue the story by further ministering God's grace to others.

In a similar way, the sacrament of the Lord's Supper engages us not simply as spectators but as participators. The current British Methodist Conference Report on Holy Communion, *His Presence Makes the Feast*, expresses this when it says, 'the language of the service recreates in words the original drama and allows the worshipper to become both participant and beneficiary in the saving act'.[20] It is not just the language of the service that makes this possible. The sacrament involves 'word, gesture, action, taste', it involves the dynamics of taking and eating and drinking.[21] In Holy Communion, as in baptism, the worshipper is incorporated within the mighty saving acts of God. The sacraments are not just dramatic re-presentations of the gospel, they are invitations to participate in the drama of salvation. In this sense they are effective in conveying the grace of God to our souls. As Kendra Hotz and Matthew Mathews have recently stated:

> We do not simply recall facts from the distant past; we remember and re-tell the stories of our faith in an identity constituting way. To remember the night on which Jesus was betrayed is to participate once again in the central drama of the faith, to be pulled afresh into the foundational story of our identities.[22]

As occasions for meeting with God

The sense in which God is present to us in the sacraments has been a cause of intense and prolonged debate throughout the history of the Church. There is not space in this chapter to revisit these debates[23] but *His Presence Makes the Feast* gives an excellent and succinct account of this aspect of understanding the Lord's Supper. It speaks of the different possible understandings of Christ's presence at the Eucharist without specifying which particular understanding or combination of understandings are acceptable in British Methodism. For Methodists, who by nature tend to be pragmatists, it is often more important to recognize the potential for meeting with God in the sacraments rather than worrying too much about how this is possible.[24]

Through the sheer power of symbol

His Presence Makes the Feast is especially helpful in exploring the power of symbol. In the report symbol is described as 'an object, event, action or person that establishes a connection – a bridge between two worlds'.[25] In this sense the simple everyday elements of water, bread, and wine can be said to convey grace to humanity as they establish a connection between the ordinary everyday experience of humankind, on the one hand, and the presence and purposes of God on the other. Water, the element of physical cleansing, refreshing, and new life is used to speak to us of God's cleansing of our souls by applying to us the merits of Christ's death and resurrection by the power of the Holy Spirit. Bread and wine, physical elements of a simple meal, convey grace to humankind as they symbolize the great banquet of the Kingdom to which Christ calls us and which he invites us to share. Through the elements of physical nutrition and sustenance the spiritual sustenance offered by God and applied to us through the working of the Holy Spirit in our lives is powerfully set forth.

Through the deepening of community

Mons A. Teig, a Lutheran professor of worship, argues that 'a private baptism is a contradiction in terms'.[26] By this he means that, because baptism is the sacramental sign of initiation into the Church, the whole Church has a stake and a responsibility in the ministry of baptism. The *United Methodist Book of Worship* emphasizes this exceptionally well in its 'Services of the Baptismal Covenant' by including the following rich responses:

> Will you nurture one another in the Christian faith and life and include *these persons* now before you in your care?

> With God's help we will proclaim the good news and live according to the example of Christ. We will surround *these persons* with a community of love and forgiveness, that they may grow in their trust of God, and be found faithful in their service to others. We will pray for them, that they may be true disciples who walk in the way that leads to life.[27]

This represents a vital aspect of the sacraments as they signify God's grace to humankind. They express to us that we are not intended to be isolated beings motivated by self-interest and content to be self-sufficient. Neither are we intended by God to exist in our own self-selected communities gathered around commonalities of race, status, ability, or wealth. Rather we are invited into the all-embracing community of God as the proper context for our existence and our growth (cf. Gal. 3.27–29). Baptism is the sacramental sign of belonging to that community through God's gracious invitation. The Lord's Supper is the sacramental meal which signifies our ongoing sharing in community with Christ and one another. Indeed, the regular sharing of the sacramental sign of the new community in Christ has the potential, when received by faith in the power of the Spirit, to constantly renew and deepen that sense of community.

The Missiological Potential of the Sacraments

The sacraments draw on story, symbol, and ritual to communicate the good news of God in Jesus Christ and, through them, God extends an invitation to human beings, beckoning us to participate in the drama of salvation. Recently, story, symbol, and ritual have been identified as key factors in society's ongoing search for meaning and identity. The British theologian Ross Thompson has suggested that a 'rite' or 'ritual' can be thought of as 'a repeated action that derives its meaning from its human context of ideas, rather than from practical needs'.[28] A good example of this is the celebration of a birthday by baking a cake, lighting candles, singing 'Happy Birthday', and blowing the candles out. These actions are meaningful because of their location within a cultural-linguistic framework and don't show forth obvious meaning at the level of physical need. This ritual is a way of celebrating and participating in the narrative of a person's life and marking a significant moment along the way. The birthday celebration will feel meaningful or meaningless depending on the love and care shown by participants for the individual in the rest of the year rather than on the ritual itself.[29] The point is that effective ritual grows out of and establishes patterns of being.

Rituals are all around us. Some of them are generally positive and life-affirming like the gathering of family and friends to show genuine love to an individual at a birthday party. Many are less positive, having their context of ideas, their narrative, located in patterns of being that are ultimately meaningless, even destructive. This has been recognized by John Drane in his book *The McDonaldization of the Church*, in which he reflects on the important place of story and narrative in contemporary society:

> The danger is that we will allow the narratives that inform our lives to be provided by the phony stories of consumerism, in which the security of true wisdom will be replaced by sporadic choices and feel good experiences. We are seeing the consequences of this all around us, as people are identified primarily by the style of their clothes, or by what they drink, or by the sort of cars they drive. Not only does this kind of story lack the power to form community, but at worst it can also encourage privatism and a destructive form of individualism. If the only thing available to us is a fragmented and meaningless story, then we inevitably become meaningless and fragmented persons ourselves.[30]

This view of popular culture has within it a measure of truth that we can see displayed in rituals all around us. There is nothing wrong with the family's ritualistic trips to the shopping mall, but when the desire to consume becomes all-consuming then there is a need for a more life-giving narrative to be introduced. There is nothing wrong with meeting friends for a drink at the local pub, but when such meetings regularly lead to excessive consumption culminating in violence or illness or casual sex, and when such patterns constitute something of a ritualized identity narrative, then the narrative and the ritual need to be addressed. There is nothing wrong with taking a holiday but when life comes to be understood as a quest in which meaning is located in seeing as many places as possible before dying, then the ritualized identity narrative can be shown to be false. Rituals like these and many others can be seen all around us.

The Christian gospel is a life-giving narrative with the power to offer people an alternative vision of reality which is rooted in the boundless love of God for God's creation. This rich narrative is set forth in word and sacrament, in ritual which is embedded in the context of ideas that is God's dramatic saving activity for human-kind. In what follows I consider the sacraments of baptism and the Lord's Supper in turn, reflecting on my experience of them in a British Methodist context and imagining how Methodism might helpfully evolve in order that the sacraments might set forth more clearly the abundant life that God offers to us in Jesus.

Baptism

At the outset of this chapter I referred to my own baptism and how I have, in recent years, started to grow in understanding the ongoing importance of that sacrament in my life as a disciple of Jesus. As I have grown in my own appreciation of baptism I have become increasingly aware of three particular challenges to our baptismal thought and practice with which the church needs urgently to engage. These are:

1 How to respond to the many requests for infant baptism received from families who would not normally worship with the church.
2 How to prepare adult converts for baptism so that they will receive the sacrament fruitfully and grow in the life of discipleship.
3 How to enable ordinary Christian people to develop a sense of the significance of their own baptism.

The missiological challenge of infant baptism

Baptism, as the sacrament of entry into the church, has very obvious relevance for mission. Indeed the sacrament finds its whole rationale in the context of mission. The *Methodist Worship Book* cites two scriptural passages at the outset of its baptismal liturgies.[31] These are Matthew 28.18b–20 and Acts 2.38b–39. These passages clearly locate baptism within the context of the missionary activity of the church as it engages in the post-resurrection mission of making disciples of Christ. The baptismal command of Christ in Matthew 28.19 situates baptismal ministry within a complex of activities intended to call new people into discipleship and to establish them in this new way of life. Similarly, Acts 2.38b–39 locates the commencement of the church's ministry of baptizing in the context of proclamation of the gospel (Acts 2.14–36) and the desire of new converts to respond to that gospel in repentance (Acts 2.37–38a). Baptism, therefore, takes place as a sign of God's reconfigured new life characterized by allegiance to the crucified and risen Jesus and empowered by the Holy Spirit. Baptism was always intended to be missiological.

The Methodist Church is committed to baptizing both converts to the faith and their children. This commitment to baptizing children 'in appropriate circumstances' has its roots in a particular interpretation of Scripture.[32] Acts 16.15, Acts 16.33 and 1 Corinthians 1.16, whilst not proving that children were baptized in the biblical period, refer to the practice of household baptisms in the earliest days of the Church. These baptisms were carried out on the profession of faith of the head of the household. By the third century, it had become the widespread practice of the Church to baptize the children of converts to the faith.[33] The reasoning for this would seem to include some recognition that the child of a disciple is nurtured in an environment of repentant discipleship; therefore the sacramental sign of belonging to the household of God is appropriate from the beginning of that process of nurture.

The notion of baptizing infants of those who choose not to be part of the community of faith is difficult to sustain from Scripture. This was recognized in the last full British Methodist report on baptism, *Christian Initiation* (1987) which stated that 'a baptismal practice which does not hold grace and faith in sufficient balance, such as "indiscriminate baptism", is much less easy to justify from the New Testament'.[34] Surprisingly it did not refer to the World Council of Churches document *Baptism, Eucharist and Ministry*. This important ecumenical document offered churches the following challenge:

In order to overcome their differences, believer Baptists and those who practice infant baptism should reconsider certain aspects of their practices. The first may seek to express more visibly the fact that children are placed under the protection of God's grace. The latter must guard themselves against the practice of apparently indiscriminate baptism and take more seriously their responsibility for the nurture of baptized children to mature commitment to Christ.[35]

This serious consideration of the church's responsibility for the nurture of the baptized to mature commitment to Christ is in need of review within Methodism. Increasingly, the culture in which we seek to minister is being described as post-Christian.[36] One manifestation of this post-Christian cultural setting is that there are many families, whom we seek to serve, who approach the church for baptism for an infant even though they have little sense of what the church understands baptism to be. For many, nurtured in a society regarded as post-Christian, there is a continuing attachment to Christian ritual without a related sense of how that ritual dramatically presents and involves us in God's saving activity. This process has been going on for some time. Consider the Faith and Order comments to Conference in 1952:

> The spread of unbelief, indifference to religion and nominal Christianity in Western Europe has created a difficult situation in relation to the administration of Infant Baptism. The mixed character of a community which is neither Christian or pagan gives rise to acute practical problems. It is notorious that many parents who do not themselves attend Church, seek baptism for their children, often with the most vague and erroneous ideas about its meaning, and with no intention of accepting the solemn obligations involved.[37]

Over 50 years later the situation is even more difficult. The Church exists in a society in which the understanding of Christianity by many is very limited. As far back as 1992 John Finney published research suggesting that for about half of the population there were no or very few Christian resonances and that this group is growing rather than declining.[38] From experience I can testify, along with many ministerial colleagues, that very often those who request baptism for their children could be described in such a way. This makes the pastoral practice of baptism very challenging. The Church of England report, *On the Way*, describes this very accurately:

> Parents may well be moved by little more than social convention or they may have profound but inarticulate feelings of their child's need of God's favour; they are likely to have very little sense of what may be expected of them. Clergy and congregation are often sharply aware of the demands as well as the joys of public Christian discipleship. The two groups have very different starting points and there is often, in the nature of things, too little time for the clash of expectations to be explored.[39]

In these challenging circumstances the church has developed ways of understanding baptism that have helped it to come to terms with responding positively to requests like these. These understandings tend to be underpinned by a commitment to the notion that baptism is a sign of God's prevenient grace.[40] This view of baptism is not inaccurate but it is partial. Baptism is not merely a sign of God's prevenient grace, it is more properly understood as a sign of God's saving grace. This saving grace of God is prevenient (in the sense that it precedes our ability to respond), it is justifying (in the sense that it is received by repentant faith through which humanity is freed from the guilt of sin), and it is sanctifying (in that it enables the believer, in the power of the Holy Spirit to grow in grace and holiness). All of this is apparent in the celebration of baptism when the children of Christian parents are baptized. The prevenience is demonstrated most clearly here as the sacrament is offered before the child can make any response. However, the justifying and sanctifying grace is also apparent as the family and the entire community of faith pledge to nurture the infant in the faith of his or her baptism. Here the sacrament of baptism is performed in a manner that is clearly connected to the context of ideas which gives it its meaning. This is simply not the case when baptism is celebrated purely as 'a rite of welcome' or as 'a good experience of the church'. Here the context of ideas in which we experience baptism is being distorted and therefore we are not practising baptism in a way that is fully God-centred and we are not taking the opportunity to speak richly of God in ways that make sense.

Earlier in this piece I referred to the importance of word and sacrament belonging together in order that sacraments can effectively convey God's grace. I referred to the sacraments as dramatic presentations of the gospel in which the worshippers are invited to participate. I referred to the sheer power of symbol to establish a point of connection – a bridge between worlds. I referred to the sense in which a natural outcome of the sacraments is a deepening of community. In all of this I suggested that the sacraments ritually present an identity narrative which has the power to subvert and replace the various meaningless and damaging identity narratives of our age. The sacrament of baptism is all of this. We need to find ways to offer it in such a way that this becomes clear to those who seek it for their children or themselves. This will not be easy and it will demand a real shift in the culture of the Church and in the way it engages with society.

The missiological challenge of baptizing adults

Our Calling defines evangelism by saying that 'the church exists to make more followers of Jesus Christ'. The American Methodist scholar William Abraham, in his book *The Logic of Evangelism*, suggests an understanding of what it might mean to make a follower of Jesus Christ. He defines evangelism as 'that set of intentional activities which is governed by the goal of initiating people into the kingdom of God for the first time'.[41] Abraham argues that this initiation into the rule of God in an individual's life will involve 'a complex web of reality'.[42] This 'complex web' involves engaging with a person in a multidimensional way. So evangelism includes:

- a certain cognitive dimension in appropriating the logic of the Christian gospel;
- a communal dimension as a person is rooted in the love and support of the church as signified through baptism;
- a moral dimension which involves the handing on of a particular moral framework;

- an experiential dimension that will involve a person in experiencing the assurance given by the Holy Spirit;
- a dimension characterized by a willingness on the part of a person to serve God in the church and in the world;
- a dimension that is focused on the transmission of spiritual disciplines to enable growth and development in discipleship, for instance, prayer, Bible reading, Holy Communion.[43]

Of course, as Abraham acknowledges, people become rooted in Christian discipleship not as a result of 'human enterprise driven simply by earthly passion and planning' but because of God's gracious action in people's lives.[44] However, the Church is called, in response to the command of Christ, to make disciples (Matt. 28.18–20). This then implies that the Church has a role to play in co-operating with God's grace such that disciples might be made. This is, according to *Our Calling*, the task of evangelism, and Abraham presents us with a comprehensive understanding of this task.

Priorities for the Methodist Church focuses our energies on 'developing confidence in evangelism' and on 'encouraging fresh ways of being church'. The outworking of these priorities in a post-Christian context will increasingly involve us in the task of initiating people into the Kingdom of God. In doing this the church will need to remember that making disciples is a complex web, a multidimensional activity. It will be important to think carefully about how we baptize new adult disciples (or help them to reflect on a baptism received in infancy). It will be important also to think through strategies for ensuring that this initiation into the people of God is also initiation into the Kingdom of God in the sense proposed by Abraham.[45]

The missiological challenge of the Church's baptismal self-understanding

Martin Luther once wrote:

In Baptism, therefore, every Christian has enough to study and to practice all his life. He always has enough to believe firmly what baptism promises and brings – victory over death and the devil, forgiveness of sin, God's grace, the entire Christ, and the Holy Spirit with his gifts. In short, the blessings of Baptism are so boundless that if timid nature considers them, it may well doubt whether they can all be true.[46]

In Romans 6.1–11, Paul writes about baptism as a baptism into the death and the resurrection of Christ. He writes in verse 11 that we must consider ourselves dead to sin and alive to God in Christ Jesus. Thus baptism is presented as a paradigm for Christian living. Reflection on our baptisms and all that they symbolize serves as a spiritual resource to enable growth in discipleship.

The ordination services in the *Methodist Worship Book* stress the importance of understanding our baptism as an initiation and calling into Christian ministry:

All Christians are called through their Baptism and by the hearing of God's word to ministry and service among the whole people of God and in the life of the world. ... All who are received into the Church by Baptism are called to proclaim the mighty acts of God in Jesus Christ our Saviour, and to serve him in the Church and in the world.[47]

Only a relatively small number of Methodists are able to attend ordinations and they are such infrequent occasions that these words are unlikely to penetrate very deeply. In addition words like these do not appear elsewhere in the liturgies of the British Methodist Church. Even the baptism and confirmation liturgies themselves do not bring out very strongly the relationship between baptism and Christian vocation.

I fear many Methodists rarely consider the meaning of their own baptism or its relevance for their understanding of and growth in discipleship. The Church needs very carefully to reconsider what it does in the practice of baptismal ministry because its actions in this respect are powerful in forming what Methodists believe about baptism. This is precisely the danger of regularly celebrating baptism as a rite of infancy, of welcome, as a good experience of the church; this is the difficulty that we store up for ourselves when we regularly celebrate baptisms as private or semi-private affairs away from the gathered congregation; this is the problem when we satisfy ourselves with the poverty of symbolism apparent in fonts of miniscule proportions scarcely applying any water to the candidate's head: what is done will inevitably shape what is believed about baptism. When we celebrate baptism as something apart from any expectation of discipleship then we shape people in a belief that baptism has little or nothing to do with discipleship. When we celebrate baptism away from the gathered congregation, for those that we have no realistic expectation will ever return to church, then we shape people in a belief that baptism has nothing to do with belonging to the community of Christ. When we content ourselves with minimalism in our symbolism then we shape people in a belief that baptism is no big deal. Baptism is a paradigm for the Christian life of discipleship; it is the sacramental sign of new birth, of new identity in God, of new vocation in the church and the world; it is incorporation into the mighty saving acts of God. All of this is big stuff. Our baptismal practice should be reconsidered so that Methodists can grow in understanding the significance of baptism for their ongoing life of discipleship.

The Lord's Supper

Often we in the Methodist Church can overlook the sense in which the Lord's Supper is a missionary sacrament. In what follows I explore some areas relating to the practice of the Lord's Supper as it relates to mission. These reflections relate to the ongoing potential for understanding the Lord's Supper as a converting, confirming and nurturing ordinance.

The missiological role of the Lord's Supper as a converting ordinance

In referring to my own experience of the Lord's Supper I reflected that to a certain extent I received Holy Communion as a converting ordinance. I don't mean by this that it caused me to make a

'Damascus Road' type leap from not believing one moment to believing the next. Rather, as part of a journey in progress, this sharing in Communion played a key role in causing me to recognize Christ, to accept him as my risen Lord and Saviour. Such an understanding of the Lord's Supper has a clear biblical precedent. Luke 24.13–35 tells the story of Cleopas and his friend, on the day of resurrection, journeying to Emmaus. They are joined on the road by Jesus, but 'their eyes were kept from recognizing him' (verse 16). As they arrived at Emmaus they asked 'the stranger' to stay and share food with them. At table he 'took bread, blessed and broke it and gave it to them' (verse 30; cf. 22.19). At this moment they recognized who this 'stranger' really was. The account concludes in verse 35, 'how he had been made known to them in the breaking of the bread'.

John Wesley saw the Lord's Supper as a 'converting ordinance' in just the way suggested by this story from Luke and experienced in my own faith journey. *His Presence Makes the Feast* summarizes this well:

When John Wesley saw Holy Communion as a 'converting ordinance', he did so in the context of a serious search for salvation. He assumed that the 'unconverted' who came to Holy Communion would be members of the societies, 'desiring to flee from the wrath to come' and would have assumed a very serious search for God. He believed that, within the context of experiencing the vividness of the sign, the 'penny would drop' for many and they would receive the necessary assurance that Christ had indeed died for them and achieved their salvation.[48]

The missiological role of the Lord's Supper as a confirming ordinance

I understand the term 'confirming' here to be equivalent to 'strengthening'. I am suggesting, therefore, that regular participation in Holy Communion strengthens believers and confirms them in their discipleship, in their relationship with God and in the household of God, the Church. This is an important aspect of thinking about the sacrament as a means of grace. It is something that many Christians would testify to in their own experience of Holy Communion. For this reason it is important that those coming to faith are introduced to the Lord's Supper, helped to understand something of its significance and encouraged to participate. As the Church grows through fresh expressions of Christian community meeting in a variety of different contexts and often in the absence of anyone authorized to preside at the Lord's Supper, the church needs to think carefully about how it can provide for the sacramental life of these communities. This is necessary if we are to help these emerging expressions of church to keep their worship and prayers God-centred and enable them to become confident in speaking of God and faith in rich ways that make sense.

The missiological role of the Lord's Supper as a nurturing ordinance

As a father of two children, aged seven and five, I have marvelled as I have seen them grow in their understanding of Christian faith as they have received communion. Both of them have received communion since their bodies were developed enough to process bread. I, therefore, rejoice in the policy of the British Methodist Church 'that it be considered normal practice for baptized children, as members of the whole body of Christ, to participate in Holy Communion by receiving bread and wine, irrespective of age'.[49] The full inclusion of children at the Eucharist has the immense benefits of helping children to feel fully a part of the community of faith and to help them in their faith and discipleship by offering them the means of grace. The American theologian Mark P. Bangert has argued that such inclusion has benefits for the whole church as it develops a culture in which children are fully included, encouraged to bring their gifts to the community and to share them in worship and mission. He suggests that 'such communities live out that eschatological vision that proclaims God's tireless gathering of all humans, young and old, no matter what their emotional, physical, or intellectual capabilities'.[50] This brings us back to the sacraments as ritual presentations of God's saving activity, offering the world an alternative life-giving and meaningful narrative in which to find its identity.

Concluding Thoughts

In this chapter I have sought to encourage the church to value the sacraments of Baptism and Holy Communion as essential components of our involvement in God's mission to the world. Sacraments are a presentation of God's saving love for the world; they are invitations to participate in the drama of salvation. The sacraments help us to keep our worship and prayer God-centred. They are laden with rich potential to help us speak of God in ways that make sense but in order to realize its present potential the Methodist Church will need to:

- ensure that sacramental policies, proclamation and practice are in tune with one another so that the sacraments can be more clearly understood as dramatic presentations of God's story in which we are invited to participate;
- reconsider its approach to baptism focussing on how baptism can be practised and experienced in ways that make clear the intimate connection between baptism and a life of faithful discipleship;
- develop a growing sense of baptism as a sacrament of Christian identity and vocation which has continuing relevance for disciples all through their lives;
- give serious and urgent attention to strategies for developing sacramental life in emerging Christian communities;
- continue to invite and encourage full participation in the Eucharist by as many people as possible, emphasizing the value of Holy Communion as a converting, confirming and nurturing ordinance.

Notes

1 Methodist Church in Great Britain Deed of Union: Section 2.4.
2 Trustees for Methodist Church Purposes (TMCP), *The Methodist Service Book*, London: Methodist Publishing House, 1975.

3 This should really be five headings of course as *learning* and *caring* are separate things – it's very easy to lose sight of the discipleship imperative to learn by allowing ourselves to focus exclusively on *caring* in order to tick the box!

4 TMCP, 'Called to Love and Praise' (1999) in TMCP, *Statements and Reports of the Methodist Church on Faith and Order, Volume Two 1984–2000 Part One*, Peterborough: Methodist Publishing House, 2000, pp. 1–62, quoting from p. 22.

5 John Wesley, 'Sermon XII: The Means of Grace' in John Wesley, *Sermons on Several Occasions*, London: Epworth Press, 1944 pp. 134–51, quoting from p. 136.

6 All historical quotes in this chapter are presented in their original gendered form but should read inclusively.

7 Wesley, 'Means of Grace', p. 136. Note, Wesley only explicitly mentions the Lord's Supper in this context. It would seem that this is because he is addressing the baptized and so there is no need to exhort them to baptism. However, in his definition of a sacrament as a 'means by which we receive the same [inward grace]' there is a strong but implicit sense that Wesley regarded baptism as a means of grace too.

8 See Wesley, 'Sermon XXXVIII: Original Sin' in *Sermons on Several Occasions*, pp. 502–13 esp. pp. 512–13; 'Sermon I: Salvation by Faith' in *Sermons on Several Occasions*, pp. 1–11 esp. pp. 1–2; 'Sermon V: Justification by Faith' in *Sermons on Several Occasions*, pp. 49–61 esp. pp. 49–52.

9 Wesley, 'Sermon I: 'Salvation by Faith' in *Sermons on Several Occasions*, pp. 1–11, esp. pp. 2 and 4; 'Sermon V: Justification by Faith' in *Sermons on Several Occasions*, pp. 49–61 esp. pp. 52–4.

10 Wesley, 'Sermon XXXV: Christian Perfection' in *Sermons on Several Occasions*, pp. 457–80, esp. p. 462; 'Sermon XXXIX: The New Birth' in *Sermons on Several Occasions*, pp. 514–26, esp. pp. 519 and 523–4; 'Sermon V: Justification by Faith' in *Sermons on Several Occasions* , pp. 49–61, esp. p. 52.

11 12 13 Wesley, 'Sermon XXXIX: The New Birth' in *Sermons on Several Occasions*, pp. 514–26, esp. pp. 522–6. Note that Wesley stops short of contradicting the prayer book which proceeds from the supposition that, in the case of an infant, baptism does achieve the grace which it signifies and removes the imputed guilt of original sin. Cf. 'The New Birth', p. 523. Though Wesley taught the need for repentance and faith in later years in order to receive justification, new birth and sanctification he did not teach the need for rebaptism at this point. His baptismal theology may have been strengthened had he referred to such adult appropriation of salvation as a growing into or claiming of baptismal grace.

14 Wesley, 'Sermon XII: The Means of Grace' in *Sermons on Several Occasions*, p. 150.

15 Wesley, 'Sermon XII: The Means of Grace' in *Sermons on Several Occasions*, p. 135.

16 See Ross Thompson, *SCM Studyguide to the Sacraments*, London: SCM Press, 2006 p. 5.

17 Kevin J. Vanhoozer, *The Drama of Doctrine: A Canonical Linguistic Approach to Christian Theology*, Louisville, KY: Westminster John Knox Press, 2005, p. 74.

18 Edmund Schlink, *The Doctrine of Baptism*, trans. Herbert J. A. Bouman, St Louis: Concordia Publishing House, 1975, p. 205, quoted in Mons A. Tieg, 'Holy Baptism: Promise Big Enough For the World' in Thomas H. Schattauer (ed.), *Inside Out: Worship in an Age of Mission*, Minneapolis, MN: Augsburg Fortress, 1999, pp. 39–58; for quote see p. 40.

19 From 'Services of the Baptismal Covenant' in *The United Methodist Book of Worship*, Nashville, TN: United Methodist Publishing House, 1992, pp. 81–114, quoting from p. 87.

20 TMCP, *His Presence Makes the Feast: Holy Communion in the Methodist Church: The Faith and Order Report to the Methodist Conference 2003*, Peterborough: Methodist Publishing House, 2003, p. 57.

21 *His Presence*, p. 57.

22 Kendra Hotz and Matthew Mathews, *Shaping the Christian Life: Worship and the Religious Affections*, Louisville: Westminster John Knox Press, 2006.

23 Good introductions are available for further study. These include: Alister E. McGrath, *Christian Theology: An Introduction*, 4th edn, Oxford: Blackwell, 2006, pp. 419–44; Daniel L. Migliore, *Faith Seeking Understanding*, 2nd edn, Grand Rapids, MI: Eerdmans, 2004 pp. 206–30; and Thompson, *Sacraments*, pp. 143–59.

24 *His Presence*, pp. 67–9; cf. Neil Dixon, *Wonder, Love and Praise: A Companion to the Methodist Worship Book*, Peterborough: Epworth Press, 2003, pp. 77–8.

25 *His Presence*, p. 55.

26 Teig, 'Holy Baptism' in Schattauer (ed.), *Inside Out*, p. 48.

27 *United Methodist Book of Worship*, p. 89.

28 Thompson, *Sacraments*, p. 5.

29 Mark P. Bangert, 'Holy Communion: Taste and See' in Schattauer (ed.), *Inside Out*, pp. 59–86, esp. p. 68.

30 John Drane, *The McDonaldization of the Church: Spirituality, Creativity and the Future of the Church*, London: Darton, Longman and Todd, 2000, pp. 136–7.

31 These baptismal liturgies can be found in TMCP, *The Methodist Worship Book*, Peterborough: Methodist Publishing House, 1999, pp. 60–113; Scriptural references found on pp. 64, 77–8, 89, 104–5.

32 The non-committal term 'appropriate circumstances' comes from TMCP, *The Constitutional Practice and Discipline of the Methodist Church*

Volume 2 (2007), Peterborough: Methodist Publishing House, 2007, S.O. 520 (3) on p. 513.

33 McGrath, *Introduction*, p. 441.

34 TMCP, 'Christian Initiation (1987)' in *Statements and Reports, Volume Two, Part One* pp. 63–101 quoting from p. 70.

35 World Council of Churches, *Baptism, Eucharist and Ministry: Faith and Order Paper No. 111*, Geneva: World Council of Churches, 1982, p. 6.

36 *Mission-Shaped Church: Church Planting and Fresh Expressions of Church in a Changing Context*, London: Church House Publishing, 2004, pp. 11–12. See also the description of this cultural shift in Steven Croft, *Transforming Communities: Re-imagining the Church for the 21st Century*, London: Darton, Longman and Todd, 2002, pp. 20–29.

37 'Statement on Holy Baptism (1952)' in TMCP, *Statements and Reports of the Methodist Church on Faith and Order, Volume One 1933–1983*, Peterborough: Methodist Publishing House, 2000, pp. 33–38, quoting from p. 34.

38 John Finney, *Church on the Move*, London: Darton, Longman and Todd, 1992; quoted in General Synod of the Church of England, *On the Way: Towards an Integrated Approach to Christian Initiation*, London: Church House Publishing, 1995, p. 24.

39 General Synod, *On the Way*, p. 85.

40 This view is put forth in TMCP, 'Christian Initiation' (1987) p. 92, though see my critique in 'Heeding the Great Commission? A challenge to Methodist baptismal theology and practice' in *Epworth Review*, Volume 34 Number 4, October 2007, pp. 38–54.

41 William J. Abraham, *The Logic of Evangelism*, Grand Rapids, MI: Eerdmans, 1989 p. 95.

42 Abraham, *Logic*, p. 103.

43 Abraham, *Logic*, pp. 99–103.

44 Abraham, *Logic*, p. 103.

45 In recent years various denominations have sought to implement a form of the ancient catechumenate designed to help new disciples grow in faith and commitment when approaching baptism or confirmation. See International Commission for English in the Liturgy, *Rite for the Christian Initiation of Adults*, London: Geoffrey Chapman, 1985; Daniel Benedict, *Baptism and our Ministry of Welcoming Seekers and Making Disciples*, Nashville, TN: Discipleship Resources, 1996; Peter Ball and Malcolm Grundy, *Faith on the Way: A Practical Parish Guide to the Catechumenate*, London: Mowbray, 2000.

46 Martin Luther, 'The Large Catechism' in Theodore G. Tappert (ed. and trans.), *The Book of Concord: The Confessions of the Evangelical Lutheran Church*, Philadelphia, PA: Fortress Press, 1959 pp. 441–2 quoted in Tieg, 'Holy Baptism' in Schattauer (ed.), *Inside Out*, p. 41.

47 TMCP, *The Methodist Worship Book*, pp. 297 and 302.

48 TMCP, *His Presence*, p. 75.

49 TMCP, *Statements and Reports Volume Two, Part One*, pp. 176–92 quoting from p. 187.

50 Bangert, 'Holy Communion: Taste and See', p. 78.

4

A Diverse Faith

SHIRLYN TOPPIN

Introduction

There is a saying in the island of Tobago[1] that 'cockroach has no rights to be in fowl party'[2] and there have been many occasions when I have felt that saying epitomizes the varied experiences that I have encountered in my ministry thus far. These experiences have led me to question the validity of acceptance of my given ministry to the congregations for whom I have pastoral oversight. Is my presence simply tolerated because it is a good reflection on the Church, which, in theory, believes in the practice and celebration of diverse faith? Contrastingly, there are times when those queries cannot be substantiated; however, they are only few. Additionally, being female brings many challenges, given the androcentric nature of the society that we exist in: however, being Black, female and an immigrant[3] raises its own set of problems, not just in society, but more so in the Church. It 'poses challenges and discomfort for some and a sense of liberation for others depending upon the personal views or assumptions one may hold'.[4] Yet, in spite of the unceasing challenges, my solace is in knowing that God is the one who has called me, equipped me, and continues to walk with me in his ministry.

Monoculturalism and monoreligiosity are not words that can be applied to Britain. It is a diverse country and that diversity is here to stay. This is most visible in some of its major cities. It is seen in every aspect of society, including the established Churches that feature a substantial minority community in their midst. This

73

resulted from the missionary activities in the Caribbean of the established churches and the mass migration of African Caribbean people to what they considered as the 'mother land'.

The effects of non-acceptance and non-welcome have plagued the Black migrant[5] generation since the early days of the fifties and sixties with their arrival on British shores. Open disapproval of their presence was voiced by some of the local inhabitants and politicians of the day and many naively sought refuge in the established churches of their homeland, only to be further awakened by the sincere greeting 'You are not welcome'.

In spite of the intolerance faced in the British churches, they were committed to maintaining their presence, demonstrating Black resistance. Through their determination to 'stay put' and persevere in their struggles for justice, 'they strove to dismantle structures, policies and practices which had an adverse effect upon their lives',[6] believing that they had every right to worship in the denomination that had nurtured their spirituality in the Caribbean. This form of Black resistance has indeed paved the way for many people, including myself, to be where I am today, ministering as a young Black female Methodist minister to three White congregations. I have the opportunity to share my theology and faith praxis learnt from my upbringing and cultural heritage, which are inextricably linked with 'the struggles of our ancestors in Africa and the Caribbean, forged in relationship with a belief in the benevolent power of the Creator'.[7]

While the blatant 'You are not welcome', spoken to a generation in the past, may not be verbalized today, it is implicit in behavioural patterns and sarcastic comments, belying the message that all can find a place in the Church regardless of colour, creed, and race. Essentially, the Church should be a 'safe haven' through its preaching and exercising of pastoral care; it should follow the pattern of the early Church community in Acts 2.44–47. In a community of grace, welcome, acceptance, love and fellowship in action became a priority, embodying the life-transforming power of God's presence. The narrative clearly displays a collective and communal concept of care, negating the notion of individualism. Conversely, many people's concept of welcome is separate from their understanding of spirituality. Although they know their spiritual life is an essential element of the Christian faith, they practice discrimination, which is not in accordance with Scripture. The Church, a place that appears to be rather welcoming, has been known to be the least hospitable, not just to people of colour, but to anyone or anything that may disturb its comfortableness.

People of varying race, class, or gender should be accepted, in accordance with Peter's declaration, 'I truly understand that God shows no partiality, but in every nation anyone who fears him and does what is right is acceptable to him.'[8] However, though many say, 'I do not see colour' as a way of defending their bias, in essence they are simply saying, 'I do not acknowledge them.' Not seeing a person's skin colour conflicts with any belief in diversity.

In spite of the achievements of the Black migrant generation, the struggle goes on and total acceptance of multiculturalism, both in the Church and society, is still a hurdle to overcome for many White people, resulting in many present-day Black Methodists feeling wounded and alienated. Despite varying measures by the Methodist Church to embrace the diversities and complexities of the given situation, it falls remarkably short of the mark, due to its inability to promote any teaching of the Christian faith that is not academically White and middle class. It forgets that biblical hermeneutics must be grounded in the context of the readers, in order that they can identify themselves within the biblical narratives.

The Eurocentric interpretation of the Bible excludes Black people from within the story and if we are not excluded, we are portrayed in a negative light, hence we are envisaged as submissive slaves. 'Interpretation of Black experiences, Scripture and other evidence about one's culture is important, in order that one's identity is preserved and affirmed.'[9] In addition, there is a need to address the issue of leadership roles that undermines and disempowers people of a different ethnicity, through sheer ignorance and arrogance. This has become a problem, not just for Black people, but for women and people of a lower class income and education. It raises many questions about the future sustainability of the Church as a diverse organization.

I hope that my exploration of the similarities and differences I have experienced will not be dismissed as that of another Black person with a 'chip on their shoulder', but will be seen as a serious attempt to address the ongoing challenges of the diverse cultural roots in both the Church and society. I will develop this discussion using personal experiences as a young Black and female minister, while contrasting them with the experiences of the Black migrant generation who live in British society yet are not fully accepted. I will further outline how the influence of Black Christian educators can assist the Methodist Church to engage in meaningful dialogues and respond practically to the needs of its diverse faith people.

Young, Female and Black Minister

'This is not a criticism of you, but we know the members of the congregation more than you, and they are not happy, because you preach with such strong convictions!' This was the statement of the senior steward in one of my congregations. I was bemused to say the least at what I considered to be 'satanically orchestrated' words. I wondered if it was a dream that had turned into a nightmare. But it was real.

Would it be preferable to hear a minister preach with strong convictions, showing how Scripture speaks to people's lived realities, or one that preached on 'holidays in France'? I am of the view that the former would be more desirable. Likewise, many Christians are willing to engage in a serious dialogue with the Bible and Christian tradition, expecting radical transformation and growth in their spiritual life that will enable them to communicate their faith with confidence.

To be challenged on the sermon contents is inevitable, but to be criticized for the integrity of my faith was disparaging of my personhood and my cultural heritage, which in effect make the saying in Tobago that I alluded to in the introduction valid in my present context. Do I have to compromise my inherited beliefs in order to fit in? Is this another way of saying 'you are not welcome'? Seeking answers to these questions is not straightforward, yet, it is clear to me that however far the Church has come in addressing issues that are detrimental to the well being of all its people, it will always be a struggle for Black people.

It seems that we are constantly expected to 'prove ourselves', despite academic achievements, in order to find acceptance, not as 'house Negroes',[10] but as human beings validated only by God. I am reminded of the question posed by Robert Beckford in his book *Jesus is Dread*: 'what kind of freed slaves worship in the slave master's church?'[11] The answer, I hope, is: the ones who are committed to the empowerment and liberation of both Black and White people from institutional attitudes that have had a negative influence on their lives, and have become a poor reflection of the *Imago Dei*.

Furthermore, the remark that 'preaching with strong convictions' was creating unhappiness for that congregation was gravely disturbing. It led me to question the congregation's understanding of its theology, ecclesiology and missiology in the light of Scripture. Surely, they are not separate entities that speak to certain people and aspects of the church, but work as a whole to inform, direct, and challenge our thought processes.

As I pondered on the incident, and reacted as I deemed fit at the time, I saw that it raised a number of issues for the church. It became clearer that I was ministering to a vast number of people with an immature faith and no depth of spirituality, who expressed what the Black British theologian Anthony Reddie terms 'theology of good intentions'.[12] Some felt that the sermons did not make them 'feel good about themselves'; instead it challenged beliefs and practices they considered as acceptable of a 'good' Christian. Interestingly, what they regarded as 'good' reflected intrinsically racist, sexist and classist attitudes in their understanding of theology, ecclesiology, and missiology. Their effort to feel good was grounded in 'a theology of good intentions',[13] which attempts to separate a vengeful and angry God of the Old Testament from the more pietistic and emollient view of the divine that is reflected in the life, death and resurrection of Jesus, in the New Testament.

When such a limited view of God is expressed, it becomes a pastoral challenge that may have an adverse impact on people who cannot come to terms with a differing perception of God, or be open to explore new possibilities. This, however, cannot be a bad thing if a modicum of sensitivity is exercised in ensuring that a critical analytic method is used in responding to the raised issues, while aiming to provide the necessary tools for ongoing theological reflection. This may be easier said than done, yet I do believe that some members of the three congregations are capable of engaging in critical theologizing.

Further dialogue with the stewards resulted in the expected comment, 'Preaching with strong conviction is your culture.' What does cultural identity have to do with preaching? However, if it does, maybe the preachers of the evangelical revival were of African-Caribbean descent, for they delivered their message born out of a strong belief in God and his salvific atonement. I am aware that there is a wide disparity in cultural forms of expressions and religious experiences of Black and White people, but the passion to preach what you truly believe is not confined to race or culture. If there is a prevailing belief that Black ministers preach with stronger convictions than those of their White colleagues then it is a reflection of ignorance.

Using cultural background as a way of justifying non-acceptance and un-appreciation of a differing style of preaching and ministry reinforces the belief of Robinson Milwood, in his book *Liberating Mission*, that the 'Methodist church does not accept Black people, but tolerates them because of the financial benefit they bring to the Church in urban areas'.[14] He believes that the Church is inherently racist, and advocates an essentialist ideology, those essential characteristics and beliefs that can be seen as an indispensable part of being Black, as the key to combat racism, believing that all White people are the 'enemy'. Milwood's approach is not the opinion of all Black people, for this 'kind of essentialist, dialectical "othering" fails to see the complex and varied levels of commitment to racial justice in both Black and White worshippers'.[15]

In spite of Milwood's inaccurate beliefs regarding some aspects of the Church, his comment about tolerant inclusion cannot be ignored simply because of his radical approach to the issue of exclusion. Milwood's theory can be closely linked with that of Miroslav Volf, who believes that

Exclusion can entail erasure of separation, not recognising the other as someone who in his or her otherness belongs to the pattern of interdependence. The other then emerges as an inferior being who must either be assimilated by being made like the self or be subjugated to the self. Exclusion takes place when the violence of expulsion, assimilation, or subjugation and the indifference of abandonment replace the dynamics of taking in and keeping out as well as the mutuality of giving and receiving.[16]

Therefore, to combine acceptance with any restricting element becomes exclusionary, for it will inhibit creative encounters with others. Exclusion is the antithesis of the practice of any church which is biased towards the dominant majority, hence 'exclusion does not express a preference; it names an objective evil'.[17] Thus, Milwood's perception of tolerant inclusion has made me pay closer attention to the phrase 'we are ready for something new', which often really means 'we are happy as we are'. Far too often injections of new concepts or new practices are either rejected or criticized, causing deep hurts and mistrust.

However, using cultural identity as a basis for remaining in a spiritual slumber and living unchallenged by God's word is fatal for church growth. Assuredly my experience is not the first, nor will it be the last, for I sense that such ill-bred views may be ubiquitous in many White-majority congregations, who often mistakenly see their 'whiteness' as a right to be disrespectful of other people's culture. Such points of view can hinder not only the bridge building of relationships, but also spiritual growth, by closing people's minds to the possibility of new experiences.

Consequently, when such opinions are expressed Black worshippers, who may already feel marginalized by their style of worship and understanding of God, may stop participating out of a desire for self-preservation. However, is such self-exclusion the answer to structures and practices that appear designed to maintain White supremacy in the Church? I deny that this approach is the way forward in dealing with influences that are injurious to one's integrity and humanity. Self-exclusion is defeatism, undermining the progress that has been made through the 'sweat and tears' of the first generation of African Caribbean immigrants who persevered in spite of the many challenges encountered.

Using the notion of inclusion to respond to racial non-acceptance is more than just words, for a willingness to include people is not just an acceptance of people's different beliefs and identities, but also an understanding of their way of being and their cultural heritage. However, there is a danger of culture becoming decontextualized, confining it to a narrow understanding of Black cultural life and in particular Caribbean culture, resulting in it becoming a 'consumable commodity'.[18] Holding such a limited idea of Black culture denies its pluralistic nature, and when only certain aspects of Black life are explored by White-dominated churches (for example, Black gospel choirs and 'Caribbean evenings') then it is being patronizing to the people for whom this is an indelible part of their identity.

On the other hand, engaging Black participation to the extent of being politically correct can also be perceived as tokenistic and not affirming, 'for it suggests that this kind of racial reasoning of placing Black people in strategic positions will assist with anti-racist struggles'.[19] Not only has this reasoning proven to be misleading, it queries the legitimacy behind the struggle for racial harmony and equality among White people. Additionally, this seemingly well-meaning idea of Black participation raises many questions when the contribution given may be ignored, for then the person is denied the opportunity to articulate their viewpoint. This can be a debilitating factor for the unsuspecting Black person in further discourse. This perception not only creates a framework of suspicion, but it highlights the need to stop the gap among Methodist communities from widening any further.

In order to realize its potential, the Methodist Church will need to:

- be open to the challenges of differing cultural expressions;
- recognize that Black presence and participation does not necessarily result in acceptance and equality;
- eradicate concepts that suggest denying of 'self' is linked with full acceptance;

- practise inclusion, not tolerance;
- address practices that are patronizing and disabling to people who are non-White.

Comparative Analysis

Comparing the experiences of the Black migrant generation and myself reveals that the acceptance of 'others' that are non-White continues to be an ordeal for every Black generation in today's multicultural Britain. The stereotypical views of Black people have not altered nor died, in spite of educational and economic advancement in society over 50 years after the *Windrush* arrival. Negative stereotypical images and expectations continue to help reinforce power structures, inhibiting further progress towards a society that is welcoming rather than being merely tolerant. Marginalized and oppressed people, because of the nature of the challenges faced, have responded by affirming diversity, rather than denying its existence. Being pretentious or ignorant of the complications of dissimilarity have more far-reaching implications than confronting the issues head on, for immigration will not disappear.

Therefore, when phrases such as 'he is articulate' or 'good educational background' are used to justify placing a Black person 'on trial' as a local preacher informs me that achieving equality and acceptance is far from reality. It suggests that many church leaders have not grasped the concept of inclusivity, nor dealt with their negative presuppositions about Black people. Likewise, when colleagues quickly substitute another word for the one that was originally intended in order to be politically correct, or apologize for using derogatory words, it suggests the mammoth task of dismantling innate perceptions. These examples not only highlight a lack of sensitivity, but also a lack of practical Christian principles, not just to people of colour but across the range of human beings who may not fit in with what might be perceived as an acceptable British society.

What is more noticeable is that the Black generation did not have the advantage of a political correctness framework. The widespread use of 'politically correct' language has somewhat lessened the impact of openly verbalized attitudes against Black people, but they continue to operate in a more subtle manner. The sense of 'unwelcome' has not been eradicated, in spite of support systems helping to contradict the ignorance and bias found in the Church and in society. While Black people are not literally turned away from the church today, with the remark 'your church is down the road', there is a sense that full participation is still a barrier to overcome, even if they hold particular roles in the church.

Maybe the problem lies with church leaders who may lack understanding in facilitating Black people in leadership roles, and who have allowed the White members to articulate the ethos of the church while disempowering others in the process. This attitude may have stemmed from the British way of life that, with its imperial and colonial past, carries an effortless 'superiority' that influences all people, including Christians. Can this mind-set be eradicated from the Church in order that its Black members may have a chance to express their humanity and spirituality? However impossible this task might seem, there are examples of Black members having effective leadership roles in White-majority congregations.

Despite the measures employed to combat ignorance and misunderstanding, Black liberation in the Church is costly. It comes at a high price, not only for the Black members, but also for the White minister committed to live by his or her Christian convictions and fulfilling a pastoral role. The minister is at risk of being sidelined by 'powerful' White members, whose attitudes have undermined the contribution or potential contribution from the Black members. While diversity may be difficult to understand, it is an empowering force to create good, signifying that all human beings have an inherent dignity, regardless of racial identity, gender disposition, and social class. Unfortunately, for the marginalized and disenfranchised of this world, gaining respect for their inherent worthiness has been costly, because of a predominant world-view that caters for the powerful.

The transformative process must begin with respect for cultural differences. The willingness to embrace others and the desire for reconciliation cannot be compelled or dictated. 'If embrace takes place, it will be because the other has desired the self just as the self has desired the other.'[20] Reciprocation is fundamental, for no community is inclined to believe it has surrendered its identity. Volf believes that 'in an embrace the identity of self is both preserved and transformed, and the alterity of the other is both affirmed as alterity and partly received into the ever changing identity of self'.[21] If we do not wish to understand people's culture, it emphasizes the impossibility of the task and illegitimacy of embrace.

Moreover, the diverse composition of the Church and of society cannot be swept under the carpet as something to be ashamed of, nor must it be treated as something merely to be tolerated, when in reality it is becoming a stabilizing force of social harmony. We should be grateful that the Black migrant generation were not willing to accept their treatment and struggled to gain recognition in both Church and society. Ironically, they should not have had to be in that situation, for no human being should have to work for acceptance. Sybil Phoenix, a Black Methodist lay woman and founder organizer of the Methodist Leadership Racism Awareness Workshops, described in an interview her regrets at having created the Southwark Diocesan Race Relations Board:

> Knowing what I know now, I feel ashamed. I regret that I was grateful, thanking bishops for setting up a priest to minister primarily to black people. I should have seen that it's people full stop, no matter what the colour, whether you are blue or green or whatever. A shepherd should be a shepherd to any sheep . . . how dare they not look after the black sheep? I should have told the bishops that they should instruct their priests that we should be welcomed and accepted into every church as a matter of right, not special privilege.[22]

The realization that expectations are not always fulfilled can be a bitter pill to swallow, and can become another obstacle. On the other hand, it can inspire us to persevere in the fight against injustice, to bring about substantial change not just for the oppressed but also for the oppressors.

Affirming diversity in all its richness and not denying it or using it to exploit and oppress is important in the continuing battle against the evils that arise from difference. Embracing and examining difference is crucial. We should not consign it to the margin and pretend it does not matter, for it can be a means to overcome barriers. Diversity should be received as a gift, not seen as a burden.

Present-day realities are different from those of the Black migrant generation of the *Windrush* period, who through sheer determination and pride endured and triumphed against the odds to chart a better path for others. However, the struggle goes on and it will be some time before diversity is truly embraced, not just theoretically, but practically.

In order to realize its potential, the Methodist Church will need to:

- affirm difference and refrain from seeking conformity;
- address the balance of Black people in leadership roles, not as a tokenistic gesture;
- examine its own understanding of diversity and the complexities it raises;
- realize that issues relating to diversity are not always a joyous undertaking, but can be quite costly;
- embrace the richness of diversity, seeing it as a bonus, not a burden.

Future Response

Some will argue that the Methodist Church has done and continues to do more with regard to race relations and tackling the issue of diversity than any other mainstream denomination. This may be the case, but providing innovative strategies and support systems without seriously addressing the responses or seeking to implement them fully in the Church is of little purpose, and can be perceived as another act of tokenism to placate its Black members. On the other hand, if these measures are put in place not as a gesture of appeasement, but with the sincere objective of fully engaging with issues of diversity regardless of the outcome, then it is free of any criticism.

The British Methodist Church's Racial Justice Office is a leading example of an attempt to address the issue of diversity in the Church. It offers training programmes to raise awareness among White people. I wonder what percentage of the Methodist Connexion has taken advantage of the Racial Justice Office for a racism awareness course? I believe there are districts and circuits who would benefit significantly from such a course, especially for those in leadership roles. Awareness of the difficulties should conscientize the unaware, possibly enabling them to challenge the status quo and generate opportunities for marginalized people to work out their liberation.

It is important to correct people when they refer to a Black person as 'coloured', because this word can inflict a lot of hurt. However, what is saddening is that the people who use this term often pride themselves on being politically correct. This raises the question of the nature of teaching or lack thereof in the Church. If there is a failure to keep abreast with what is current in our multicultural society, more than likely there is a dearth of ongoing critical Christian thinking. Yes, the world may have gone 'PC-crazy', but we still need to be respectful and open to correction.

Ongoing learning is an imperative discipline and the Church is not exempt from this nor should it shun new theological thoughts. It is critical that the Church be open to employing differing approaches and not be constrained by White Eurocentric ideologies which maintain White power at the expense of Black people. To counteract the negativity inherent in such ideologies, Black people must also be receptive to new theological reflections that draw upon their experiences and cultural heritage.

The emergence of Liberation theology prompted marginalized people to think theologically in their own context. Black theology has responded to the exclusion of Black people from the biblical narratives and has enabled them to identify positively with the emancipatory powers of God. James Cone explores how God sides with the oppressed of the world; Cone takes as his starting point the ethnicity of Jesus as a marginalized Jew. 'Jesus is not a human being for all persons', he says; 'he is a human being for oppressed persons, whose identity is made known in and through their liberation.'[23] Cone's helpful insight not only restores hope to the excluded, but it has created a framework that others could implement in their own theological reflections, like Womanist theologians and Black Christian educators.

With the advent of contextual theology, it has become clearer how misinterpretation has resulted in the pernicious subjugation of Africans as slaves and the internalization of racism that is symptomatic of many Black people because of the negative connotations of the word 'Black'. Reddie reminds us that 'the psychological repudiation of the Black self, implanted and perpetuated by White power and authority, has led countless generations of Black people to see White as superior to Black in every sense'.[24] With this notion, a clear link between representation and oppression is visible. African slaves have been portrayed in a negative light and treated as inferior beings to be dominated. Stuart Hall expounds further in his essay 'Cultural identity and diaspora':

> The ways in which Black people were positioned and subjected in the dominant regimes of representation were the effects of a critical expertise of cultural power and normalisation. Not only, in Said's 'orientalist' sense, were we constructed as different and other within the categories of knowledge of the West by those regimes, they had the power to make us see and experience ourselves as 'Other'.[25]

It may be tedious to go on confronting representations which have an adverse effect on Black people, but it is necessary for the celebration of Black identity. This has far-reaching implications for both Black and White people, highlighting the need for edification. Some may argue that the key component in bridging the cultural divide is simply acceptance over and against the implementation of education. This argument cannot be substantiated for the process of acceptance must begin with self, celebrating the image of God within one's self. Reddie points out how crucial this is for Black people. He states:

The importance of Christian education, as a corrective to the ongoing psychological denial of the Black self, cannot be overstated. Christian education directed towards people of African descent must assert the importance of self-esteem. The teaching and learning process must be concerned with enabling Black people to have a profound appreciation and love of self. This self-love can be fostered by reminding Black youth that God, in whose image they are created, loves them and desires all that is good for their continued existence.[26]

Christian education is another way of tackling issues of diversity in the Church and society. This education, however, is not one-sided, for minorities only, but for each person willing to respond fittingly. This is far from easy for people to take on board, given the years of negativity in relation to Black people and the dominance of White people. For many Black people the opportunity to embrace and express their God-given dignity and diverse faith may be viewed with some scepticism, causing them to cling to practices and beliefs that deny their personhood. Yet, the greater challenge is to the majority White congregations: can they embrace new concepts that may change their practices?

This was very clear when I led two of my congregation in a discipleship course and in particular a session on 'Who is Jesus?' There were a number of images of Jesus to choose from, yet most gravitated to the traditional Eurocentric image, blue eyes and blond hair. I was not surprised, but was disappointed, by the response of one participant who felt that in spite of the historical origins of Jesus, she was most comfortable with a childhood Western portrayal. Reflecting on her comment, I had to come to terms with the fact that the introduction of new perspectives was just as daunting as abandoning unhelpful old theories, for both Black and White Christians.

The idea of holding to a childhood image of Jesus led me to explore growth in faith for many in the Church whose spirituality seems to be at a plateau and those who are inclined to believe that advanced age and ongoing learning are poles apart. Is the Church in danger of maintaining childhood faith and childhood notions of diversity, in spite of its relevance for the minority in its midst? If this is the case, then the Church needs to examine those practices that are detrimental to the survival of a diverse faith.

Another key element of Christian education is the use of oral tradition. This practice has been passed down from our forebears of African origin, who have always employed oral technique for the retelling of their history in order to preserve their traditions and morale. If this aspect of Black cultural life is deemed unimportant then the experiences of Black people are diluted and lack authenticity. The United Methodist minister Edward P. Wimberly in his book *African American Pastoral Care* speaks of the importance of faith stories as an educational tool. He states:

> These narratives suggest ways to motivate people into action, help them recognize new resources, enable them to channel behaviour in constructive ways, sustain them in crisis and bring healing and reconciliation in relationships, heal the scars of memories, and provide guidance when direction is needed.[27]

He believes that the retelling of faith stories highlights God's nature and presence, bringing healing, wholeness, and liberation. The experiences of Black people cannot be sidelined, but must be adopted as a mechanism to educate their offspring in the continual struggle for justice as the stories are passed down from generation to generation.

However, the oral tradition is manifest in a variety of ways, such as 'storytelling, festivals, celebration, parties, role-playing and acting, through to religious worship'.[28] This legacy is also normal in African Caribbean family life, where stories and folklore are an intrinsic part of child rearing, not just for amusement but also as moral guidance. The use of oral tradition can be a positive source for Christian education, not only for the empowerment of Black people, but to illustrate how the sharing of stories can be a link in other people's narrative, transposing time and place, yet finding commonality. By engaging in this exercise of linking stories we hope to create openness in place of suspicion, thus forging new relationships and enriching existing ones.

If the Church is not ready to accept that Christian education is multifaceted and should not be restricted to Eurocentric practices and traditions that are advantageous for the White, middle and upper class, then it continues to fail the minority population of the Church. It is good at offering 'lip service', but not faithful in ensuring that issues which inhibit the development of marginalized people are assessed with effective recommendations.

In order to realize its potential, the Methodist Church will need to:

- review the purpose of the Racial Justice Office;
- examine the teaching manuals used in the Church, especially in the edification of the younger generation;
- be more pragmatic in its theological discourse, adopting ideas from different traditions;
- create educational programmes that address the inherently damaging ideas of both Black and White people;
- employ and celebrate the contributions of Black Christian educators and the use of Black educational tools such as oral tradition.

Conclusion

Diversity was a complex issue for the African Caribbean generation of the *Windrush* period and continues to be a complicated subject today. Despite many changes, which have occurred since the arrival of people from the British colonies, the situation for many Black people worshipping in the established churches is still far from ideal. There are no signs saying 'not welcome', but the established practices and attitudes of some imply that a sign would be best, eradicating any disingenuous mannerisms. Black people continue to worship and are part of the Church, but they may feel excluded when difference is not affirmed and celebrated.

The present situation may seem bleak, but steady progress has been made in hearing Black voices, such as that of Anthony Reddie, and in taking their contributions seriously. It can be argued that the Methodist Church has been sympathetic to the plight of

Black people, thereby creating new initiatives and support networks to help alleviate the hurt. It can be equally argued that such justification should not be necessary and that equality and not sympathy should be the basis of acceptance. An interesting example is the Black Methodist Youth Conference, which meets separately from the Methodist Youth Conference mainly to create a 'safe' place in which Black youths can affirm their identity without fear of ridicule and stigma. Although I recognize there are times when separation is necessary for rejuvenation or spiritual development, I am concerned that this type of disconnection is in danger of creating a benchmark for future generations. Diversity does not mean conformity, or exclusivity. In theory, diversity should strive to recognize, celebrate, and accept differences, rather than criticize, negate and label.

On the other hand, exploring the subject of diverse faith and delving into my present experiences juxtaposed with those of the African Caribbean generation highlighted that many White people hold erroneous beliefs of 'others' which are deeply rooted in their psychological composition, which cannot be easily dismantled. The experiences of the past and present hold much in common and cannot be readily denounced or categorized as a matter of ignorance on the part of those who have not encountered difference. The media and global travel have dealt with such perceptions by making people aware of other races and cultures.

It may be easy to deprecate the domineering activity of White people, but such pigeonholing prevents rational dialogue. Reflecting on the conversation I had with the stewards, I had failed to see the genuineness of those who appreciate my ministry. I responded by excluding myself from the congregation, as an act of self-preservation. Despite my attempts to practise self-exclusion from the congregation, it had proved to be difficult, for I was still expected to fulfil my role as minister and pastoral carer.

I cannot stress too much the importance of education, mainly for people of African Caribbean origins and future generations in Britain, enabling them to draw upon their experience and heritage as a basis for empowerment and liberation. Therefore, the work of Anthony Reddie has much to offer by informing the churches of practices that have contributed negatively to the self-identity and self-love amongst Black people. He counters this by promoting a practical theology of Christian education, adopting an African theory, which places all Black religio-cultural discourse within a broad interpretative framework.

Using oral tradition will help to combat negative and stereo-typical views that have hindered the growth of Black people by denying them the opportunity to articulate their stories in light of their experiences, their understanding of God and the use of Scripture. Thus, Scripture becomes a pastoral aid, offering hope, sustenance, empowerment, direction, and liberation for the marginalized whose stories are often neglected. Sharing stories works on two levels: first, it provides a structure for pastoral care where support and nurture are inextricably linked within its framework; second, it challenges and overturns distorted notions of Black people, which regard them as inferior, subordinate beings with little or no value. However, the emergence of contextual theology has enabled many Black people to become aware of their self worth and be proud of their skin colour and cultural heritage.

In spite of all the difficulties that the subject of diversity raises for both Black and White people, denying its influence on the Church reduces its potential as a tool for revitalization. Likewise, hoping that it may go away is impractical; hence, the only choice is to listen to cries for justice, equality, and sincere acceptance.

Notes

1 Tobago is part of a twin island republic known as Trinidad and Tobago and is situated in the southernmost part of the Caribbean. Tobago lies 21 miles (33km) north-east of Trinidad, with a population of over 50,000 (primarily of African descent) and a flourishing tourism industry.

2 Cockroach is one of the insects that the fowl/hen eats. Therefore, it becomes vulnerable and is at risk of being eaten or ignored if it should be at a fowl's party. Applying that saying to myself as a Black female Methodist minister sometimes evokes feelings of being in the wrong place amidst people who are not of my culture or racial identity.

3 Relating to those who have come to settle in another country.

4 Shirlyn Toppin, '"Soul Food" Theology: Pastoral Care and Practice through the Sharing of Meals: A Womanist Reflection', in Anthony G.

Reddie (ed.), *Black Theology: An International Journal*, Wiltshire: Equinox Publishing, 2006, p. 44.

5 Relating to those who have moved from one country to another, often for employment or economic improvement.

6 Toppin, '"Soul Food" Theology', p. 50.

7 Anthony G. Reddie, *Faith Stories and the Experience of Black Elders*, London: Jessica Kingsley, 2001, p. 15.

8 Acts 10.34–35.

9 Toppin, "Soul Food' Theology', p. 51.

10 Black folk who preferred to be around White folk because they loved Whiteness more than Blackness. Robert Beckford, *Jesus is Dread: Black Theology and Black Culture in Britain*, London: Darton, Longman and Todd, 1998, p. 43.

11 Beckford, *Jesus is Dread*, p. 42.

12 The source for a 'theology of good intentions' is found in the paternalistic and patrician attitude that is often manifested in the life of historic mainline churches and in wider British society. This attitude flows from a particular narrow reading of the Bible, coupled with a limited understanding of God. Anthony G. Reddie, *Nobodies to Somebodies: A Practical Theology for Education and Liberation*, London: Epworth Press, 2003, p. 155.

13 Reddie, *Nobodies to Somebodies*, p. 155.

14 Robinson Milwood, *Liberating Mission: A Black Experience*, London: African Resource Centre, 1997, p. 89.

15 Beckford, *Jesus is Dread*, p. 50.

16 Miroslav Volf, *Exclusion and Embrace: A Theological Exploration of Identity, Otherness, and Reconciliation*, Nashville, TN: Abingdon Press, 1996, p. 67.

17 Volf, *Exclusion and Embrace*, p. 68.

18 Black choirs are constantly asked to perform 'the spirituals', as if the experience within the songs were a consumer commodity for emotional titillation. Similarly, White churches want to put on Caribbean evenings to get a taste of the Caribbean. It is easier to eat Caribbean food than to read the history of English slavery, colonialism, and imperialism in the region. Beckford, *Jesus is Dread*, p. 36.

19 Beckford, *Jesus is Dread*, p. 53.

20 Volf, *Exclusion and Embrace*, p. 143.

21 Volf, *Exclusion and Embrace*, p. 143.

22 Clarice Nelson and Sybil Phoenix, 'If the church was what it professed to be . . . ' in P. Grant and R. Patel (eds), *A Time to Act*, Nottingham: Russell Press, 1992, p. 20.

23 James H. Cone, *A Black Theology of Liberation*, New York: Orbis Books, 1986, p. 85.

24 Reddie, *Nobodies to Somebodies*, p.145.

25 Stuart Hall, 'Cultural identity and diaspora', in Bell Hooks (ed.), *Black Looks: Race and Representation*, London: Turnaround Press, 1992, pp. 64–5.

26 Reddie, *Nobodies to Somebodies*, p. 146.

27 Edward P. Wimberly, *African American Pastoral Care*, Nashville, TN: Abingdon Press, 1991, p. 12.

28 Reddie, *Faith, Stories and the Experience of Black Elders*, p. 32.

5

A Shared Faith

LUKE CURRAN

One of my earliest political memories is the trouble Margaret Thatcher found herself in after declaring that 'there is no such thing as society'.[1] As a teenager, like many of my generation, I wasn't particularly interested in politics but there was something about this statement which seemed profoundly wrong, something that disturbed the socialist, trade unionist, and ex-Primitive Methodist value base that I had inherited from my father and which, at least in part, I subscribed to.

To be fair to Margaret Thatcher, what she was actually suggesting was that we need to be in charge of our own destiny. We need to look after ourselves and our family and behave generously towards those in need but this isn't something those in need have a right to expect. Or to put it another way, there shouldn't be a 'nanny' society who will solve my problems for me.

To what extent this message of individual advancement, familial responsibility, and prudent giving was itself a result of Thatcher's own rather more Wesleyan Methodist upbringing[2] is a discussion for elsewhere but it raises an interesting question which I'll return to later about the extent to which whose of us who were 'Thatcher's children', brought up in a culture of increasingly postmodernist individualism and now in our 30s, will ever be truly at home expressing a shared faith within Methodism.

I'll use the idea of shared faith in three different, but interlinked, ways in this chapter; all have deep roots in Methodism but also pose particular contemporary challenges. The first is the proposition that we are called to share our experience of faith with other

Christians as a potential means of grace, growth, and account-ability. The second is that as local church communities and as a denomination we hold particular understandings in common, so that a shared faith is a common but distinctive understanding of what it means to be Christian within a particular congregation or tradition. The third recognizes that a shared faith needs an organizational structure to sustain it.

But I want us to start at a different point.

At the heart of our shared faith are the relationships we have with others and the concept of belonging. Being part of groups is a dominant factor in our lives; we are born into families, educated together in schools and often work in businesses with other em-ployees. We derive structure, stability and a system of authority from these group associations and they constantly influence our thinking and our behaviour. Sociologists often talk about two dis-tinct types of group both of which involve regular interaction with other members and where there is an expectation that you will fol-low the groups' 'norms' while accepting that other people might not.[3] These are 'primary groups', which involve an emotional commitment to the other members (such as family or friendship groups) and 'secondary groups' which tend to be more impersonal and focussed on a practical end (such as a sports club or business organization). In reality most groups are a mixture of the two and for a church congregation these are more like poles on a spectrum than distinct categories. However, the usefulness of this distinction is that it begins to suggest that there might be different reasons for belonging and certainly different levels of commitment.

The *Oxford Reference Dictionary*[4] suggests that to belong is 'to be rightly placed'. Continued, long-term involvement in a Method-ist church is likely to happen when we feel 'rightly placed'. This may result from socialization,[5] a sense of acceptance by others, or a conviction that this is where we are called to be. Being rightly placed helps promote a positive self-image and therefore a sense of well-being. It meets two basic psychological needs: the need for certainty and the need for the acceptance and approval of others. The technical term for this is the 'dual process dependency model'.[6]

The need for certainty arises from a need to feel we are right, that we have an accurate perception of reality. We join groups that share our view of the world because their positive reinforcement reduces our own uncertainty. This is particularly important in situations that might challenge our world view in which we need to look to others to support our own position.

The need for acceptance and approval arises from a need to gain social approval and avoid rejection by others because of their ability to reward or punish us, both materially and psychologically, and therefore we comply with the group norms or viewpoint, at least in public.

The practical upshot of all this is that we join groups who make us feel welcome and share our views. However, in doing so we often create church communities with distinctive characteristics which a new member must either conform to or leave. Conformity is achieved either through internalization, where private belief changes to become consistent with public belief, or compliance, where individuals choose to compromise their private beliefs in public because the benefits of doing so outweigh the cost of leaving the church community. These distinctive characteristics may relate to tradition, theology, or faith form. For example, if you take a medium-sized circuit like the one I live in you will find churches with distinctive traditions, often based on their roots in Wesleyan or Primitive Methodism,[7] and which are evident in the role of the presbyter, the exercise of power and governance (whatever our Standing Orders say!) and even what constitutes a good sermon. You will also find churches with distinctive theologies; in my circuit this relates to a tendency to be evangelical or liberal, demonstrated in the local preachers they like and dislike. You will also find local churches with distinctive faith forms.

This last category arises out of the work of theologians and psychologists of religion such as James Fowler[8] who suggest that at different stages on our Christian journey the way we 'faith' changes. 'Faithing' isn't about the content of our faith (for example, how much we know about the Bible) but how we believe and think about faith issues. In Fowler's model, people with a 'conforming faith'[9] think about their faith and are able to draw together different content into a cohesive pattern to support their world view, but they do so without much analysis and are therefore likely to swim with the tide and accept the beliefs of those around them. This is in stark comparison to those at the 'choosing faith' stage whose faith is very self-directed; everything is open to examination and analysis as they search for explanation and meaning, demythologizing as they go.

People at different stages on their faith journeys tend to be attracted to churches which meet the needs of their particular faith stage (sometimes called faith form). A person with conforming faith is likely to join one with strong leadership and a message of assurance; people with a choosing faith are likely to be much more dismissive of this type of church and look for one which supports their individual quest.

While Fowler identifies seven stages of faith, the majority of the adult population have either a 'conforming' or a 'choosing' faith.[10] Neither of these faith forms is better than the other and for a denomination to be healthy we need to have congregations which nurture people at both these stages. Conforming congregations will support the faithful and transmit a fairly generalized form of Western European protestant Christianity. Choosing congregations will, in the words of the Fred Pratt Green hymn,[11] enable a denomination 'beset by change but spirit led' to 'claim and test its heritage and keep on rising from the dead' as they question its value and rework it in their quest for meaning.

My worry is that Methodism no longer has a critical mass of 20- to 50-year-olds with a choosing faith to sustain the denomination's future development in Britain, but I'll return to this later.

Christian belonging is more than simply a sociological or psychological phenomenon. It has deep scriptural and doctrinal roots. Perhaps the strongest image and metaphor for Christian belonging is contained in Paul's first letter to the Corinthians[12] where our life in Christ is described as like being parts of a single body, each with a different purpose yet interdependent. The slight irony is that the letter also had to contain a plea about the need to get on with each other.

The significance of the metaphor is that it identifies a number of characteristics of the early Church which are born out elsewhere in Acts and the Epistles. First, there was a Christian community that you joined. This may seem unsurprising for us, but in the context of a Jewish world where the religious community existed simply by the fact people were born into it, Paul was making a significant statement about the nature of belonging: in theory at least, Christian is something you become and in doing so you join the community.[13] Second, joining is through the specific act of baptism and that is available to all. Third, there is an expectation that you will play an active part in the community and that failure to do so diminishes the whole as bodies have no extraneous parts. Fourth, by the same argument, your commitment to the Christian community is life-long. Body parts don't usually come and go.

Perhaps unsurprisingly given the context of the early Church, this model of church feels very much like a community under persecution that needs to be clear about who is in and who is out and which attempts to minimize internal dissent. It has also formed the basis for the dominant form of ecclesial community for the last two millennia, but it is not the only model offered by Scripture.

The model of Christian community offered by the gospel is much more fluid. Jesus called people to be part of the community without any entry rite or even confession of faith,[14] appointed people variously for lifelong tasks and for short-term strategic purposes,[15] and while constantly challenging people to a deeper commitment accepted all those who wanted to belong to his fellowship for however long they wished to be part of the group. The attractiveness of this model for contemporary Methodism is that it recognizes the likelihood of belonging before believing which is increasingly central to many contemporary approaches to mission.[16]

However, this dynamic of belonging and believing is complex. Methodists, along with all other Christians who subscribe to the Nicene Creed, 'acknowledge one baptism for the forgiveness of sins' and recognize that 'baptism marks the entry into the One Holy Catholic and Apostolic Church, of which the Methodist Church is part'.[17] Baptism is a response to faith and requires a profession of faith, given either by the person themselves or in the case of young children by their parents and godparents. Whether these children then grow into an active faith or not, the fact of their baptism and therefore baptismal membership of the Church remains. Whether this membership bestows any form of individual faith or sense of belonging is more debatable.

The general membership of the universal Church which is granted to Christians at baptism is very different from membership of the Methodist Church. Arguably, the roots of Methodism as a movement which you could join may be traced back to an incident that John and Charles Wesley highlight at the beginning of the 'General Rules of the United Societies'.[18] John recalls that towards the end of 1739 a group of eight to ten came to him seeking their own salvation and that he formed them into a group which met weekly to pray together, to receive a word of exhortation, to watch over each other in love and to help each other work out their personal salvation. Similar groups, called 'societies', quickly grew up in many of the places Wesley preached and initially the only condition of membership was 'a desire "to flee from the wrath to come, to be saved from their sins"'.[19] However by the time the General Rules were written in 1743 Wesley had extended this, recognizing that members should demonstrate their desire of salvation and growth in holiness through three actions: 'First, by doing no harm, by avoiding evil of every kind; especially that which is most generally practiced' (this point is then followed by a list of 23 examples of such evil); 'Secondly, by doing good' (and another list of examples); and 'thirdly, by attending upon all the ordinances of God'.[20] Failure either to comply or later to repent for transgressing these rules would ultimately lead to expulsion from the society.

Echoes of some of these original rules are still present in Methodism's contemporary understanding of the duties and privileges of membership recorded in the Deed of Union:

It is the privilege and duty of members of the Methodist Church to avail themselves of the two sacraments, namely baptism and the Lord's Supper. As membership of the Methodist Church also involves fellowship it is the duty of all members of the Methodist Church to seek to cultivate this in every possible way. The weekly class meeting has from the beginning proved to be the most effective means of maintaining among Methodists true fellowship in Christian experience. All members of the Methodist Church shall have their names entered on a class book, shall be placed under the pastoral care of a class leader or pastoral visitor and shall receive an annual ticket of membership.[21]

It's interesting to note that the very strong theological messages that Wesley was giving about the nature of salvation, evil and grace in the 1743 Rules have today been almost exclusively replaced by functional requirements. In part this is because the doctrinal material appears elsewhere in the deed of union but it also reflects a loss of focus on why people should belong to Methodism. We are no longer called individually, at least by our Discipline, to work out our own salvation and grow in holiness. Nor are we called to assist others in doing so, and while the Conference encourages us as members to develop our discipleship in line with our current faith experience and for local churches to offer opportunities for this to happen,[22] it hardly has the urgency or vigour of Mr Wesley's Rules.

The deed of union also raises the rather fraught issue of fellowship and meeting in class as a means of belonging. Wesley's 'Plain Account of the People Called Methodist'[23] is contained in a letter written to the Revd Mr Perronet, the vicar of Shoreham, in 1748 and outlines the establishment of the classes. Wesley had a problem: the debt resulting from the building of the New Room in Bristol was large and he needed to find a means of clearing it. An unnamed member of the society at Bristol suggested that the members of the society should be grouped into classes of 12, with a leader who would visit each member weekly for the purpose of collecting a penny towards the debt until it was paid off. Special provision was made for those too poor to pay. After a while the class leaders started telling Wesley that they had found on their visits members who 'did not live as they ought' and the role of class leader was quickly expanded from a collector of pennies to that of a pastoral carer whose duties during the visit were to 'inquire how their [the members'] souls prosper: to advise, reprove, comfort, or exhort, as occasion may require; to receive what they are willing to give towards the relief of the poor'.[24]

It fairly soon became evident that home visiting wasn't the most expedient way of organizing the classes. This was because it took up more time than the class leaders could offer; many members lived with relatives or had masters who would not let them be visited; there was no privacy to the conversations in many homes and 'one affirmed what another denied'.[25] Therefore it was decided that the class should meet all together; 'advice or reproof was given as need required, quarrels made up, misunderstandings removed: and after an hour or two spent in this labour of love, they concluded with prayer and thanksgiving' and in doing so 'they began to "bear one another's burdens" and naturally to care for each other'.

Whether this process was as idyllic as Wesley attempts to make it sound is questionable and both in Wesley's own lifetime and throughout the nineteenth century the issue of mandatory attendance in class as a condition of membership was repeatedly raised until it was finally modified by the New Connexion in 1889 and the Wesleyans in 1890. The Primitive Methodist Church retained it, at least in their General Rules if not in practice, until Methodist union in 1932.[26] The difficulties fell broadly into three categories: about leadership, about holding office, and about process. Many people complained that the class leaders were not up to the job 'having neither the gifts nor graces for such employment';[27] the requirement that all members regularly meet in class as a condition of membership was precluding some, occasionally for good reason, from membership and therefore from holding office, and many felt uncomfortable and ill equipped to offer the prayer, testimony and to 'speak of the things of God'[28] that were required in a class meeting.

This last point was one that particularly exercised the Wesleyan special Conference committee set up to consider Church Membership and the Class Meeting, reporting in 1889.[29] They recognized that the class meeting was 'pre-eminently a method for sheltering, encouraging and developing the spiritual life' and that this process linked into a range of other activities including the provision of pastoral care and 'the first training' for prayer leaders, mission workers, Sunday-school teachers, Local Preachers and Ministers because it is through 'the practice of simple and fervent utterance in the class meeting ... [that the] ... finest evangelical instruments have been shaped and tempered'. In highlighting this, the report unintentionally forewarns of the necessity, just over a century later and in a Methodist Church where class meetings are little more than a folk memory, for the 2005 Conference Report *Time to Talk of God: Recovering Christian Conversation as a Way of Nurturing Discipleship*,[30] which encourages people to learn again the skills necessary to share their faith with others.

We also need to remember that for Wesley at least, the class meeting was a prudential means of grace,[31] a point of need where God makes his love for us known so as to sustain and empower our Christian life, our working towards salvation and Christian perfection.

The class meeting therefore had a central function in the promotion of belonging, in offering opportunities for Methodists to share their faith and in doing so create a 'shared' faith, a common understanding. It also provided the mechanism by which Methodists remained accountable to each other for their Christian journey. While not unique among Christian groups, the denomination-wide practice of weekly recounting our Christian experience and sometimes being reproved for our transgressions was distinctive. Yet the decline in the class system was marked, and probably inevitable, after the decoupling of attendance and membership. By the 1920s Newton Flew estimated that 'half the London members of the Wesleyan church met regularly in Class',[32] although some historians would view this figure as high, and by the 1970s when the term 'class leader' was replaced by 'pastoral visitor' the class meeting had all but disappeared, at least as a weekly feature of Methodist life.

My second worry therefore is that Methodism has lost its emphasis on an individual journey of faith for which we were held accountable not simply before God but also our fellow Christians, whether in class or elsewhere.

Methodism likes counting, and while we should be mindful of the saying that 'there are three types of lies – lies, damn lies, and statistics',[33] they do offer a useful insight into contemporary patterns of Methodist belonging. The tri-annual 'statistics for mission' (or membership returns to use a more familiar Methodist phrase) have recently been reported for the period 2005–07.[34] At face value, they potentially paint a stark picture of a doomed denomination. In that period adult attendance fell by 10 per cent, membership by 7 per cent, involvement of young people (13–19) by 30 per cent and by children (under 13) by 32 per cent.

But this is not as gloomy as it first might appear. Leaving the figures for children and young people aside as this could easily form a chapter in itself, we need to put this into perspective by considering what they mean for an average local church. In many places local churches are still in good heart: for a church of 20, this means a loss of two people and a church of 18 is realistically just as viable as a church of 20. This is also true for a church of 10 dropping to 9. And the results are not uniform, with one in five churches actually growing between 2005 and 2007.

Extrapolating from statistics is always difficult, particularly where there are legitimate concerns about the accuracy of past data and continuing uncertainties over some of the reported numbers in the latest figures,[35] but the tendency, from at least the 1960s, to view British Methodism as in terminal decline is probably still unfounded. Any statistics need to be considered in the light of two other factors: first, Methodism has an older age profile than any other Christian denomination in the UK and a significantly older age profile than the general population;[36] second, we have a large number of numerically small churches. I think it is not unreasonable to extrapolate from our current position that the steady decline in membership and church attendance will continue without significant change for the next decade. It is in the following decade that we will see a radical reshaping of British Methodism as our demographics finally catch up with us: the membership will drop significantly and local church closures will begin to be widespread. I recognize though that Methodism has a particular propensity to keep small causes going, even when their closure would be a relief to all concerned, so I'm not too certain of the timescale of chapel closures.

The result of all this is that in 20 years' time we have a much smaller, say half our current, membership/attendance with perhaps two-thirds of our current number of churches, but still a viable denomination. The challenge is to ensure that those churches that remain are vibrant worshipping communities which retain the Methodist emphasis on evangelism and social engagement and that they are not dragged down by the very connexionalism that has historically been the strength of British Methodism.

While not wishing to rehearse the complex and at times bitter arguments of nineteenth-century Methodism about whether power should be local, central or connexional,[37] we need to recognize that in organizational form the Methodist Church is a bureaucracy. Rosemary Stewart, who before her death was an influential business theorist, suggested that the four main features of a bureaucracy can be summarized as: specialization, hierarchy of authority, system of rules, and impersonality. All four are clearly visible in contemporary Methodism.

We have a high level of specialization of role: stewards, pastoral visitors, local preachers, presbyters, deacons, lay workers, evangelism enablers, the list could go on and on and in some areas of church life we are becoming even more specialized as we consider specialist callings related to leading fresh expressions of church[38] and appoint youth enablers and participation workers to deliver the Youth Participation Strategy.[39]

We have a hierarchy of authority. Bureaucracies make clear distinctions between leaders and led and while recognizing that our leaders are democratically appointed, either by straight election (e.g. church stewards) or a committee-based decision (e.g. in accepting candidates for their future leadership role of presbyter) and that they remain accountable through our governance and scrutiny processes, we do still actually expect them to offer leadership, even if we try very hard to avoid the word itself.[40] The danger is that even a democratic bureaucracy can easily collapse into an oligarchy, where control is exercised by an often self-appointing few. This is very close to the fly sheet controversy of the nineteenth century[41] when the then Secretary of the Conference, Jabez Bunting, was viciously accused of centralizing power in the hands of a few ministers based in London.

We love our rules. The old adage that Methodists are people of the book and that book is our Constitutional Practice and Discipline rather than the Bible is perhaps slightly unfair but it does emphasize that we have the kind of system of rules designed for the efficient operation of the organization envisaged in Stewart's functions of a bureaucracy: they are relatively stable, although often tinkered with; at least some knowledge of them is a requisite of holding a position of authority; and they are impersonal, in the sense that they apply to all from the newest member to the President of the Conference.

Finally, we have impersonality which simply extends the last point, recognizing that the allocation of privileges and the exercise of authority should not be arbitrary but in accordance with the laid-down system of rules.

The danger for Methodism in the next 20 years is that we retain unquestioningly this bureaucratic expression of connexionalism while not recognizing either its dangers or that there may be alternatives. The dangers are those associated with any bureaucracy: an overemphasis on rules, procedures and paperwork which become a means to an end rather than enabling mission; officers who become dependent on status rather than the exercise of individual gifts and graces; the stifling of initiative through complex approval mechanisms; a tendency by officers to conceal administrative procedures from outsiders until you have inadvertently got them wrong; and a general lack of responsiveness to new ideas.

Most Methodists who have been involved in any significant way in the life of their local church or the wider connexion are likely to identify all of these dangers in what currently happens, but significant progress has been made in the last 20 years. Generally the deregulation in the mid 1990s (when the divisional structure and associated committees at circuit and district level were removed) has been a good thing and freed up resources (not least of people's time) for use in other ways. The principle of moving decision making over the use of resources more locally, for example through the emphasis on grant-making to local churches by districts rather than a connexional body, or the organization of learning and development on a regional basis through the new Methodist Training Forums, is to be welcomed. The reduction in size of the Connexional Team and its refocussing on things which 'are best done or can only be done by the Team in pursuit of the Priorities [of the Methodist church]'[42] is also a positive move although the final outcome of this process is unlikely to be as radical as it could, or perhaps should, have been.

However, we need to seriously question whether simply reforming a bureaucratic based understanding of connexionalism is sufficient to sustain a shrinking denomination. The answer to this may be 'yes', in which case we have to ensure a continuous evolution of our rules and style of leadership. The answer may be 'no', in which case we need to consider the alternatives after first identifying the key values of connexionalism, rather the outworking of those values, which need to be preserved. Whatever answer we eventually choose, we need to do it consciously rather than by default and this discussion is becoming urgent.

But what does all this have to say about belonging? While the discussion about shape, structure, and size are important when considering the future of Methodism as a denomination, the reality is that most members are only really concerned with their local church, the group of people they are in regular contact with and where personal relationships have developed. About a third of these members will meet with each other for prayer or Bible study, almost 75 per cent will have a specific role within the life of the church, most contribute financially and there is a consistent and sometimes growing sense of belonging.[43] Wider Methodism tends only to affect them when there is a financial crisis, they are committed to a property scheme, the minister is up for re-invitation or stationing, or where there is a commitment (often historic) to support a project which enables them to feel as though they 'live on a larger map'. The annual Easter Offertory for the Fund for World Mission is a good example of this.

This form of 'local' belonging to Methodism will, I suspect, continue to be the primary expression of our belonging into the foreseeable future for established congregations. It is too early to tell if the Fresh Expressions movement will result in any radically different models although I suspect that while the outward form of church might be different, the form of commitment, and therefore belonging, may be remarkably similar. Except, and this is a big except, I wonder if anything that is distinctly Methodist will be left.

My pessimism about the continuation of a shared faith which is distinctively Methodist is based on two things. First, anecdotally at least, there is a growing tendency for people to identify themselves as Christian rather than Methodist. In one sense this is both theologically and scripturally sound; we are, after all, as Paul puts it, one body, but in another sense this rather misses the point. To identify ourselves as Christian signifies a relationship with God, that we acknowledge the Scriptures as a revelation of truth (however you might interpret this) and that we give some broad doctrinal consent to the faith of the Church as expressed in the historic creeds. This is the minimum required to be 'in' but does not adequately recognize that within God's general purposes for creation he causes, by grace, specific expressions of those purposes to be raised up in particular times and places. The doctrinal statement of the British Methodist Church strongly acknowledges this: 'in the providence of God Methodism was raised up to spread scriptural holiness through the land by the proclamation of the evangelical faith'.[44] It isn't a general call to be Christian but to a specific theological expression of Christianity necessary to God's mission. Therefore in identifying ourselves simply as Christian, rather than Methodist, we need to ask the somewhat unpalatable question whether this is simply a cop-out from what God is calling us to do and be or whether the original purpose for which Methodism was 'raised up' has been fulfilled and therefore it is no longer part of God's purpose for this place and generation.

My second reason for pessimism is the growing number of members, deacons, and presbyters whose knowledge of Methodism, and in many cases passion for it, is limited and whose natural instincts are either essentially congregationalist and/or ecumenical rather than Methodist and connexional. This isn't the fault of any of these individuals but our collective error over many years in neither ensuring that the religious socialization of children brought up in Methodist families was specifically Methodist (rather than more generically Christian, if it happened at all) nor insisting that proper preparation happened not just for confirmation but also for admission to membership within our tradition, including the knowledge and understanding that should accompany that. As I argued in the last paragraph, the Methodist bit is not an optional extra, although our emphasis in recent years on confirmation as the adult commitment to faith rather than membership gives the impression that it might be.

My third worry therefore is that Methodism has lost and fails to communicate its distinctive theological reason for being and there is little energy to try and recapture it.

Finally, I want to look at who might belong to the Methodist Church in 20 years' time, not so much the demographics but the type of believer, and then return to the issue of 'Thatcher's children'. Methodism is reasonably good at attracting people in their 50s and 60s who are looking essentially to support a fairly conforming type of belief, be that following some form of 'conversion' experience, re-engagement with an earlier pattern of attendance (although clearly as our numbers of young people and children dwindle this will become less frequent) or simply because they are looking for a community to which they can belong and feel a part of. This group will remain an important part of the church. We will also still attract younger evangelicals and families who find an affinity with events such as Pentecost[45] and who will cluster together into a more limited number of like-minded congregations. There will also be a remnant of increasingly elderly 'good and faithful servants' who will retain at least a folk memory of the Methodism of their youth. However, to return to what I said earlier, my worry is that as Methodism has few people with a choosing faith in their 20 to 50s now and there is no evidence to suggest that they will be attracted back into the Methodist Church in later life, so in 20 years' time they will all be gone.

Working with these questers is never easy; they disturb the equilibrium of the groups they belong to. Yet in my parents' generation they managed somehow to find a place and remain in Methodism in a way which simply hasn't been true for my generation and below. Symptomatic of this is the decline of the METHSOC movement.[46] The need for an open, challenging and non-judgemental approach hasn't changed, but patterns of belonging have and perhaps my greatest worry of all is that Methodism failed to find a way to engage questers who were also 'Thatcher's children' and it is now almost certainly too late.

The origins of the phrase 'Thatcher's children' are unclear, although it is now widely used for those of us whose formative years in terms of social and political awareness coincided with Margaret Thatcher's term of office as prime minister. It's shorthand for two distinct but interlinked phenomena which had a profound effect on our lives and thinking. The first was the rapid growth of individual consumerism linked to late capitalism and the second was the loss of certainty associated with the postmodern debate. Both had a profound effect on potential questers.

Increasing individualism, greater choice, and emerging economic stability opened up a range of possibilities for questers to do things, both literally and metaphorically, that their parents never could. For questers, debate is central and where once that took place in the church youth fellowship or the working men's institute, it could now take place through experience. Why discuss world poverty when you could go and experience it for yourself during a gap year, or perhaps more fundamentally, why think about God when the media are bombarding you with a hundred and one other experiences to think and talk about, with the seemingly urgent issues gaining attention rather than perhaps the important ones?

This coincided for us with the fashion of postmodernism. While the term 'postmodern' has its roots in an academic description of a particular style within the arts, it quickly spread in the 1980s to encompass a wide range of actual and exaggerated shifts in contemporary culture and society. As a teenager, I was much attracted by its underlying philosophical model which was suspicious of both authority and reliability and which wanted to challenge the idea that rationality could act as an arbiter of either truth or of objective, ahistorical, universal knowledge. To put it another way I was with Pilate when he asks in John's Gospel 'and what is truth?'[47] and Methodism was sadly lacking in its ability to provide any answer that spoke to what I saw as my postmodern reality.

And it missed a trick. If Methodism had used its own tradition of small groups to engage us in debate about our experience and teach us its theological understanding of grace and holiness it may well have kept many of my questing contemporaries who left Methodism, and usually the Church. The message of a personal relationship with God achieved through his grace but which needs to be worked at (to somewhat simplify Wesley's position) would have been a far more helpful message for this group of postmodern questers than the 'believe and be saved' message based on a confidence in the truth – which, then and now, seems to be more typical of our contemporary preaching and teaching.

But part of me wants to ask, 'Does any of this matter?' In a global sense it should, as the Church must be concerned with the salvation of all humankind, but more locally it probably doesn't. Most Methodist churches could happily survive without any questers, and do. Those questers under 40 who are still around often find other ways of engaging: for some it's through ordination, for others active engagement with the connexional church and for a few through academic theology; rarely it is simply in a local church.

So Methodism began as a movement that you joined. You became a member as an expression of your belonging and you were expected to take an active part in its class meetings, to share and be accountable for your individual faith to your fellow Christians. It became a Church and slowly the emphasis on sharing individual faith and its theological emphasis on grace and personal holiness waned and so it has lost two of the primary points of distinctiveness through which it could have engaged in dialogue with the contemporary world. Methodism will still be here in 20 years' time, smaller and with a narrower theological and faith form focus but still here, although for questing liberals like me, I think it will very much be a case of 'Thank you for sharing and will the last one left please turn out the light?'

In order to realize its present potential, the Methodist Church will need to:

- recover and communicate its distinctive theological reason for being;
- find contemporary ways of engaging people who have a choosing faith as well as a conforming faith, recognizing that most have left;
- own the bureaucratic nature of connexionalism and re-imagine it for contemporary mission;
- recognize the fluid nature of Christian community but also our accountability one to another for our individual faith journeys;
- be proud of being Methodist, recognizing that 'in the providence of God Methodism was raised up to spread scriptural holiness through the land by the proclamation of the evangelical faith' and that our purpose is still incomplete.

Notes

1 Margaret Thatcher, interview for *Woman's Own* 23 September 1987 and widely quoted at the time.

2 Margaret Thatcher was the daughter of a devout and active local preacher and spent her childhood attending the Wesleyan Methodist Chapel in Grantham, having been baptized there on 28 December 1925.

3 See, for example, Anthony Giddons, *Sociology*, Cambridge: Polity Press, 1989, pp. 275–6.

4 *Belong v.* in *Oxford Reference Dictionary*, Oxford: Clarendon Press, 1991, p. 75.

5 For more information on socialization see, for example, Benjamin Beit-Hallahmi and Michael Argyle, *The Psychology of Religious Behaviour, Belief and Experience*, London: Routledge, 1997, pp. 97–112.

6 See, for example, Richard Gross, *Psychology – The Science of Mind and Behaviour*, 4th edn, London: Hodder & Stoughton, 2001, p. 387.

7 And the other pre-union Methodist denominations.

8 James Fowler, *Stages of Faith: The Psychology of Human Development and the Quest for Meaning*, new edn, San Francisco: Harper, 1995.

9 Fowler's terms for these stages are Synthetic-conventional Faith for conforming faith and Individuative-reflective for choosing faith. These shorter forms are used in the British publication *How Faith Grows* (see note 10).

10 For a brief introduction to all seven stages, see Jeff Atley (ed.), *How Faith Grows*, London: National Society, 1991.

11 *Hymns and Psalms*, number 804.

12 1 Corinthians 12.12–31.

13 See Acts 2.41 'So those who welcomed his message were baptized, and that day about three thousand persons were added.'

14 For example Philip (John 1.43).

15 Mark 3.13–19 and Luke 10.1–20.

16 See, for example, the work of Brian McLaren or Dan Kimble.

17 *The Methodist Worship Book*, Peterborough: Methodist Publishing House, p. 60.

18 Reproduced in Rupert Davies, Raymond George and Gordon Rupp (eds), *A History of the Methodist Church in Great Britain*, volume 4, London: Epworth Press, 1996, pp. 59–61.

19 John Wesley and Charles Wesley, 'The Nature, Design and General Rules of the United Societies', reproduced in Davies, George and Rupp, *A History of The Methodist Church in Great Britain*, volume 4, p. 60.

20 For Wesley these ordinances were: public worship of God; the ministry of the word, either read or expounded; the supper of the Lord; family and private prayer; searching the Scriptures; and fasting or abstinence.

21 *Constitutional Practice and Discipline of the Methodist Church in Great Britain*, volume 2, Peterborough: Methodist Publishing House, pp. 208–37. Quote on page 215.

22 'Membership and Christian Discipleship Report', in *Conference Agenda 1999*, volume 1, Peterborough: Methodist Publishing House, 1999, p. 358.

23 Reproduced in Davies, George and Rupp, *A History of The Methodist Church in Great Britain*, volume 4, pp. 92–102.

24 John Wesley and Charles Wesley, 'The Nature, Design and General Rules of the United Societies', reproduced in Davies, George and Rupp, *A History of The Methodist Church in Great Britain*, volume 4, p. 60.

25 John Wesley, *A Plain Account of the People Called Methodists*, reproduced in Davies, George and Rupp, *A History of The Methodist Church in Great Britain*, volume 4, p. 95 (para. 6).

26 When the Wesleyan, Primitive and United Methodist Churches merged to form what is now the Methodist Church (in Britain).

27 John Wesley, *A Plain Account of the People Called Methodists*, para. 12.

28 *Church Membership and the Class Meeting*, Wesleyan Conference minutes, 1889, appendix XI, extract reproduced in Davies, George and Rupp, *A History of The Methodist Church in Great Britain*, volume 4, p. 571–4.

29 *Church Membership and the Class Meeting*, Wesleyan Conference minutes, 1889.

30 'Time to Talk of God: Rediscovering Christian Conversation as a Way of Nurturing Discipleship Report', Methodist Conference, *Conference Agenda*, volume 1, Peterborough: Methodist Publishing House, 1995.

31 For a helpful introduction to Wesley's understanding of grace, prudential and otherwise, visit http://wesley.nnu.edu/wesleyan_theology/theojrnl/31-35/32-1-5.htm (accessed May 2008).

32 Quoted in John Munsey Turner, 'Methodism in England', in Davies, George and Rupp, *A History of The Methodist Church in Great Britain*, volume 3, London: Epworth Press, 1982, p. 315.

33 Variously attributed to Mark Twain, Benjamin Disraeli and others.

34 'Statistics for Mission 2005–2007' in Methodist Conference, *Conference Agenda*, Volume 2, Peterborough: Methodist Publishing House, 2008, pp. 578–602.

35 'Statistics for Mission 2005–2007'.

36 Phil Escott and Alison Gelder, *Church Life Profile 2001, Denominational Results for the Methodist* Church, Churches Information for Mission, 2001, section 3.1, p. 3.

37 In this context, centrally means a small group in one location (e.g. in London) and connexionally in one body, the Conference.

38 See for example 'Fresh Expression Working Group' in Methodist Conference, *Conference Agenda*, volume 1, Peterborough: Methodist Publishing House, 2007, pp. 564–77.

39 'Youth Participant Strategy for the Methodist Church', in Methodist Conference, *Conference Agenda*, volume 1, Peterborough: Methodist Publishing House, 2007, pp. 219–34.

40 For example in the report *What is a Presbyter?* we talk about them participating, co-ordaining and equipping which sounds very much like leadership to me but the word isn't obviously used. It lurks as one part of a long list of tasks of a presbyter.

41 For a fuller explanation of the flysheet controversy see O. A. Beckerlegge, *The United Methodist Free Churches*, London: Epworth, 1957, pp. 30–34.

42 'Team Focus Report', Methodist Conference, *Conference Agenda*, volume 2, Peterborough: Methodist Publishing House, 2005, p. 363.

43 Caricature based on information in section 5 of Phil Escott and Alison Gelder, *Church Life Profile 2001, Denominational Results for the Methodist Church*, Churches Information for Mission, 2001, pp. 17–23.

44 *Constitutional Practice and Discipline of the Methodist Church in Great Britain*, volume 2, Peterborough: Methodist Publishing House, pp. 208–37. Quote on page 213.

45 Replacement for Easter People, a large annual evangelical event, begun in 2008.

46 METHSOC (or Methodist Societies) in universities.

47 John 18.38.

6

An Ecumenical Faith

KAREN JOBSON

At my Connexional interview when I was a candidate to be a Methodist presbyter, I was asked to give a presentation on 'The Future of Methodism'. I confidently announced that Methodism did not have a future in Britain, at least not in its current form. The future of Christianity was post-denominational, and if we were lucky, we might just claim our stake in that. Two of the panel members looked traumatized, the others vaguely amused.

The background to this was that I had spent seven years worshipping ecumenically at St Lawrence's Church in the Stantonbury Ecumenical parish and abroad. A young person from St Lawrence's had rung me just before the interview in confusion; she had recently become involved in a university chaplaincy but she was not sure to which denomination she was supposed to subscribe. After all, she had only ever known ecumenical congregations with ministers from a variety of denominations, and had experienced adult baptism and confirmation in the same service. I had also recently spent two years living in Namibia working for Voluntary Service Overseas; in my time there I had ended up leading a house church for a disparate group of expatriates who were from seven different countries and ten different denominations. What united us was our inability to speak the local language with any competence, and the desire to worship in our own tongue. I was asked to start leading an act of worship because I had a 'preaching certificate'.

I had to quickly learn the parts of our traditions that unified, and find ways of celebrating those, while recognizing that we each had our own church language and customs that had helped us to encounter God in deep ways. These could be enriching and alienating for others in the group in equal measure. So I learnt to feel comfortable leading liturgy, silence, guided meditations, discursive sermons, and using various stimuli for prayer. I had been able to experiment with few of these tools within the traditional Methodist churches where I had done my preaching training, long before I had heard the phrase 'Fresh Expressions of Church'.[1]

The experience felt like church as it should be: it gave space for us to worship God, to strengthen our faith and to deepen our fellowship with one another (which led to some very tangible pastoral care when a crisis arose), and it gave opportunities to do theological reflection on our work and the reality of being expatriates in a post-apartheid country. I knew then that I would have to commit to a denomination when I returned home at the end of my contract to offer for ministry, but it was with a great deal of sadness: I had learnt that each denomination must learn from the others if we are to benefit from the fullness of the Christian heritage.

Since then I have become more entrenched in my Methodist roots, have become more confident about the role of Methodism on the world stage and discovered that although British Methodism might be bad, many of the other denominations seem to be worse, especially for women. Yet I belong to a generation of ministers that must bridge the gap between the inherited Church and the emerging Church. At times it results in living with the dialectic of trying to create something new, relevant, and appropriate for post-Christian generations for whom denominational allegiance is largely meaningless, and still remain committed to maintaining the practice and traditions of the Methodist Church in which we grew up and that we represent. In putting energy into maintaining that balance, many of my peers have given up on the ecumenical movement, asking what it has really done for British Methodism other than drain resources and detract energy, enthusiasm, and commitment from the real work of making disciples. The language of ecumenism feels dated and excessively institutional, the detail involved is not something that concerns the majority of ministers or lay people and it often feels that most formal ecumenism is done in theological ivory towers, divorced from the realities of real-world Christianity.

I have found more formal ecumenical engagement challenging at times, but I do believe that it is an essential element of the process of being part of the body of Christ. It is always very tempting to remain in the company of other people whose theology and worldview is similar to our own: there is comfort and affirmation, we feel a safe sense of belonging and we can kid ourselves that our perspective of God is right and other people just need to adapt to our way of seeing things. Enticing though it is to stay with people who are like us, it does not bode well for a healthy Church. I am immensely sympathetic to those who have become disillusioned with the ecumenical movement, with those who find the process frustrating and insular. Yet I do believe that ecumenical engagement, at every level, is important in helping us to be challenged to redefine our theology and ecclesiology; it is an essential part of the process of discernment in helping the Church to develop and grow.

Historical Background

Methodists often cite Wesley's sermon on a 'Catholic Spirit'[2] as a starting point for an ecumenical paradigm. He was clear that 'as long as there are various opinions, there will be various ways of worshipping God' but he also suggested that it is unnecessary to get too stuck in the detail of the differences, for though they might prevent an entire external union, they do not need to prevent a union of love and good works. Wesley emphasized that a true Catholic Spirit also necessitated being confident in the religious principles to which one subscribed, worshipping in a way that was felt to be most acceptable, and experiencing the fellowship of a congregation, not being indifferent to the differences and not trying to 'blend them into one'. The emphasis on conscience was significant; it was to become central to the separation from the Church of England.

From the first Methodist Conference in 1744 it was apparent that the Anglicans had not extended a 'Catholic Spirit' to those who associated with the Methodist movement and there had been many accusations of preaching false doctrine. Wesley had maintained that though the bishops must be respected, conscience had to determine the extent to which they must be obeyed. In his approach Wesley modelled something of what we would recognize as the contemporary post-denominational Christian; he was secure in the doctrines that defined his faith yet, when it came to attitude and even to practice, he and those who were part of the movement were flexible and adaptable. This was especially apparent when he was in Ireland where denominational allegiances were, and still are, hugely divisive. His brother Charles reported: 'The Presbyterians say that I am a Presbyterian; the church-goers that I am a minister of theirs; and the Catholics that they are sure I am a good Catholic in my heart.'[3]

Since the death of the Wesleys, Methodists have divided from the Anglican Church and divided again within the Methodist tradition. Yet ironically, given that was it was the desire to be effective in mission and to be true to conscience that caused the break from the Anglican Church, it was also those same desires that stimulated the start of the current ecumenical movement. Many missionaries were being sent abroad into countries that had gained links with Britain through the expansion of the empire. There was a plethora of missionary societies, including the Methodist Missionary Society, often trying to convert the same people and frequently seen to be in competition with one another. This led to increasing frustration and ineffectiveness and triggered the desire to bring together the different missionary organizations at a conference that would give a forum for discussion and debate and hopefully lead to a more coherent mission strategy.

The result was the World Missionary Conference in Edinburgh in 1910. What is striking about the transcripts of the speeches made at that conference is how contemporary they seem. The emphasis was very much on the common quest to communicate God's love to 'our generation', and there was an acknowledgement that one of the greatest hindrances in doing that was the divisions between them. Thus there was a recognition that mission and unity needed to go hand in hand and it developed the base for the ecumenical dialogues that were to follow.

Methodists have always played a key role in those. John R. Mott, a Methodist from the USA, for example, gave the closing address at the World Missionary Conference; 38 years later he preached at the opening service at the World Council of Churches in 1948.[4] During those intervening years, even before World War Two had totally redefined the sociopolitical landscape, the ecumenical movement had gained a different momentum. Ecumenical dialogue was no longer perceived solely as something to facilitate more effective mission; rather, different strands began to emerge with a greater emphasis on the importance of full visible unity between Christians and within the Church both practically and theologically.

In 1925, in Stockholm, there was the first conference of the Life and Work movement that brought Christians together to enable a common response to poverty, oppression, war, and natural disaster. This was followed in 1927 in Lausanne by a conference for the Faith and Order movement that focussed on theological issues and sought to find ways of overcoming the differences surrounding baptism, eucharist, ministry, and membership. Mission also remained an important element, and in 1928 there was a meeting of the International Missionary Council in Jerusalem that endeavoured to continue the work of the earlier World Missionary Council. This focussed on how best to communicate a common witness and encouraged co-operation in mission and evangelism.

The two World Wars inevitably had an impact on the ecumenical process and the churches felt a responsibility to be involved in reconciliation in a broken world; their actions needed to mirror their rhetoric. The United Nations was formally constituted in 1945 to give a secular vehicle for communication and convergence. The World Council of Churches (WCC) had its first official meeting in Amsterdam in 1948 to serve the same purposes for churches. For both organizations the shadow of the war gave a strong imperative to work for unity so that such a situation would never arise again. The churches recognized that

We are divided from one another not only in matters of faith, order and tradition, but also by pride of nation, class and race. But Christ has made us His own, and He is not divided.[5]

Unity was worth seeking for its own sake and for the sake of the world that the Church sought to serve, rather than just as a missionary tool. Following a time when the majority of the world had been scarred by profound cruelty and evil as a result of corrupted human ideology, it was understandable that the churches sought to be a source of unity and that unity had to be visible and evident to those both inside and outside the ecclesiological structures. The dominant theological paradigm was one of a Church united by a belief in Christ crucified and risen and although this was the same principle that underscored the missionary motivation for ecumenism, after World War Two it became more reflective and much more energy was invested in exploring theological and ecclesiological differences and trying to find ways of bridging them. There was also a strong emphasis on social justice and over the years gender, racial, and economic justice have been central themes for the work of the WCC. Member churches of the WCC affirm that they

are called to the goal of visible unity in one faith and one eucharistic fellowship, promoting the common witness in work for mission and evangelism, engage in Christian service by serving human need, breaking down barriers between people, seeking justice and peace, and upholding the integrity of creation and to fostering renewal in unity, worship, mission and service.[6]

The contemporary ecumenical movement has attracted much criticism, particularly within the evangelical tradition. It has been suggested that too much emphasis has been placed on the commitment to the quest for visible unity and eucharistic fellowship; momentum and effort that should have been put into evangelism and mission have been lost on internal politics. Full visible unity is perceived as unrealistic and unachievable, and though some level of eucharistic fellowship is a helpful tool when Christians are working together, it is largely irrelevant. None of the many ecumenical reports that have been produced have helped to regenerate the Church and they are often seen as the desperate clinging of churches to one another for mutual support in the face of their demise. So the ecumenical movement has been a source of disillusionment for those who would much rather concentrate on communicating the 'good news' of the Christian faith and are not concerned with the intricate details of theological divergence, particularly when the pace of progress to overcome them is so painfully slow.

Though I have considerable empathy with this perspective, my own experiences have challenged my thinking on this. While I was at theological college I spent a semester studying with the World Council of Churches' training centre, the Bossey Institute. I was on the course with 32 people from 23 countries and a variety of Christian traditions. I found the time that I spent there immensely challenging. I am comfortable with regarding myself as a feminist theologian, had a very deep sense of call to ordained ministry, and had the arrogance to believe that having spent two years living in Africa I actually knew something about Liberation theology.

All of those things that were such crucial parts of my Christian identity were severely questioned. At least two-thirds of the people on the course did not believe that, as a woman, I was called to ordination. At a service I led where I referred to God as mother and father I so upset an Orthodox colleague that he accused me of 'raping' his God, and I learnt from listening to the stories of those who lived in the developing world that actually, from my privileged Northern European perspective, my opinions on Liberation theology were trite and limited.

I came back to the UK feeling depressed, demoralized, and bruised; more aware than ever of the realities of trying to move towards full and visible unity; and deeply questioning whether the immense nature of the task warranted the effort and engagement. I desperately wanted to be back in a world that was safe and comfortable and populated by people more like me who would affirm my understanding of my faith and my self.

During those months on my return I was immensely challenged by reading Dietrich Bonhoeffer's *Life Together*:

> Just as surely as God desires to lead us to a knowledge of genuine Christian fellowship, so surely must we be overwhelmed by a great disillusionment with others, with Christians in general and if we are fortunate with ourselves... God is not a God of the emotions but a God of the truth. Only that fellowship which faces such disillusionment with all its unhappy and ugly aspects, begins to grasp in faith the promise that is given to it.[7]

I understand that engagement with other traditions in real depth is demanding and time consuming. However, if Methodism is to have a future, it cannot afford to let the theological dialogue with people from other traditions dwindle; it is too important in keeping us accountable and preventing theological stagnation. Other traditions hold up a mirror to us in which we can see our own failings and limitations. I question whether we will ever develop full and visible unity, but in a sense that destination is less important to me than the journey towards it. The ecumenical process becomes more crucial, not less, when we are facing increasing secularization.

One aspect of my experiences at Bossey that gave me immense hope was talking with the Orthodox students who had grown up in Eastern Europe during communism. As an oppressed church they had to hold on to what was elemental about their tradition and find ways of communicating it against the odds. In ecumenical discussions, that was apparent. There was a deep sense of confidence in their tradition and that could mean a large degree of inflexibility of thinking, and little tolerance for theological divergence. Yet it was born from the knowledge that their tradition had survived every conceivable attack on it during the past two thousand years, and it remained.

Any church participating in ecumenical dialogue needs to have, at its heart, that deep confidence in its tradition but I would also suggest that it needs an openness to the aspects of the church that are given by God and those which are human constructs.

The first will endure the crucible of challenge and of time, the second should not. The changes that do come are often subtle, though positive: they are characterized by a clarifying of thought and a reassertion of the essential elements of the tradition. Those who denominationally are relative newcomers have much to learn about endurance from those traditions that have survived for much longer. They too have something to learn about flexibility and responsiveness from us. In the same way those Fresh Expressions of Church that survive the test of time will in turn look to the lessons learnt from the eighteenth and nineteenth centuries, those fresh expressions of which Methodism was one. Our faith does not exist in a historic vacuum. It is built upon more than 2000 years of evangelism and mission by previous generations. We need reverently to bear our collective Christian memory of how God has brought us to this moment. Though we are commanded to make disciples, let us not forget all the work that has gone before.

Over recent years there have been many examples of how engagement with ecumenism has helped to shape Methodist theology. The World Council of Churches Faith and Order Paper number 111 *Baptism, Eucharist and Ministry* (BEM – the 'Lima Text') published in 1982 was the product of 50 years of discussion and exploration. The methodology involved moving away from comparative theology in which differences were highlighted and reinforced, to recognition that no one Christian tradition held the whole truth and that each was interpreting the same Scriptures in different ways. There was much hyperbole surrounding the document: the moderator of the Faith and Order Commission, John Deschner, a Methodist theologian, likened it to a deep relationship between a man and woman that would inevitably lead to marriage, while Jurgen Moltmann stated that as a result of the work there were 'no longer any doctrinal differences which justify the divisions of our churches'.[8] Sadly history would suggest that their enthusiasm was misplaced.

Yet for the British Methodist Church it did provide an unparalleled opportunity for churches on a local level to become involved in theological debate. Synods, Circuit Meetings and

Church Councils were invited to discuss the document and a year was given to the process. It became clear from the final report compiled from the feedback that there were some aspects of British Methodism that were not to be compromised in the quest for unity. These included the importance of the calling of the whole people of God, not just those who are ordained; the belief that the call of women to ordained ministry was of God; and the centrality of the active pursuit of justice and peace as an integral part of the apostolic faith.[9] It conceded that other elements of Methodist theology needed more thought; these included our understanding of authority, sacramental theology, and some other aspects of our ecclesiology.

From the discussions a response document was drawn up. Much of what it affirmed became the basis of further dialogues and led to more structured theological thought from within the British Methodist tradition, including two substantial reports: *Called to Love and Praise*[10] on the nature of the Church and *His Presence Makes the Feast*[11] on the Eucharist.

Called To Love and Praise

In 1999 the British Methodist Conference adopted as a Conference Statement[12] *Called to Love and Praise*. It was the result of ten years of work that sought to develop a definitive text on the ecclesiology of the British Methodist Church. In it the biblical basis for models of church are explored and there is recognition that even from the earliest times there has never been one single structure. Moreover, there is also an emphasis on the nature of the unity of the different parts of the early Church: the shared belief in the life, death, and resurrection of Jesus; the common heritage shared by the Church and Israel, and finally the life of faith which Christians share expressed in fellowship, worship, mission, and service. The statement maintains a strong ecumenical focus throughout and it concedes in its conclusion that the British Methodist Church as a separate denomination may soon cease to exist, though it hopes that some aspects of its heritage will remain.

The statement celebrated the work done by the World Council

of Churches and the slow, but continued, progress in facilitating a deeper understanding of what both temporal and transcendent unity in Christ can be. This focussed particularly on the *koinonia* model, which has at its heart the call of the church to hold together, the call to be in relationship with God and, through fellowship and ministry, with one another. Central to it is the emphasis on shared existence:

> a common sacramental life entered into by one baptism and celebrated together in one eucharistic fellowship; a common life in which members and ministries are mutually recognized and reconciled; and a common mission witnessing to all people to the Gospel of God's grace and serving the whole of creation.[13]

With regard to the gifts that the British Methodist Church is able to offer, it develops the thinking that was done in response to the BEM document, self-critically recognizing the distinct contribution of Methodism towards an understanding of holiness, Holy Communion, and ordination, while also acknowledging the areas of ambiguity and dissonance within Methodist theology and practice.

The ecumenical model presented is still that of moving towards full and visible unity for the different inherited denominations. Yet it glosses over some of the very real barriers in moving towards that. The writers of *Called to Love and Praise* state clearly: 'injustice and inequality based, for example, on race, gender or age have no place here [within the *koinonia* model]'.[14]

Many people living in postmodern Britain would agree with that statement, but it is not something that they associate with the churches. At the heart of a number of the denominations with whom we seek to enter into unity is the deeply held, scripturally based and theologically legitimate belief that inequality with regard to ordination and oversight is acceptable and even essential. Though the document might affirm that the Christian tradition is fluid and experiential rather than static, many within Methodism and in the other churches would fundamentally disagree with this statement; for them there is much within the Church that is absolute and not open to change. Meanwhile those on the fringes and outside of the Church struggle to understand the contradictory messages that we communicate and they disengage as a result.

An Anglican–Methodist Covenant

The bilateral ecumenical discussions that both the British Methodist Church and the worldwide Methodist Church have been involved in have been marked by greater candour with regard to barriers and bridges towards unity.

The Anglican–Methodist Covenant,[15] produced in 2001, is the work of one of the most significant ecumenical dialogues that the British Methodist Church has engaged in. Attempts in 1972 and 1982 to move the Methodist Church and the Church of England towards greater unity faltered when the proposals failed to achieve the support required at General Synod. Again much of the stated motivation for the covenant was the recognition that 'our separation damages the credibility of our witness in the world to the reconciling purposes of God ... and it weakens our mission and evangelism in this country'.[16]

Mission was the motivator for it, but theology and ecclesiology has formed the basis of much of the discussion. As a result of the work on the Covenant, the Churches were able to make a number of affirmations that recognize the validity of each of the Churches and their baptism and eucharistic rites, the authenticity of the call of the ordained ministers in both Churches, and that episcope is exercised in different forms in each Church. Several commitments were also made which included working towards full visible unity, one mark of which would be united, interchangeable ministry and oversight. The subsequent recommendations centred on ensuring that the document was discussed and debated at every level in the two Churches and that a Joint Implementation Commission be established with a specific brief of exploring the question of the interchangeability of ministries.

The Joint Implementation Commission has since produced two interim reports that explore the progress of the Covenant: *In the Spirit of the Covenant*[17] (2005) and *Living God's Covenant*[18]

(2007). The 2005 Interim Report is a predominantly descriptive document in which the differences in eucharistic practices and the implications of interchangeable ministries are explored. The 2007 report develops this further with a particular focus on the differences between the Churches in their understandings of the relationship between Church, state and establishment; lay ministry; and the Eucharist. It also gives more consideration to the practical implications of the Covenant and considers how it is being applied within churches.

As working documents both reports have interacted with the ongoing internal discussions within the churches, especially regarding women bishops within the Anglican Church and *What Kind of Bishops?* within the Methodist Church. Those feeling impatient with the slow, painstaking progress of the discussions would have not have taken comfort from the recognition that 'We are in this for the long term. Clever human plans to create a "quick fix" merger between our two Churches are not what our Covenant is about.'[19] However, it does reflect the reality that ecumenical work takes time; any attempt to rush it or push too hard is detrimental in the long term.

There was much excitement, within some circles, about the Covenant when it was first launched. Yet the reality for most people is that it has made very little impact. Martyn Atkins has noted the attitudes of different generations of ministers towards the Anglican–Methodist Covenant. He suggests that there are three distinct approaches. First, those who had lived through the disappointments of other attempts at ecumenical relations see such moves as positive and the answer to prayer. The second group adopt a pragmatic approach: ecumenism is a positive thing but let us not get too entrenched in the detail, we need to get on with it. The final group tend to be those newest to ministry who see ecumenical advancements as 'nice' but irrelevant, confident in their own denominational identity and what it can contribute to the mission of the whole Church. They are people that will work with whoever share the same approach to mission. This approach recognizes that we are living in a post-denominational age, and in trying to minister to those under 40 who have had no previous experience of any denomination, it is a waste of energy to try to persuade them that one is preferential to another.[20]

This is a reasonable generalization; however attitudes also vary a great deal according to the local context. As was noted in the second interim report there are many different forms of Anglicanism and the question often arises: 'To which Anglican Church are we supposed to relate?' Some branches of Anglicanism relate much more easily to Methodism than others. Within some areas Anglican–Methodist relations are very natural and often they existed long before the Covenant was ever signed. Shared services and common mission activities flow from a common Christian presence within communities. In other areas the relationships are much more strained and Methodists often find themselves in more comfortable partnerships with other denominations. The reality for most congregations is that the Covenant has had very little real impact.

At the time of writing, I minister to two Methodist/Anglican Local Ecumenical Partnerships (LEPs). What is very apparent even when the congregations and clergy are deeply committed to shared working is that there are still disparities. My Anglican colleague sits on the Circuit Meeting with full voting rights; I attend Deanery Synod as an observer. He is authorized to serve within the whole of the Methodist circuit; no equivalent is extended to me. The buildings too are regarded in different ways; while the Anglican building is on consecrated ground and therefore subject to infinitely more bureaucracy, the Methodist building is not. There is still a sense that the Methodist Church is the inferior partner at every level and this causes frustration and resentment throughout. This local example is replicated throughout the country and can be observed in most of the practical efforts to engage with the Anglican Church.

The roots of these current partnerships go back to 1964 when Churches were asked to designate areas in which there could be 'experiments in ecumenical group ministries, in sharing of buildings and equipment, and in the development of mission.'[21] The result was Local Ecumenical Projects. They were regarded as transitory and given only very tentative support by the mainstream

Churches. Those experiments have gone on to redefine local ecumenical possibilities, something recognized within the BEM report and the Anglican–Methodist Covenant. Yet over the years they have become institutionalized and often find themselves boxed in by excessive legalism and bureaucracy, unable to be responsive to their localities in the ways that they would like to be. I have a deep concern that the same will happen with denominationally funded Fresh Expressions. Though the Covenant is intended to reduce the barriers to effective working, the structures in neither the Anglican nor Methodist Church are flexible enough to accommodate this. It is this lack of structural flexibility that will prevent the Covenant from working for ordinary Christians, not the theological differences.

The Covenant and interim reports that followed are important in helping us to develop a more coherent theological understanding of the differences and in providing an academic framework for dialogue on which our churches can build. However, if it is to be meaningful for the majority of church members we need to be much more effective in providing Christian education so that congregations themselves can be confident in the doctrine and history of their own denominations. In the LEP to which I was recently appointed as minister, my Anglican colleague and I did a series of sermons on our different denominational understandings of Holy Communion. I was assured afterwards that for the majority it was the first time that they had been told why we do things in a certain way, yet most had been going to church for more than 60 years. Ecumenical relationships need to be built on a shared understanding and mutual respect. This can only come from denominational self-knowledge and confidence.

Living With Contradictory Convictions

One of the most useful theological frameworks offered for dialogue in recent years is the 2006 report to Methodist Conference, *Living With Contradictory Convictions*.[22] British Methodism itself is not a monolithic tradition; within it every expression of Christianity is represented. The work done on the 'Pilgrimage of

Faith', which explores the issues surrounding sexuality within the Church, highlighted some of these deeply held differences. This led to the Faith and Order Committee being asked to explore the implications of being a Church that must 'contend with different and mutually contradictory convictions'.[23] Central to the report is the use of 'Wesley's quadrilateral': Scripture, reason, tradition, and experience. It suggests that any theological discernment must be done in the light of each of these components. Accordingly, there is emphasis on the importance of listening to one another's stories in order to discern where God is at work. This demands vulnerability and the ability to listen to viewpoints that can often diverge from our own. It recognizes that diversity is inevitable within the Church and there is a need to engage with it in a prayerful, respectful, and informed way. In common with *Called to Love and Praise* it affirms a dialogical relationship with God and one another, which embraces fluidity, challenge, and change. That can be threatened by excessive dogmatism and a desire for absolutes.

Though it was written specifically to better enable internal dialogue, it is equally applicable to ecumenical dialogues. I am immensely thankful for the report and the value it gives to experience and story when balanced with the other aspects of Scripture, reason, and tradition. This represents a positive move forward for the Faith and Order Committee, which has frequently given more credence to a historical-critical methodology that has too often become divorced from the reality of people's lived experiences of God.

The report resonates with my own experience of grass roots ecumenism, which is ultimately relational. This does not detract from the need for more theological education for the laity, to empower them to understand the issues better, but it does affirm the day-to-day experiences of God at work through the relationships that are developed. This approach is consistent with a view of ecumenism that values the journey more than the destination, and recognizes that God is still at work through the process. The need to listen carefully to one another and actually hear the stories of joy, hurt, and pain is essential in effective discernment and this becomes particularly crucial when relating to Christians who have a different cultural background to us.

Global Methodism and Ecumenical Dialogues

It is apparent that even within a small Church such as the British Methodist Church there are fundamental differences of opinion and theology. Worldwide, churches associated with Methodism make up one of the largest denominations, and consequently it encompasses a great deal of cultural and theological diversity. In an attempt to address this, in 1881 the first Ecumenical Methodist Conference brought together delegates from 30 Methodist bodies to encourage dialogue and understanding. The conference continued to meet about every ten years (though the pattern was interrupted by World War Two) and in 1951 it became known as the 'World Methodist Council' and started to meet every five years. The Methodist Church has grown to include around 37 million members worldwide. It is therefore not surprising that there are quite profound differences that divide the community, but the World Methodist Council provides an important forum in which these differences can be explored.

As a newcomer to the Council, what is striking is the way in which history and experience fundamentally define relationships between members. In addition to theological differences there is an ongoing need to bridge the divisions caused by race, gender, wealth, and power. Though our history is a unifier, it is also immensely divisive. Our historical link to Wesley is what draws us together, but this cannot be divorced from the secular context of colonialism and slavery, which have affected all of our churches. The World Methodist Council is providing a forum for intra-Methodist dialogues as churches attempt to explore some of the painful aspects of history that divide them and find ways of growing together. I am convinced that though Scripture, reason, and tradition will inform those dialogues, it will be the ability to hear one another's stories respectfully that will transform them, and move us closer to one another and towards God.

The World Methodist Council also provides an agency for international bilateral dialogues. Formal dialogues have taken place between Methodists and the Roman Catholics, the Lutheran World Federation, the Anglican Church, the World Alliance of Reformed Churches and most recently the Salvation Army. Each dialogue is unique, but all have sought to consider the essence of what Methodism is in relation to the other Church and explore ways of productively moving towards a more united ministry. With regard to the dialogue between the Roman Catholic Church and the World Methodist Council this has meant doing some very detailed theology on the Holy Spirit, the Church, and the Apostolic Tradition. The dialogue between the Salvation Army and the Methodists was underscored with a celebration of our shared history and an exploration of how each presently perceives the other. Again it is interesting to note the value that each of the reports places on the individual relationships that develop between participants and how crucial they are in developing trust.

The international bilateral dialogues, by their nature, are based on the perceived essence of denominations; there are considerable regional differences in the ways that denominations are structured and express their faith. These dialogues do not always express regional concerns in the ways that some would like, and ultimately it is the local churches that must be the practical agents of ecumenical change. In some circumstances that can be very difficult, especially when other denominations are much stronger and more dominant. However, the dialogues are helping us to progress further in our understanding of one another and laying the foundations for further work together.

A rapidly changing global context also means that many see interdenominational dialogue as less important than interfaith work; particularly, as has been well documented, there are increasing tensions between Christendom and the Islamic world. Though the need to engage with other faiths in a non-tokenistic and meaningful way is essential, this can give more impetus to the ecumenical dialogues and can provide an external focus that may well prove to be a helpful unifier. The learning that can be gained from working towards understanding and greater unity within our own Church and in relation to other Churches is able to inform how we approach the much greater challenges of inter-faith dialogues. Some might suggest that this too is detraction from our core mission. Yet we are called to be God's people in the world where the need for mutual understanding and respect between people of different theological convictions and none has never been greater. We cannot afford not to put energy and effort into this.

Conclusion

I am under no illusion that for the majority of Methodists, the formal ecumenical movement is an irrelevance. Regardless of what happens with bilateral discussions either in Britain or on a global scale, what concerns them most is their local Church. If there are positive local ecumenical relations it is probably because the clergy or some dedicated lay people have an enthusiasm and commitment to it. For those who do actively pursue partnerships they will find that the structures for ecumenical work are cumbersome, time consuming, and disabling. Yet despite all of this, God calls us to be part of the broken Body of Christ. We cannot turn around and say to the other Churches that we do not need them, for we do. Clinging together because we are drowning in a sea of secularization stimulates ecumenical interdependence but it should not be the primary motivation for those relationships. Whether we like it or not, we are tied by history to the same God and the same Jesus Christ, we are called to discover together what God wants for the future Church.

In the longer term it might mean that denominations become defunct, but there will always be differences in theology, worship and practice. Because of this, one united Church seems like an impossible dream. Yet the world has much to teach us about how seemingly impossible dreams can be realized: a united Ireland, a united Germany, and a united South Africa. Thirty years ago all of them seemed impossible; now, though there is still much work to do in each of those places, the dreams are becoming reality.

Somebody once suggested that 'hell is other people'. My concept of hell is other people who are just like me. I have come to equate uniformity with predictable sameness, sterility, and unfruitful-ness. Imagine if the only church in the world were the Methodist Church, we would lose so much of the richness of Christianity. But diversity does bring challenges and does demand of us great humility. Commitment to work meaningfully with those who dif-fer from us theologically does tie us to a slow, painstaking process if it is not to be superficial. Working together in practical ways is important, but so too is doing the hard thinking and listening. Undoubtedly the ecumenical movement will continue to progress in fairy steps rather than giant leaps, but provided it is giving us the opportunity to tell our faith stories and to listen and learn from those stories of others, then it is a movement that I believe still demands investment.

In order to realize its present potential, the Methodist Church will need to:

- continue to commit time and resources to ecumenical dialogue;
- develop a greater self-confidence about what Methodism has to offer and be clearer about what can be compromised on and what cannot;
- encourage people in local congregations to learn about the his-tory of Methodism and develop their confidence in engaging with theology;
- remain committed to exploring theological differences within our own denomination and be open to helping others to learn from our journey;
- celebrate the fact that we are part of a strong world Church: learn from Methodist Churches around the world and remem-ber that though British Methodism is in decline, globally the Methodist Church is still strong.

Notes

1 See www.freshexpressions.org.uk for an explanation of this term.
2 *John Wesley's Forty-Four Sermons*, London: Epworth Press, 1985, pp. 442–56.
3 Cited in Kenneth Cracknell and Susan J. White, *An Introduction to World Methodism*, New York: Cambridge University Press, 2005, p. 247.

4 Speech by John R. Mott. Cited in Michael Kinnamon and Brian E. Cope, *The Ecumenical Movement: An Anthology of Key Texts and Voices*, Geneva: WCC Publications, 1997, p. 10.

5 Cited in Kinnamon and Cope, *The Ecumenical Movement*, p. 21.

6 Quoted from the World Council of Churches website www.oikumene. org/who-are-we.html.

7 Dietrich Bonhoeffer, *Life Together*, London: SCM Press, 1954, p. 15.

8 Michael Kinnamon, *Why It Matters: A Popular Introduction to the Baptism, Eucharist and Ministry Text*, Geneva: World Council of Churches, 1985, p. 16.

9 Max Thurian (ed.), *Churches Respond to BEM Volume 2: Official Responses to the 'Baptism, Eucharist and Ministry' Text*, Geneva: World Council of Churches, pp. 210–29.

10 Faith and Order Committee, *Called to Love and Praise*, Statement of the British Methodist Conference, 1999, para.3.1.11. Download from www.methodist.org.uk/downloads/conf99_called_to_love_and_praise.

11 *His Presence Makes the Feast: Holy Communion in the Methodist Church. The Faith and Order Report to the Methodist Conference 2003*, Peterborough: Methodist Publishing House, 2003, p. 57.

12 A Conference Statement expresses the mind of the British Methodist Conference on a particular subject.

13 *Called to Love and Praise*, para. 3.1.11

14 *Called to Love and Praise*, para. 3.1.8

15 *An Anglican–Methodist Covenant: Common Statement of the Formal Conversations Between the Methodist Church of Great Britain and the Church of England*: Methodist Publishing House and Church House Publishing, 2001.

16 *An Anglican–Methodist Covenant* para.65

17 The Joint Implementation Commission, *In the Spirit of the Covenant: Interim Report (2005) of the Joint Implementation Commission between the Methodist Church of Great Britain and The Church of England*, Peterborough: Methodist Publishing House, 2005.

18 Joint Implementation Commission, *Living God's Covenant: Second Interim Report (2007) of the Joint Implementation Commission under the Covenant between The Methodist Church of Great Britain and The Church of England*, Peterborough: Methodist Publishing House, 2007.

19 *In the Spirit of the Covenant*, para. 4.5.

20 Martyn Atkins, *Resourcing Renewal: Shaping the Churches For The Emerging Future*, Peterborough: Inspire, 2007, p. 41.

21 Cited in Maxwell Craig, *For God's Sake Unity: The Church Is Called to Be One*, Glasgow: Wild Goose Publications, 1988, p. 123.

22 Faith and Order Committee, *Living With Contradictory Convictions*,

Report to the British Methodist Conference 2006. Download from www.
methodist.org.uk/downloads/Conf06_Faith_and_Order_committee_pt2.
23 *Living With Contradictory Convictions*, para. 1.1.

7

A World Faith

DION FORSTER

'Thursdays are "Manyano" days...,' a lay preacher from my township Church told me. For years I had noticed the women and men in their bright red uniforms walking the streets of the townships but somehow it had never dawned on me that these were Methodists like me! In large part this was because I was brought up in a traditional, almost entirely white, Methodist Church in suburban South Africa. The Church of my youth might as well have been situated in one of the suburbs surrounding London. Now, for the first time, I realized how out of place it seemed in Africa. I had never considered that the largest contingent of our Church, connexionally, belonged to the 'Manyanos'. Here they were converted, discipled, cared for, and found expression for their calling and faith through the vibrant men's and women's organizations of the Methodist Church of Southern Africa. What was significant about my realization was that I had never considered just how diverse, and even different, Methodists were here in South Africa, let alone what Methodism must look like, and sound like, throughout the rest of the world. In the years since that day I have enjoyed experiencing and discovering new, and unique, expressions of our Methodist identity in many different contexts and forms. Yet for some reason, whenever I am with Methodists I feel a sense of common identity, in spite of the styles of worship, or the structure of the institutional Church. There is something about Methodist identity that runs through all of these varied expressions.

The creeds affirm that the Church universal has a common

theological character and mission mandate throughout the world. Emilio Castro, a Methodist from Uruguay and the fourth General Secretary of the World Council of Churches, gives the following wonderful summary of that universal character and mission:

> The church is called ... to be an anticipation of the kingdom; to show in its internal life the values of justice and supportive love; to develop a priestly servant vocation in interceding in Abrahamic tradition for the whole human community; to celebrate liturgically, in anticipation, the coming of the kingdom; to watch like the virgins of the parable for the coming of the Lord; and then to be the missionary people of God, called and sent all over the world to proclaim and serve, announcing and manifesting the kingdom of God.[1]

Yet as Bishop Graham Cray commented, the gospel must also be 'constantly forwarded to a new address because the recipient is always changing his place of residence'. Few theologians would disagree with the understanding that the common character and mission mandate of the universal Church takes on particular, and varied, forms and expressions in the wide array of contexts into which the Church has been planted throughout the world. In some instances these forms and expressions are pragmatic, adapting the central identity to fit into a particular cultural identity. In other instances the contextual challenges that are faced are significant enough to warrant a change in the fundamental identity of the Church itself.

As Methodism spread from Britain throughout the world in the eighteenth and nineteenth centuries it faced similar pressures to change in order to adapt to the new contexts into which it was entering. In the centuries since those first missionary outreaches the religious character of the world has shifted dramatically. Whereas Europe, and particularly Britain in the case of Methodism, was the birthplace of missionary activity throughout the world, the twentieth century has seen Christianity gain much greater support and fervour among those territories and nations into which the Church was born. The largest group of Methodists in the world are no longer in Britain. Rather, they are to be found in nations such as Korea,[2] Africa, and Latin America.

The question that this chapter considers is whether these contextual expressions of Methodism, born of missionary work from Britain, still maintain an identity that is akin to the central theological emphases of Wesleyan Methodism. It would not be possible to consider all of the varied Methodist and Wesleyan traditions that have arisen across the globe within the scope of this chapter. What I shall do, however, is to present and consider one expression of world Methodism, namely that of the Methodist Church of Southern Africa. In doing so I shall examine the notion of a common Methodist identity as it takes shape in a particular context, that of contemporary Southern Africa, a context that is quite different from that in which Methodism was birthed.

The Methodist Church of Southern Africa (MCSA) is the largest mainline Christian denomination in Southern Africa. This Church offers insights into the necessary adaptation of the global Methodist identity in order to meet the contextual differences, and particularly the contextual challenges, that Methodism faced as it was planted on the southern tip of Africa. In order to consider the unique identity of Methodism in Southern Africa it will be necessary to consider how the unique contextual challenges of Southern Africa adapted the central tenets of Methodist theology in the nineteenth and twentieth centuries. Having presented insights that sketch this background (with particular reference to South Africa's apartheid history), five seminal historical examples of Southern African Methodist theology and mission will be presented. These events show how the Church sought to respond pragmatically to the social crises that arose in Southern Africa, and in so doing adapted Methodist identity to meet the needs of this context. From a theological perspective this section will show how these efforts were understood as attempts at achieving the goal of Christian perfection – the central thrust of early Wesleyan Methodist theology. The chapter then concludes with some consideration of the relationship between the identity of world Methodism and that of Methodists in Southern Africa.

Struggle, Opportunity, and New Life

Planting the seeds of Methodism in Southern African soil

What is the most important theological trait in Methodist identity? In order to establish this one would need to consider the central theological emphases of the founder of Methodism, John Wesley.

Most Methodist scholars agree that the order of salvation was central to John Wesley's theology. The following quotation from 1746 shows what Wesley himself understood:

> Our main doctrines, which include all the rest are three: that of repentance, of faith and holiness. The first of these we account, as were the porch of religion, the next the door; the third religion itself.[3]

However, within the order of salvation Wesley regarded one element as more important than the others, namely the goal towards which all faith is oriented in the order of salvation – Christian perfection. He believed that Christian perfection was a peculiar emphasis and heritage that had been given to the Methodist movement by God. In 1789, just two years before his death, Wesley writes in defence of his emphasis on Christian perfection,

> This doctrine is the grand depositum which God has lodged with the people called Methodists; and for the sake of propagating this chiefly He appeared to have raised us up.[4]

Sadly, Wesley's emphasis on Christian perfection has been largely misunderstood and forgotten in popular Methodist circles, particularly so among its adopters in the holiness movements in recent history. He writes of true religion, and true holiness (as opposed to false religion and false holiness), that the

> gospel of Christ knows no religion but social; no holiness but social holiness. 'Faith working by love' is the length and breadth and depth and height of Christian perfection.[5]

This form of Methodism came to South Africa soon after John Wesley's death in 1791. The very first record of a Methodist (lay person) in the Cape was that of an Irish soldier of the English Army, John Irwin, who held prayer meetings at the Cape as early as 1795.[6] The first record of a Methodist preacher in Southern Africa was that of a soldier of the 72nd regiment of the British army, George Middlemiss, who had been stationed in the Cape of Good Hope to secure British interests there in 1805 as a result of the war between Britain and France.[7] Middlemiss soon gathered a small group of Methodists in the Cape around himself for prayer and fellowship. This work quickly grew. By the time Sergeant Kendrick, a Methodist class leader and lay preacher, arrived in 1812 the congregation numbered 142 persons, of which 128 were of British descent and 14 were of mixed race.[8] So when the British settlers arrived at the Cape in 1820, Methodism was already well established in Southern Africa.

In subsequent years missionaries were despatched from Britain to establish and spread Methodist work throughout the subcontinent.[9] They did this with great courage, sacrifice, and faith.[10] By 1860 there were 132 Methodist ministers and missionaries in the Eastern Cape and Natal, and their combined congregations numbered around 5,000 members.[11]

From the very beginnings Methodist work was multiracial, and while some other Churches and mission organizations concentrated almost exclusively on one racial group, working either among the white settlers, or among indigenous African peoples, the Methodists established joint works. In part this led to the Methodist Church of Southern Africa having more black members than any of the other mainline denominations in Southern Africa.[12] Moreover, at the same time the Methodist Church became the largest English-speaking denomination in the country.[13] Methodism continued to spread and grow in Southern Africa throughout the nineteenth century.

However, even at this early stage there was a clear sense of the need to inculturate the mission and identity of British Methodism, and particularly Wesley's emphasis on Christian perfection as social holiness, in this new African context. Thus the early missionaries placed a strong emphasis on the need to engage not only in the proclamation of the gospel and the fostering of personal piety, but also in the work of social transformation and development within the mission communities. Naturally some of the attempts at social transformation and development had a decidedly western, and even blatantly colonial, slant to them, as was common among nineteenth-century missionaries.[14] The emphasis on social holiness, which was influenced by the missionary identity of Christian work in England in these early years, included projects such as:

- the establishment of schools and skills development projects;
- the translation of the first complete Bible into an African language (1859);
- offering medical care to all, and the establishment of hospitals;
- the establishment of homes for orphans and senior citizens;
- the development and publication of Christian literature;
- facilitating racial reconciliation among the settler population and the 'native' population;
- working for reconciliation and peace in areas that were subject to conflict.

The social and political climate of the day played a significant role in the development and appropriation of Methodist theology on African soil. The rise, implementation, and eventual demise of the racial ideology of 'apartheid' was one of the most significant social and political forces that the Church had to contend with in Southern Africa during the twentieth century.[15] This significant social threat would be the most important tool in reshaping Southern African Methodist identity and mission in subsequent years. I would argue that in many ways apartheid caused Methodism in Southern Africa to take on new characteristics in its structure (for example, episcopal leadership), yet in other ways it helped Methodists in Southern Africa to hold more tightly to their true identity, namely to be agents of Christian perfection, with a particular emphasis on social holiness.

Implementing this system of racial segregation and oppression from the early 1940s meant that many native South Africans were forcibly removed from their ancestral lands, the land itself was expropriated and either put to use by the government or sold to white South Africans. In order to maintain this system of segregation, and force black persons to remain in the black homelands, various apartheid laws were employed to oppress black South Africans systematically. Economically they were disenfranchised through job reservation and Bantu education.[16] Moreover, health care, civil service, and even freedom of movement were all curtailed for black South Africans. The violent and systematic implementation of this evil ideology had considerable and damaging effects on Southern African society as a whole and particularly on the individual South Africans who suffered under it. The effects of apartheid are likely to be felt for many generations to come.[17]

In the process of conducting this research I found that the Methodist Church of Southern Africa made statements, protested, and worked against apartheid in many ways between the ideology's formal adoption in 1948 and its downfall in 1994. Every copy of the minutes of Conference in this era contained evidence[18] of the Church's struggle to undermine the false theology that supported the apartheid system and the evil consequences that resulted from it.

Neville Richardson, principal of the Methodist Church of Southern Africa's theological college, notes just how influential and significant this ideology of systematic oppression was for the operation and identity of the South African Church:

the church under apartheid was polarized between 'the church of the oppressor' and 'the church of the oppressed'. Either you were for apartheid or you were against it; there was no neutral ground. Given the heavy-handed domination of the minority white government, those who imagined themselves to be neutral were, unwittingly perhaps, on the side of apartheid. This complicity was especially true of those Christians who piously 'avoided politics' yet enjoyed the social and economic benefits of the apartheid system ... While young white men were conscripted into the South African Defence Force, many young black people fled the country to join the outlawed liberation movements that had their headquarters and training camps abroad. What could the church do in this revolutionary climate? And what should Christian theology say now?[19]

It is in this social context that the Methodist Church of Southern Africa sought to bring about its brand of Christian perfection, a perfection that is shaped by social justice. Naturally one can see that the identity and functioning of the Church would need to be changed and adapted from its roots in eighteenth-century England in order adequately and effectively to address the needs of Southern Africans in the twentieth century.

What was required was a measure of flexibility that allowed for an interaction between orthodoxy and orthopraxis, an approach to faith that recognized and celebrated the truth of who God is (personal piety) yet was expected to enact God's will for individuals and society (social holiness). Accordingly, Attwell can affirm that 'Methodism seems peculiarly well-adapted to meet the spiritual and social needs of [a] changing Africa.'[20]

Five Important Markers in the Journey to the New Land, And Beyond

A theological evaluation of Christian perfection, as social holiness, in the Methodist Church of Southern Africa

The Wesleyan heritage has allowed Southern African Methodists to face one of the most dehumanizing and destructive systems of abuse in our time, namely the sin of apartheid. Peter Storey, in his book on revisioning Wesleyan heritage in the new Southern Africa, is correct when he notes that John Wesley said little about the great obsession of Southern Africa – race. Yet it would be a mistake to think that this was not a matter on which Wesley had an opinion. Wesley was certainly not ignorant of the forms of racial abuse that were prevalent in his time and context.

The word 'racism' had to wait until the 20th century to be invented, indicating how long the European world remained supremely unconscious of any pathology in its attitude to people of colour. Nevertheless, Mr. Wesley did have passionate things to say about slavery, the most brutal expression of that pathology ... In his opposition to this most degrading of all racist practices Wesley moved from simply seeking the conversion of the slaves, and the amelioration of some of the horrific conditions under which they laboured, to joining those, led by the Quakers, who were working for the total abolition of slavery itself.[21]

Wesley was public about his opposition to slavery. In his 1744 pamphlet *Thoughts upon Slavery*, he not only denounced those who justified slavery on the grounds of European superiority, but said that they were even less civilized than their victims. More pointedly in relation to the Southern African context, it is clear that Mr Wesley had some apparent sensibilities about the tyranny and evil of racism. Storey records that in his famous letter to William Wilberforce (1791) he refers to the racism of the colonial legal system: 'it being a law in all our Colonies that the oath of a black against a white goes for nothing. What villainy is this!' Storey goes on:

> When Wesley said that liberty is 'the right of every human creature as soon as he breathes the vital air', there is little doubt that in his mind, this genuinely embraced *every* human creature, regardless of race.[22]

John Wesley's heritage of practically addressing both the needs of persons and the abusive and oppressive structures in society that bring about these needs, carried through the development of Methodism in the years after Wesley's death. They remained important in the new contexts into which Methodism was planted as a result of missionary work.[23]

This groundwork of social engagement and practical care laid a firm foundation on which Southern African Methodists could work against the system of apartheid. The Group Areas Act of 1950 was to be the first significant political challenge to the structure and identity of Southern African Methodism. This quite easily could have been the attack that destroyed the spirit and intent of Christian perfection on Southern African soil.

'One and Undivided' 1958 – a Movement from Above

The MCSA's stand against the structural sin of racial segregation

Up to this point in Southern African history the Methodist Church had been a single denomination in which black and white Methodists studied together in Methodist schools, worshipped together in Methodist churches, and ministered together in Methodist communities. There were some exceptions where conservative communities sought to align themselves with the 'petty apartheid' ideologies of separation according to race, but on a structural level the MCSA was a racially integrated denomination.[24] However, the 'Group Areas Act' of 1950 and the 'Separate Amenities Act' of 1953 not only made this unity difficult (due to geographic separation), but also made it illegal for Methodists of different races to worship together. The Methodist Church was facing significant pressure, both from conservative (mainly white) members within its ranks and from the Nationalist Government, to segregate along racial lines, having separate churches for black Methodists and white Methodists. Many other denominations had already given in to this pressure, and some others had been segregated from their missionary beginnings.

In response to this pressure the minutes of the Conference of 1958 record the following statement:

Like other parts of the life of our country, the Church is facing choices which will determine her future development, and in particular the choice between unity and division. The Conference, in prayer and heart-searching, expressed its conviction that it is the will of God for the Methodist Church that it should be *one and undivided*, trusting to the leading of God to bring this ideal to ultimate fruition.[25]

This radical stance, often referred to as the Church's resolution to be 'one and undivided', has seldom been remembered within its original *theological* context. Because of the overbearing power of apartheid it has most often been seen primarily as a social response to the political abuses of the day. However, the context within which this statement took shape was fundamentally linked to the Southern African Methodist understanding of Christian perfection, as a central tenet of Methodist identity and mission. That is, what it means to strive to live as God intended, the kind of holiness found in Scripture, and to strive towards it in perfect love, in spite of the pressure of government laws from without, and personal prejudices from within. The minutes of Conference record:

> We do not pretend that there are no difficulties; barriers not only of prejudice but of real difference will have to be subordin-ated to the love which the Holy Spirit implants in our hearts. But this will be an expression in life of the message for which Methodism was created, the message of Scriptural Holiness and Perfect Love, whereby we follow our Lord in stretching out our hands to all men that they may be saved from all evil, and may be brought into the unity of the household of God.[26]

From this it is clear to see the line of identity that linked twentieth-century Methodism in a racially divided nation to the founding principles of identity in eighteenth-century England. Christian perfection as social holiness is the binding principle.

This resolution was a truly significant and courageous one not only for its time, but also for the decades to come when the pres-sure to segregate would increase many times over.

One of the most vivid examples of how the 1958 statement of intention was applied in a local church context was the exemplary struggle of Peter Storey between 1956 and 1981 to work against the Nationalist Government's forced removal of 'coloured' people (mostly Methodists) in Cape Town. Central Methodist Mission in Buitenkant Street, a multiracial congregation, was significant-ly disrupted by the government's forced removals. The Church

naturally opposed the removals in every possible way. Yet when
the removals were eventually enacted in 1966 the congregation
decided to remain united in spite of the forced removals. Ministries of care and support for those who had been removed were
set up. Transport was arranged to bus the congregants the many
miles from the settlement areas to the church so that multiracial
services and meetings at the church could continue unabated. A
plaque was put on the front of the church, facing the busy Green
Market Square, that read:

All who pass by remember with shame the many thousands of
people who lived for generations in District Six and other parts
of this city, and were forced to leave their homes because of the
colour of their skins. Father forgive us.[27]

It was during this period that some stark theological divisions
began to surface within the mainline denominations in Southern
Africa. While the Methodist Church maintained the principles of
unity and inclusiveness at its highest levels, and drew attention to
it in their official statements, this was sadly not the case in most
local congregations and was not adequately reflected in the leadership of the denomination.

In conclusion, the 1958 statement had set the tone for the
Church to work pragmatically, through the vehicle of social
holiness, towards the Christian ideal of scriptural holiness and
perfect love. Yet while the top structures of the Church officially
addressed the evils of apartheid and opposed the state, there were
not many congregations on the local level that were truly racially
integrated, or directly fighting against government-led segregation. This led to the next significant marker in the development of
social holiness in the MCSA, the formation of the Black Methodist Consultation in 1975.

The Formation of the 'Black Methodist Consultation' 1975 – a Movement from Below

The MCSA's stance for a Church that reflects the true nature of Southern African society

The next radical movement towards social holiness in the Methodist Church of Southern Africa was the formation of the Black Methodist Consultation (BMC) by Revd Ernest Baartman in 1975. More than 75 per cent of the membership of the Methodist Church of Southern Africa is black, yet by the early 1970s the leadership of the Church did not reflect this reality. Black Methodists were largely excluded from the decision-making processes of their Church. Of the 12 districts in the MCSA at that stage, ten were led by white Methodist Chairmen; only two districts were led by Black Methodists.[28]

Conversely, it must be noted that the very first mainline Church to be led by a black person was the MCSA with the election of Revd Seth Mokitimi as the President of Conference in 1964. This was a bold statement of intent that sent a clear message from the Church to the apartheid state. Sadly, however, the reality of the internal racial struggles in the Church, and an inability to follow through with similar leadership choices at lower levels of Church government, meant that the racial transformation of Church leadership was haphazard and slow.

This legacy of white leadership had arisen out of the missionary movements of the nineteenth century. It needs to be noted that not all elements of British Methodist identity were laudable. Some did need to be discarded and developed to keep pace with changes in society and theology. The time had thus arrived for the MCSA to come of age and to find leadership under the authority of African Christians. Theilen explains the purpose in the formation of the BMC:

> The BMC's mission was to ensure that white domination was progressively reduced and the entrenched hierarchy transformed. The BMC also saw the need for political life in the church. It's [sic] membership was open to both clergy and laity. Further

the BMC laid the ground for a necessary self-examination, for a 'Black awareness'; its aim was to undo any psychological oppression born out of existing structures.[29]

While black Methodists were never officially unequal to white Methodists within the Church, the reality was quite different on the ground, and in fact still is today.[30] What the BMC has done for Methodism in Southern Africa is truly significant. First, they have engaged in the process of bringing the Church to more adequately represent and reflect the voices of black South Africans. The MCSA currently has nine black Bishops (of which one is a woman) and three white Bishops. Second, they have helped to re-appropriate the values, tradition, and religion of Africa in the Methodist Church. Sadly, missionary imperialism often sought to eradicate elements of African tradition and religion. The BMC has significantly helped the MCSA to reinvent itself as an African Christian denomination, through education, publication, and the presentation of the value and necessity of black and African theologies.[31] Third, the BMC has ensured that politics, often viewed by conservative Christians as the exclusive responsibility of the state, were dealt with as part of the official agenda of the Church.

The BMC still exists as a formidable and respected movement with the Methodist Church of Southern Africa. What is important to note in the context of this chapter, however, is that the BMC was formed as a movement within the Church that sought to honour God by being both black and African in a Church that was largely controlled by white liberals in a nation that faced massive oppression at the hands of conservative white Christians. We should never forget that the large majority of Nationalist government officials were active members in Dutch Reformed Churches, and that approximately 80 per cent of the ordinary white South Africans that kept the system of apartheid in power for over 40 years declared that they were Christians of one form or another.[32] Yet, from within the Church there arose this movement that seeks to work against the sin and evil of segregation and the lies of apartheid.

The critical work of social holiness, as undertaken by the

BMC, led in large part to the next milestone in the Methodist Church of Southern Africa's appropriation of Christian perfection – Obedience '81.

'Obedience '81' – a Movement from Within

The MCSA's radical stance for costly and painful shifts in power relations and cultural adjustment, within the Church

At the height of the violence and oppression of the late 1970s, after the deaths of so many in the 1976 student uprisings, and the rising temperature of the armed struggle for liberation, Methodists of all races, ages and genders gathered for the most representative consultation ever held in the denomination's history up to that point. Such brave steps came at a great cost to the Church's official image in society and its ecumenical relationships with other Christian Churches in South Africa. The Church-led marches against state-sanctioned oppression, violence, and abuse, together with the official statements against apartheid created a great deal of animosity against the Methodist Church as a denomination, and Methodist clergy and laity as individuals. Many Methodists were banned by the state, persecuted, and prosecuted for their stance against apartheid. Moreover, some Churches openly opposed the stance of the MCSA on apartheid. For example the Hervormde Kerk taught in its Catechism that the Methodist stance against apartheid was heretical, and thus the MCSA was itself a heretical movement. It is in this context of pressure from within and persecution from outside that Obedience '81 was envisioned. The gathering itself was in open defiance of the prevailing powers and was a further pledge to unity within the Church amidst great struggle.

Storey writes of the gathering, 'This time they acknowledged how difficult it was to achieve [unity], and how painful togetherness could be, requiring significant shifts in power relations and much cultural adjustment.'[33]

The outcome of this engagement was the *Message of Obedience '81*, in which the theology and cost of true transformation was clearly understood:[34]

When we spoke and wept, argued and agonised, [God] was there. He met us in our hurt and anger, humility and shame. Because God in Christ was in the midst, he brought us to repentance. He opened our eyes to the wounds we inflict on each other by our insensitivity, bitterness and fear.[35]

With particular reference to the shape of social holiness that was required in opposition to apartheid, the 'message' of *Obedience '81* noted that

every Methodist must witness against this disease which infects our people, our church and our country. We have experienced how hard it is to abandon long-held prejudice and long-felt bitterness, but we have seen God work this miracle. It happened because we continued to search for each other even at our times of deepest division. We now declare to all South Africans that there is a *third way where people who discovered their love for each other, translate it into justice for all.*[36]

The way of perfect love was clearly understood to be the path to justice. Once again, one can see the strong emphasis on Christian perfection as social holiness – Southern African Methodists understood that it was both their task and a missionary imperative to enact this element of their identity. The promise that members of the consultation made read:

Therefore we promise before Almighty God and each other that we will henceforth live and work to bring into reality the concept of an undivided Church and a free and just Southern Africa.

Pragmatically Obedience '81 achieved the aim of further cementing the notion that the Methodist Church in Southern Africa is one and undivided. Even if society was segregated, the Church would remain fundamentally one. The work of creating unity across racial lines was both costly and difficult, partly because of the powerful laws that restricted movement and forced separation, but also because of the strong psychological effects of almost 300 years of racial ideology that permeated all aspects of Southern Africa society. Storey recalls that

> those congregations that sought to demonstrate Methodist one-ness by deliberately [racially] integrating their memberships were relatively few, but they were prototypes of a future that apartheid claimed was impossible and had an impact far be-yond their numbers of size.[37]

Such acts of social engagement, moments of deliberate and care-fully brokered discovery, were the building blocks of the new South Africa. What is notable is that these prophetic acts took place long before the end of apartheid had even begun to dawn. Surely, these are signs of the Kingdom of God that were being evidenced in local Christian churches.

The 'Journey to the New Land' in the Early 1990s – a Movement Outward

The MCSA's decision to reconstruct the Church to help facilitate the birth of the new South Africa

The Presiding Bishop's addresses to Conferences of the MCSA from the late 1980s into the early 1990s all began with a note of concern about escalating violence and tension that had beset the country. It was hard to imagine in the late 1980s that apartheid would ever end, and if it did, many imagined that it would al-most certainly be as the result of a brutal and bloody revolt. Yet in spite of those fears there was a relatively peaceful transition to democracy in 1994. The MCSA, as the largest denomination in a predominantly Christian country, played a significant role in this process. The 1992 Conference, under the leadership of Bishop Mvume Dandala, agreed to the formation of a Church-initiated peace force that would help to monitor and quell violence throughout the land.[38] It had become clear that the Church had a central and significant role to play in preventing total anarchy and collapse in Southern African society. If the Church was to be effective both in eradicating and overcoming the structural sin of apartheid, and also in offering support and care for the increasingly impatient and militant victims of apartheid, it would need to restructure itself to take its members, and the wider society, on this 'journey to the new land'.

What was required was not just another statement of unity and solidarity, but rather a bold and courageous restructuring of the Church that could best position the institution to support and encourage its members to make the changes required for renewal and change. As such the Conference of 1993 in Benoni gave four of its eight days to a convocation called the 'Journey to the New Land'. The convocation was once again attended by representatives of varying ages, races, and genders. 'Listening was a feature of this Convocation, as we sought to hear God's Word and the cry of the community. We listened as Methodists spoke of their pain and their dreams.'[39] The Conference's attention in its decision-making was focussed on

- the call to be a priesthood of all believers;
- growth in spirituality evidenced by contextual worship and lifestyle;
- a return to the values of *ubuntu*,[40] family life and servant mission.

The issues that were addressed covered both personal piety (the development and encouragement of contextual African-Christian worship and lifestyle), and social holiness (the values of *ubuntu*, family life and servant mission).

The call for the priesthood of all believers to be accepted as the model of ministry in the Church was an expression of the desire that the Church should be democratic and representative at all of its various levels of governance and ministry. Lay leadership and ministry had been, and continues to be, a strong characteristic of Southern African Methodism. Naturally this is directly related to the structure of early Methodism in Britain. The desire in South Africa was that the Church should not reflect the oppressive, disenfranchising structures of Southern African society, but rather that it should lead the way in equality and transformation. All of the calls were to find their fullest expression in the call to servant mission. It was recognized that the Church had become 'maintenance' focussed, caring only for its own needs, its own members, and dealing only with its own concerns. If the Church was to participate actively in God's plan for the renewal and transformation of Southern African society it would need to engage far more actively in practical acts of servanthood and ministry outside of the confines of the traditional church. As an expression of this ideal all ordained Methodist clergy were encouraged to spend one day a week labouring in some form of social or community ministry (for example working as a peace monitor, or doing counselling for victims of violence and abuse, monitoring the work of the police, visiting detainees under the Security Act in their prison cells, and later serving as electoral officials, helping to ensure that all South Africans had identity documents, and engaging in voter education to ensure that intimidation and electoral fraud did not occur).[41] Such 'practical divinity' was to be the mark not only of Southern African Methodism, but of every Methodist.

After the peaceful democratic elections of April 1994 the function and responsibility of the Church had to change from that of a prophetic activism against apartheid to a role of reconstructing and developing society. This led to the dawning of a new era, and expression, of social holiness in Southern African Methodism.

The 'Mission Congress' 2004

The MCSA's stand to deliberately position itself to bring about 'healing and transformation' of both individuals and society to work towards a 'Christ healed Africa for the healing of the nations'

Under the leadership of Bishop Ivan Abrahams the Church struggled to reposition itself for reconstruction and development. During apartheid the enemy seemed so obvious and the goal so clear. However, ten years after the dawn of democracy very little had changed in Southern African society. Poverty and segregation were still rife. The cause of this segregation was now economic disenfranchisement, a high rate of HIV / AIDS infection, and the slow pace of service delivery by the new government.

As a result, in 2003, the Church adopted the vision of working towards *'a Christ-healed Africa for the healing of nations'*.[42] Clearly this statement was grounded in the understanding that African Christianity was both valid, and valuable, as an instrument for achieving God's mission in the world. By this mission it was understood that 'God calls the Methodist people to proclaim the gospel of Jesus Christ for healing and transformation'. The subsequent mission strategy was divided into four clear areas of development, ministry, and growth:

- spirituality;
- justice, service, and reconciliation;
- evangelism and church growth;
- development and economic empowerment.

It is evident that the contents and thrust of this initiative struck a strong balance between personal piety and social holiness. Through an examination of the priorities of this mission strategy one can clearly see how the concept of Christian perfection, as social holiness, took on a rich expression in the context of Southern African Methodism. Among the priorities highlighted by the Conference of 2005 were:

- a mission consciousness shaped by the imperatives of spirituality, evangelism and church growth, justice and service, development and economic empowerment;
- the liberation of the laity, to be facilitated by the clergy, that will enable their full participation in the life and witness of the church;
- the revamping of our structures that they may serve our vision, mission thrust, and transformation strategies;
- the eradication of racism, prejudice, and inequality in institutional life;

- taking seriously the call to a healing ministry, especially in our response to the HIV/AIDS pandemic;
- a clear understanding of Church/State relations within the socio-political realities of our time, and the jealous guarding of the duty to be ready to speak with a prophetic voice when necessary.

The MCSA is still engaged in addressing the social and spiritual needs of Southern African society, working not only for the salvation of individuals, but also the healing and transformation of society at large.[43]

The five milestones discussed above display the clear emphasis that Christian perfection is understood as social. There is little doubt that there is still a great deal of work left to do in Southern Africa, for the problems of HIV/AIDS, the collapse of the rule of law and the economy in Zimbabwe, and the slow pace of transformation and change in South Africa still loom large over the subcontinent. However, an approach of social holiness is surely the most God-honouring means towards Christian perfection in this context.

As the contextual and social needs have changed over time the central thrust and identity of Methodism has needed to be adapted to address the concerns the Church encountered. However, there is no doubt that Methodism in Southern Africa has a clear line of identity that links it with both the founding Church in Britain and other expressions of Methodism throughout the world.

Concluding remarks on a global Methodist identity and contextual variations

Identity is a complex phenomenon. This chapter has taken the perspective that there are certain 'core' elements, or characteristics, of Methodist identity that can be maintained and adapted in a different context without losing the true identity of Methodism. It has been argued that Christian perfection is a central element in Wesleyan mission and theology. Without some understanding and appropriation of this core doctrine one could not rightly consider oneself a Methodist. However, what has also been shown is that differing contexts will require some measure of flexibility from the Methodist institution, allowing change to take place in order to meet the ministry needs of that context.

In the Southern African context social holiness has necessarily been a strong emphasis in both the character and ministry of the Church. In other contexts, however, personal piety may feature more prominently. This does not mean that there is no common ground between these two contextual variations of Methodism. Rather, what it shows is that the goal of Methodism, Christian perfection, requires creative commitment and insightful application in order to be effectively achieved.

It was suggested that the order of salvation, with an emphasis on Christian perfection, is central to Methodist identity; repentance, living in faith, and growing in holiness are wide enough and deep enough to warrant subtle, and complex emphases that allow Methodists in a variety of contexts to engage their world effectively with the Good News of Jesus Christ. Some may argue that one can measure the effectiveness of a Church in its context numerically. I think that is too simplistic since smaller denominations and Churches have frequently been known to have a far more significant impact upon societies than some numerically larger Churches. But the rapid growth of Methodism in the 'global South' and two-thirds world does point to some measure of success in those contexts.

Clearly, persons will align themselves with faith movements that meet their real or perceived needs. The Methodist Church of Southern Africa is the largest mainline denomination in South Africa. According to the 2001 national census 79.8 per cent of the population in Southern Africa are Christian, of which 7.3 per cent were Methodist, 7.2 per cent Reformed, 7.1 per cent Roman Catholic, 5.5 per cent Congregational, 3.8 per cent Anglican, and the remaining 48.8 per cent belong to independent and African-initiated Churches.[44] One could conclude that among many other complex motivators, South Africans have favoured the pragmatic approach of Southern African Methodism with its balance between personal piety and social holiness. Of course there are many other historical, theological, and practical reasons for the statistical dominance of Methodism among mainline Christians in South Africa.

However, while the previous conclusion is speculative, what cannot be denied is that these statistics show that Southern Africans are still largely Christian, yet they long for new and different expressions of the Christian faith. Many are no longer satisfied with a Church that seems more Western than African – while the identity of the 'Mission Churches' from which they come are recognized and appreciated, there is a real desire to appropriate the core of the faith for their own context. The African renaissance is teaching us to appreciate our richness as Africans, and that richness must surely find expression within our faith.

I am left with two thoughts: in order to reach its present potential the Methodist Church will need to do two things. First, Methodism in Southern Africa, the rest of the global South (and in many other parts of the world) will need to continue to develop, change, and accentuate the unique elements of their Methodist identity in order to be effective instruments of God's mission in their respective contexts. Methodists throughout the world need to create space for this to happen. Moreover, we should celebrate new developments, fresh expressions, and changes born of God in our missional identity. Second, with the advent of globalization, the dominance of European and western church models may lose their prominence and priority in global Methodism. We have already begun to experience the immense interest that the global Church has in the revival and passion that is evident among Southern African Christians, and Christians in many other parts of the African, Latin American, and Asian world. We are finding that elements of African, Indian, Asian, and Latin American Methodist Churches have started to influence positively the traditionally dominant Methodist Churches in Europe and America. Perhaps identity is something that is shared and dynamic? It develops over time, and will continue to change, yet at the same time it is vested in those who make up the characteristics of that identity. In Africa we have a saying *umuntu ngumuntu ngabantu* – 'we are who we are through other people'. In order to realize its present potential, the Methodist Church will need to discern and accept new moves of God from unlikely places and people. We shall have to return to the pragmatism, and practical divinity, of our Methodist roots in order to be effective agents of God's mission in the world.

Notes

1 Emilio Castro, *Freedom in Mission: The Perspective of the Kingdom of God*, Geneva: World Council of Churches, 1985, p. 62. Quoted by J. A. Kirk, in *What is Mission?*, London: Darton, Longman & Todd, 1999, p. 36.

2 The world's largest Methodist society (i.e., a single congregation that meets in one building) is to be found in Seoul, South Korea. The Kumnan Methodist Church, which hosted the 19th meeting of the World Methodist Council in 2006, has a membership of approximately 110,000. See www.kumnan.org/english/.

3 Wesley in Henry D. Rack, *Reasonable Enthusiast: John Wesley and the Rise of Methodism*, London: Epworth Press, 1989, p. 286.

4 Wesley in C. Williams, *John Wesley's Theology Today: A Study of the Wesleyan Tradition in the Light of Current Theological Dialogue*; Nashville, TN: Abingdon Press, 1988, p. 238.

5 Wesley in the preface to the 1739 Methodist Hymn book.

6 D. Forster and W. Bentley, *Methodism in Southern Africa: A Celebration of Wesleyan Mission*, Kempton Park: AcadSA Publishers, 2008, p. 30.

7 D. Balia, *Black Methodists and White Supremacy in South Africa*, Briardene: Madiba Publications, 1991, p. 14.

8 See W. G. Mears, *Methodism in the Cape*, Cape Town: Methodist Publishing House, 1973, p. 6.

9 Forster and Bentley, *Methodism in Southern Africa*, pp. 13–39.

10 A superb account of early Methodist missionaries who lost their lives in Southern Africa is J. Jackson, 'Methodist South African Martyrs – Are They also Saints?' Unpublished paper presented at the Theological Society of South Africa annual meeting, 2007, John Wesley College, Kilnerton.

11 It is not necessary to discuss the details of the work of these missionaries in this paper. This topic has been well covered elsewhere. In particular it would be worth reading A. Attwell, *The Methodist Church*, Cape Town: Methodist Publishing House, 1995, pp. 3–6, for a succinct historical overview of Methodist mission in Southern Africa.

12 J. W. Hofmeyer and G. J. Pillay (eds), *Perspectives on Church History: An Introduction for South African Readers*, Pretoria: Haum Publishers, 1991, p. 253.

13 John de Gruchy and Steve de Gruchy, *The Church Struggle in South Africa*, 3rd edn, 25th anniversary edn, London: SCM Press, 2004, p. 14.

14 Please refer to Grassow's superb chapter on the Methodist missionary William Shaw in Forster and Bentley, *Methodism in Southern Africa*, pp. 13–25. In his chapter he offers critical insights into the different missionary styles among missionaries, some favouring work among the settler population, others working predominantly among the 'native' population.

15 It would not be possible to chart all of the significant shifts in society and politics in Southern Africa in a study of this scope. For an insightful and scholarly account of the social and political trends from the first colonies at the Cape through to the dying days of apartheid in South Africa see A. Sparks, *The Mind of South Africa*, New York: Ballantine, 1990.

16 This refers to the Bantu Education Act of 1953 (No. 47) which enforced separation on racial grounds in all educational institutions.

17 For a basic, accessible, introduction to the history of apartheid, see en.wikipedia.org/wiki/Apartheid (accessed 17 July 2007). For a succinct outline of the crimes of apartheid, see en.wikipedia.org/wiki/Crime_of_apartheid.

18 In order to establish this information I simply read the address of the President (later Presiding Bishop) to Conference, the resolutions, and the reports to the British Conference (when the Southern African conference still reported to Britain) from the Minutes of Conference for each year between 1948 and 1994.

19 G. L. Jones, R. Hutter and C. R. V. Ewell (eds), *God, Truth and Witness*, Michigan: Brazos Press, 2006, pp. 231–2.

20 A. Attwell, *What Wesley Believed and Taught: The Essentials of Wesley's Theology*, Cape Town: Methodist Publishing House, 1994, p. 4.

21 See P. Storey, *And Are We Yet Alive: Revisioning our Wesleyan Heritage in the New Southern Africa*, Cape Town: Methodist Publishing House, 2004, p. 77.

22 Storey, *And Are We Yet Alive*, p. 78.

23 For more information on this development I would suggest three sources: first, for a Southern African perspective P. S. Grassow in N. R. Richardson and P. Malinga (eds), *Rediscovering Wesley for Africa*, Pretoria: Education for Ministry and Mission Unity, 2005, pp. 87–96. For a truly superb, and scholarly, account of this emphasis in both Britain and America see Rack, *Reasonable Enthusiast*, pp. 381–449, 471–88. For a further perspective on developments in Methodism in Latin America and South Africa after Wesley's death see R. L. Maddox (ed.), *Re-thinking Wesley's Theology for Contemporary Methodism*, Nashville, TN: Abingdon Press, 1998, pp. 169–96. Finally, there is the exceptional work by R. P. Heitzenrater, *Wesley and the People Called Methodists*, Nashville, TN: Abingdon Press, 1995, pp. 261–80, 311–16.

24 Storey, *And Are We Yet Alive*, p. 78.

25 *Minutes of the 75th Annual Conference of the Methodist Church of South Africa*, Cape Town: Methodist Publishing House, 1958, p. 202.

26 *Minutes of the 75th Annual Conference of the Methodist Church of South Africa*, Cape Town: Methodist Publishing House, 1958, p. 202. [in original gendered form].

27 From U. Theilen, 'Gender, Race, Power, and Religion: Women in the Methodist Church of Southern Africa in Post-apartheid Society', unpublished doctoral thesis, Philipps-Universität, 2003, p. 33.

28 Theilen, 'Gender, Race, Power, and Religion', p. 28.

29 Theilen, 'Gender, Race, Power, and Religion', p. 28.

30 The current debate on equitable stipends in the MCSA, as well as the stark reality that a black Methodist minister will serve on average 3,000 members, and 12 societies, whereas a white Methodist minister will serve on average 350 members and a single society, show that there are still very different standards for black and white Methodists.

31 For a detailed discussion of this see D. A. Forster, 'Validation of Individual Consciousness in Strong Artificial Intelligence: An African Theological Contribution', doctoral thesis, University of South Africa, Pretoria, 2006, chapters 5–7. Also, D. A. Forster, 'Identity in Relationship: The Ethics Of Ubuntu as an Answer to the Impasse of Individual Consciousness' (Paper presented at the South African Science and Religion Forum), published in C. W. du Toit (ed.), *The Impact of Knowledge Systems on Human Development in Africa*, Pretoria: University of South Africa Research Institute for Religion and Theology, 2007, pp. 245–89.

32 See J. W. de Gruchy and Villa-Vicencio, *Apartheid is a Heresy*, Cape Town: David Phillips, 1983.

33 Storey, *And Are We Yet Alive*, p. 78.

34 For a full copy of the message of Obedience '81, see Forster and Bentley, *Methodism in Southern Africa*, Appendix A, pp. 168–73.

35 Storey, *And Are We Yet Alive*, pp. 5–6.

36 Storey, *And Are We Yet Alive*, p. 79.

37 Storey, *And Are We Yet Alive*, p. 79.

38 *Minutes of the 110th Annual Conference of the Methodist Church of South Africa*, Cape Town: Methodist Publishing House, 1992, p. 434.

39 *Minutes of the 111th Annual Conference of the Methodist Church of South Africa*, Cape Town: Methodist Publishing House, 1993, p. 392.

40 For further insights into the African concept of *ubuntu* see Forster, 'Identity in Relationship', pp. 245–89.

41 *Minutes of the 112th Annual Conference of the Methodist Church of South Africa*, Cape Town: Methodist Publishing House, 1994, pp. 389–93.

42 The Mission Unit of the Church published a detailed document entitled *Mission Congress 2004: Report on the Key Outcomes of the Mission Congress*, Cape Town: Methodist Publishing House, 2004. This was

followed by the *Mission Charter* that was tabled and adopted by the 117th Conference of the Methodist Church of Southern Africa in Johannesburg. See *2006 Yearbook of the Methodist Church of Southern Africa*, Cape Town: Methodist Publishing House, 2006, pp. 3–22.

43 A detailed discussion of the Mission Congress by the then Mission Director (Revd Gcobani Vika) can be found in Forster and Bentley, *Methodism in Southern Africa*, pp. 57–69.

44 See T. Stone, 'Building the Church' in *The Methodist Newspaper, Dimension*, June 2007, p. 1 and SA Government, Statistics SA, *The 2005/6 Christian Handbook*, Johannesburg: WITS University Library, 2005. These statistics are also available online at www.statssa.gov.za/census01/html/default.asp (accessed 10 July 2007). A theological critique of this data is available in J. Hendriks and J. Erasmus, 'Religion in South Africa: 2001 population census data', *Journal of Theology for Southern Africa* 121 (2005), pp. 88–111.

Part Two

8

Wesley and the People Called Methodists

The Potential of a Tradition

RICHARD HEITZENRATER

Many present-day critics of Methodism are quick to say that Wesley would not recognize his movement if he could see it now. But that offhand judgement begs the question of how one should define or determine 'faithfulness' to a tradition. Worldwide Methodism is certainly different from the societies that Wesley nurtured during his lifetime. And although there are signs of dead wood here and there, the movement still manifests a great deal of spiritual energy in many of its branches, providing some hope that the roots are still providing nourishment.

Every generation finds itself at a series of embarkation points into the future. Methodism has now had more than two hundred years of peering toward the looming future, while glancing back to the fading past and looking in the mirror at itself in a tumultuous present. Trying to understand and define itself in such circumstances results in a range of different approaches to the use of the tradition or heritage from the past as a touchstone of self-identity in the present, much less a resource to help confront the future.

The earlier chapters in this book virtually all, at some point, contain multiple explicit references back to the Wesleys in developing a rationale for interpreting the present and looking toward the future.[1] That probably would not have happened as recently as 20 or 30 years ago. Alex Haley's book *Roots* signalled a rising interest in genealogy, as people became enchanted with the lives of their ancestors and the stories of their heritage as a means of trying to understand themselves in the present. The family genealogist, however, has a much easier task than the spiritual genealogist for worldwide Methodism. Nevertheless, the current attempt at understanding Methodism in the present as containing great potential for the future necessarily harks back to Wesley.

While the authors in this study generally approach the founder John Wesley as a recognized authority within the tradition and attempt to be relatively faithful to that heritage, they manifest a variety of approaches to the Wesleyan heritage that displays a typical spectrum of interpretive angles. That spectrum ranges across several possible approaches[2] that treat the past with varying degrees of authority for understanding the present or designing the future – using the tradition as either (1) normatively prescriptive, (2) significantly instructive, (3) somewhat supportive, or (4) simply suggestive. Each level, of course, has a range within itself, and a clear demarcation is seldom evident between categories.[3] This typology will provide the framework for our discussion in this chapter.

Tradition and Change

All traditions change over the years, as James Russell Lowell illustrates with his familiar phrases, 'new occasions teach new duties' and 'time makes ancient good uncouth'.[4] The first phrase is often true; the second raises some uncomfortable questions. The real conundrum is to sort out the eternal dimensions of goodness and truth from among the time-bound elements that must give way to change. The epistemological and philosophical centralities of this issue were becoming increasingly apparent in the Enlightenment of Wesley's century. The constant challenge of new situations in the present forces the issues: when is change appropriate, what is most vulnerable to alteration, and what templates are best suited to create the future?

A Methodist student from the Philippines recently talked with me about his Central Conference's discussions about becoming an autonomous Methodist Church. His own concern centred on the issue of whether that church would be explicitly Wesleyan. His question for me was therefore, What would they have to put in place, in doctrine, polity, or mission, for their church to be considered 'Wesleyan'? That is another way of asking a question that has appeared over the ages – what is the essential core of the ongoing Wesleyan heritage? Another way to ask the question is: How does a church exhibit faithfulness to the Wesleyan tradition?

Almost immediately, a secondary list of questions begins to roll forth: Are there timeless elements within the tradition? How do we know when something is time-bound or secondary? Who sets the criteria for 'faithfulness'? Is it necessary for Methodists to be Wesleyan? Will being Wesleyan necessarily result in being vital? Are the answers to these questions the same for every group in every place in every time? Wasn't Wesley himself in favour of having few prerequisites and exhibiting broad toleration? Doesn't his belief in the reality of witchcraft undermine many of his other ideas? Have we outgrown the need for denominations? For Christianity?

Let me stop there, because the list is getting out of hand already. Certainly we hear these and more questions every day, but that doesn't mean they all deserve equal treatment. What is especially interesting to me is the variety of ways that serious people make reference to their heritage, in this case, the Wesleyan tradition. Let me disclose my bias from the beginning and say that I believe there is a place for all four types of reference back to the past. To limit the scope of viability to just one or two or these is to limit the usefulness of the historical enterprise and to devalue the meaning of tradition as a dynamic reality.

The Challenges to Tradition

Most traditions contain some core of principles and practices that hark back to their origins. For Methodists, that includes some elements that are basically Christian, some that are specifically Protestant, and some that are distinctively Wesleyan. In various

Methodist groups, these core ideas and actions provide a measure of orthodoxy and orthopraxy – right thinking and right acting – that help define the central nature of the organization. At any given time and place, members are expected to conform to these core identification markers.

Over the centuries, this approach to tradition – based on prescriptive conformity to past norms – has become less universal or pervasive. Even in Wesley's day, the list of 'essential' beliefs and actions was somewhat short, and the tendency to promote tolerance was a practical means of survival for non-Anglicans within an autocratic establishment of Church and state in England.

The inherent tension between the openness and the discipline of the early Methodists heightens the issue of what is essential. Supporters of openness and tolerance often cite the second half of Wesley's sermon on 'Catholic Spirit', which reiterates his tolerance for varying 'opinions' from people, if their heart is right. But such supporters usually fail to notice that in the first half of the same sermon, Wesley talks against theological indifference, stresses being as 'fixed as the sun' in one's beliefs, and lists more than fifty questions that one must answer positively before being considered as having a 'right heart'.

Doctrinal standards contain one of the most prescriptive elements in a denomination. And yet, Methodist denominations have no single set of doctrinal standards that prevail around the globe. The British tradition tends officially to stress the use of Wesley's *Sermons on Several Occasions* and his *Explanatory Notes upon the New Testament,* although the enforcement of these standards appears to be quite slack. Some Churches in this British tradition, such as the Methodist Church of New Zealand, explicitly require that nothing contrary to the *Sermons* or *Notes* is to be done within the church at any level including the local. As recent court cases have demonstrated, however, there are many ways to skirt this requirement.[5] Other Methodist denominations follow the American model of citing Wesley's *Articles of Religion* as the standard of doctrine. But in some of those groups, other materials also share the spotlight.[6] In the area of polity, some Methodist Churches have bishops, some have presidents, some have archbishops under a prelate. The historic debates within each denomination have often exhibited opinions that this or that form is what Wesley intended to prescribe, but no universal form of polity has emerged. And as for Wesley's focus on the mission of Methodism to 'spread scriptural holiness', his followers in recent generations have also taken on a number of foci, such as 'to make disciples of Jesus Christ', in varying degrees of excitement or lethargy.

Some Methodists over the years have settled on one or another of Wesley's 'methods' as part of a definitive prescription for authentic Wesleyanism. One common measure used among Methodists these days to signal an authentic Wesleyan approach is the so-called 'quadrilateral' – to examine an idea or action according to its conformity to Scripture, tradition, reason, and experience. At one point, every proposal made to boards and agencies in the United Methodist Church had to be accompanied by a rationale that was based on this 'Wesleyan' theological methodology, even though the actual Wesleyan nature of this method continues to be challenged.[7] Additionally, the inherent fallacy of this measure of orthodoxy, of course, is that different groups define and use these four guidelines differently. The main problem, however, is to assume that this approach of using the 'four-fold guidelines' is somehow unique to Wesley or Methodists. As I have often pointed out, nearly every Christian body uses some variation of this approach as part of their methodology for theological reflection. Prescribing the use of the quadrilateral as part of theological reflection does not make the result authentically Wesleyan.

The same would be said for a number of valuable Wesleyan methods that are part of the Methodist way. Elements of his scriptural hermaneutic that are useful – seeing the wholeness of Scripture, interpreting passages in the light of the 'analogy of faith' (the general tenor of the whole Bible), measuring the hard passages by the easy ones, and so forth – are also used as critical approaches by many people who are not within the Wesleyan fold. Conforming to these methods therefore does not make one a Wesleyan.

But perhaps an examination of Wesley's use of the Bible does in some ways help Methodists approach these writings usefully. Wesley was willing and able to cull from Scripture those ideas and actions that were timeless, that still had meaning for meeting the challenges of his own day, and recognized that transporting some biblical ideas from the past by way of proof-texting could lead to problems. Remembering and developing this approach could help Methodists to release the potential highlighted by Dean in his chapter in the present book and appreciate the 'primacy of Scripture' without holding fast to some of Wesley's own time-bound interpretations, such as his belief in the reality of witchcraft, his agreement with Paul on the matter of women speaking in church, or his adoption of Bengal's view that all popes since Gregory I represent the 'antichrist'.

So the debate goes on, but as Toppin makes all too evident, the number of people who hold fast to a set of prescriptive norms that define 'Wesleyan' seems to be decreasing within Methodism around the globe. The concept of 'dogma' has taken on a negative connotation, but not everyone would agree that 'truth' is a totally relative concept. In spite of Curran's personal preference, some people still desire absolutes, just as some groups thrive with a prescriptive list of beliefs. Although a firm dogmatism based on absolutes can be destructive, so also a tendency toward indifferent fuzziness based on universal relativism can be harmful.[8]

Prescriptive Uses of Tradition

Nevertheless, I might be so bold as to suggest that contemporary Methodists, including those referred to by the contributors of this volume, do exhibit certain features that reflect some degree of conformity to the essentials of the Wesleyan scheme of doctrine, organization, and mission from the eighteenth century. For instance, Wesley continually referred to the three 'grand doctrines' of Methodism: repentance, faith, and holiness. This trio of doctrines appears under other terms as well, such as original sin, justification, and sanctification. In any case, as the centrepiece of the Wesleyan focus on soteriology, these grand doctrines continue to define the basic Methodist doctrinal emphases in our time. To these 'essentials', one might add other doctrines that Wesley felt were central to the Christian message, such as a belief in the Trinity, a stress on regeneration, the necessity of scriptural Christianity, the centrality of grace, and the role of the Holy Spirit. There is no magic number or list of beliefs as such, since the configuration and expression of these ideas comes in a variety of formats, as they developed during Wesley's lifetime and as they are expressed in the lives and thoughts of his successors to the present day.

Certain characteristics of Wesley's organization also persist in most Methodist denominations, conforming very closely to the principles that Wesley himself emphasized. The nature of itinerant ministry and its basic reflection in the connexional principle is a central part of the Wesleyan scheme in his day and is still evident in most Methodist denominations. The idea of a thorough commitment to a common mission, exhibited in a covenantal fellowship among the preachers, has also persisted down through the years. The Wesleyan method of talking through the nature and mission of the movement in regular conferencing among the leadership, helping to get everyone on the same page, has been a common element of the connexional approach for generations. And the Wesleyan scheme has always had a shallow organizational chart – the large percentage of people participating in leadership positions has long been one of the secrets of its vitality.

And although much of Methodism has forfeited the terminology of 'holiness' to more conservative denominations, the basic duality of Wesley's view of scriptural holiness – to love God and to love neighbour – is still the motivation behind much of the mission of the Wesleyan movement. Methodist denominations incorporate a variety of programmes and subsidiary organizations that promote liturgical concerns, biblical and devotional studies, outreach to marginalized persons at home and abroad, social programmes for the disadvantaged, and educational agenda for all ages. In doing so, Methodism tries to exhibit the Wesleyan method of holding to a middle way that avoids fascination with an extreme position on either side, but rather that brings together knowledge and vital piety, social concern and holy living, spiritual vitality and moral integrity, faith and good works in an effort to proclaim and live the wholeness of the gospel.

Most importantly, perhaps, Methodism at its best has recognized that God is the central figure in the drama of salvation and the transformation of the world. The sort of synergy that Wesley promoted, acknowledging the necessity of human effort but relying upon the sovereignty of God, has been a central feature of the Wesleyan movement from the beginning. The ultimate reliance upon God's presence and power (grace) undergirds both the confidence of faith and the efficacy of good works in the Methodist tradition.

While these more or less prescriptive elements of the tradition have persisted strongly within the continuing forms of Methodism, other features of the Wesleyan scheme, while still important, have played a slightly different role over the years.

Instructive Uses of Tradition

The Wesleyan heritage has provided Methodists with a number of traditional guidelines for thought and action that are open-ended in their application, then and now. They may not be unique in themselves, but they represent part of a distinctive Wesleyan approach to the Christian life. The details of application are necessarily supplied in the context of the times, but the methods in themselves have proved to be instructive over the years. Their use helps prevent the excesses of enthusiasm, spiritism, antiquarianism, and biblicism by encouraging the use of a broader range of contemporary criteria when trying to understand Christian life and thought.

One of the themes co-opted by Methodists over the years has been the 'Catholic Spirit'. Although this phrase means many different things to a variety of people and groups, the core of its usefulness as an instructive guideline is its insistence that one must distinguish between the 'essentials' of the faith on the one hand and those matters that are secondary matters of 'opinion' on the other. Wesley was convinced that believers should be 'fixed as the sun' in their own basic beliefs, but that they should be able to be tolerant of other traditions that vary in secondary matters, such as types of worship and modes of baptism. He would have agreed with the Dissenters of his own day who encapsulated this concept with the motto, 'Unity in essentials, tolerance in non-essentials, charity in all things'. The central issue for continuing debate between groups, however, is the determination of just where that dividing line between essentials and opinions should fall.

Some elements of the Methodist tradition that were originally prescriptive can be understood as more helpful if understood within this 'instructive' level of application. An example might be the General Rules, a Wesleyan stipulation that has some form of constitutional presence in many traditions. The Rules in their general expression – to avoid evil, to do good, and to use the means of grace – are unquestionably applicable in any age. Some people have difficulty with the specific examples given under the category of avoiding evil, however, and therefore disregard the whole document. The three general rules, nevertheless, are indeed central to the Wesleyan tradition and can be instructive of the basic level of expectations for Christian living.[9] For these rules to be most relevant in any given age, the specific examples of evils to be avoided would need to be updated. In that way, they can be appropriately instructive to continuing generations of Methodists.

The Wesleyan heritage also contains some fascinating paradoxes. It might seem, for instance, that Wesley was being prescriptive when he said that he was *homo unius libri*, 'a person of one book'.[10] His intention was to stress the importance of the Bible. But later, when his preachers tried to explain their lack of wide reading by saying that they only read the Bible, throwing his own prescription back at him, Wesley replied with a strong exhortation to broad reading (citing the Apostle Paul in the process).[11] So the more sophisticated expectation included not only regular reading of the Scriptures, but also the examination of other important books as well. For those who had any doubts about how broadly he expected spiritual leaders to read, his *Address to the Clergy* listed a broad and demanding programme of subjects that would instruct the mind.[12]

The Wesleyan approach to Scripture itself provides another instructive guideline for followers of any age – that any particular questions arising from difficult or conflicting passages should be resolved in the light of the 'analogy of faith' or the 'whole tenor of Scripture'. This approach encourages a holistic view of Scripture that includes Old and New Testaments, hard and easy passages, familiar and unfamiliar stories. Wesley would assume that the major themes that tie the Scriptures together would be their focus on the drama of salvation. But the use of this scriptural hermeneutic by successive generations in different contexts does not necessarily provide prescriptive answers for interpretation in every instance. It does, however, provide a traditional Wesleyan method by which readers of the Bible can work through questions that arise and derive instructive results that will fall within a range that is appropriate to the heritage.

Supportive Uses of Tradition

A third level at which tradition operates within the Wesleyan heritage is by supporting and encouraging contemporary ideas and actions that support the intentions undergirding the original principles and practices. Such appropriation and adaptation of traditional approaches help keep Methodism vital in successive generations.

One such use might be seen in the contemporary understanding of itinerancy as being inherently associated with connexionalism. Rather than prescribing that 'travelling preachers' must move to a new assignment every year or two in order to be true itinerants, Methodism in present-day society recognizes that the requirements both to keep a preacher moving around a circuit and to change circuits regularly was a method especially appropriate to a rural and far-flung population. To the small Methodist societies scattered throughout the hills and dales, these spiritual leaders on horseback represented a spirited Wesleyan movement extending its arms and incorporating them into the community of faithful believers. Itinerancy in terms of constant rotation of preachers who were committed to a common mission of spreading scriptural holiness was a method of implementing the Connexion, the Wesleyan movement. The basic principle was the connecting element, not the travelling aspect. So in a more urbanized and settled society, while itinerancy can still include the practice of moving preachers fairly regularly, the core of the concept is the common commitment to mission that ties preachers and people together in a Connexion with conviction.

Another shift in understanding in which the tradition still plays a supportive role is a more contemporary understanding of the concept of 'social holiness'. I have frequently criticized people for confusing this Wesleyan idea with the practice of exercising works of mercy or in developing programmes of social concern. Wesley does use the term primarily to indicate that true religion is not solitary religion, as the mystics might claim. Rather, he would say that true religion is social religion – true holiness is social holiness. At its core, then, this concept encourages thoughtful Christians to nurture their faith in community, to worship together, to study together, to sing together, to pray together. Such an understanding of the Christian faith, however, also supports the idea of working together. If, as Wesley says over and over, 'faith worketh through love', then a faithful community will act together in exercising that faith not only through acts of piety but also through works of mercy. Therefore, the step from the original principle of social holiness as the communal nurture of faith to a contemporary understanding of it as mission to the marginalized in society is a short step that is strongly supported by the tradition itself.

Another practice that has supportive roots in the tradition is the use of a rite for remembering our baptism. In Wesley's day, the main debate was between the idea of infant baptism as a means of regeneration and entrance into the Church and the idea of adult baptism as a conscious expression of faith and therefore the channel for actual regeneration as the person entered the Church. For Wesley, the debate was more theoretical than practical – one should not challenge theologically the capacity of the Holy Spirit to cause real change in the life of an infant. But practically speaking, by the time children are old enough to be responsible young adults, they have sinned and stand in need of continued forgiveness and regeneration.

The reality of such backsliding, however, did not cause Wesley either to discourage the practice of infant baptism or encourage the practice of adult baptism (or rebaptism). Infant baptism still played an important role in releasing the child from the guilt and punishment of original sin. Therefore, one need not be rebaptized. But given that his interest was in promoting life-long faithful discipleship, one can understand that for many people, a conscious remembrance of the vows made at their baptism and a recollection of God's forgiving mercy exercised in that sacrament could provide powerful encouragement to continued living as a faithful disciple of Christ. The Wesleyan tradition therefore is very supportive of the practice of contemporary Methodists of nurturing their long-time relationship to Christ by consciously remembering their baptism, something that will no doubt reassure and affirm the stance taken by Ramsden in his chapter.

The supportive use of tradition would find a number of manifestations in the present agendas of Methodism around the world. The programmes of evangelism, from revivals to the use of small groups, are certainly encouraged by the Wesleyan heritage, as are prison ministries, frequent administration and participation in the Eucharist, the utilization of the latest biblical scholarship, the promotion of life-long learning (perhaps even distance education), the employment of publishing enterprises, and many other parts of the contemporary Methodist mission, without prescribing a singular approach that must be followed.

The various ways that the Wesleyan tradition has become indigenized around the world has resulted in a variety of practices within the pan-Methodist community. Their inherent unity is expressed partly through their membership in the World Methodist Council, which has existed for over a century and a half. One of the most important functions of this body is to encourage conversation and sharing of insights among the representatives of the various groups, trusting that each group will learn from other manifestations of the Wesleyan heritage. This continuing dialogue around the world represents one of the finest methods by which various expressions of the tradition can discover new expressions of lasting principles within the heritage.

Suggestive Uses of the Tradition

One of the most exciting developments of recent years is the recognition that the faithful passing on of a tradition entails creative
appropriation of the old principles in a new context. Traditions
grow into the future by incorporating constructive thinking and
actions that are on the cutting edge while still faithful to the
basic principles of the heritage. These 'fresh expressions', as mentioned by Deigh in Chapter 1, represent the application of new
approaches that are not simple reiterations of the past but are
creative approaches to new problems yet are certainly congruent
with the best thought and practice of the previous generations.

One of the bequests of the ecumenical movement of the last 60
years is a lively sense among many people that before a denominational heritage can make a worthwhile contribution to the life
and thought of the wider Christian Church, it must first fully
understand and appreciate its own tradition. Jobson makes this
point most effectively in her chapter. She correctly discerns that
lively engagement with other traditions depends upon a clear self-
consciousness and understanding of one's own heritage.

Wesley himself provided a good model as one who was willing to adapt to new situations while cognizant of the need for
maintaining continuity and congruence with his ancestors in the
faith and the recognized standards of authority. He was not hesitant to express his own point of view on matters of theology,
organization, or mission, which often seemed to be somewhat
less than 'orthodox' by some observers. But he was also quick to
assert his willingness to be taught, to be proved wrong, if anyone
cared to point out a better way or position based on Scripture or
reason.[13]

This type of constructive 'pushing the edge of the envelope'
is often seen as a risky venture, especially in the Church, where
innovation often leads to internal controversy. But even in the
field of Wesley studies itself, ingenuity and creativity are necessary to move the field ahead. At the 1983 Oxford Institute of
Methodist Theological Studies, Albert Outler analysed the field
as having gone through three stages. Stage One, grounded in the

hagiographical biographies of the nineteenth century, was trium-
phalist and treated Wesley as a hero. Stage Two in the twentieth
century began to look at Wesley in terms of his similarities with
or borrowings from one or another tradition of his day, such as
Puritanism, Lutheranism, Moravianism, Roman Catholicism,
Calvinism, and the like. Stage Three, which exemplified the best
of the later twentieth century, not only examined the whole of the
Wesleyan corpus, but also saw Wesley against the backdrop of
the multiplicity of his sources. Since then, scholars have taken the
field of Wesley studies one step further. In what I like to call Stage
Four, those who work in the fields of theology, ethics, political
theory, social work, evangelism, preaching, and so forth have
started from the base of the previous state, a critical and holistic
approach to Wesley and his sources, and have ventured forth in
constructive ways to shape new ideas for the present age in ways
that go in directions that Wesley could have never conceived but
would appreciate.[14]

In this sense, constructive approaches to the tradition can often
vary quite significantly, depending on the context and circumstances, while still being faithful to the basic historic principles of
the Wesleyan tradition. An example would be to show the basic
idea behind one of Wesley's most famous sayings ('I look upon all
the world as my parish') and show how it might be applied today
in quite different ways from the typical interpretation, which has
often been to promote world missions. That is not what Wesley
had in mind at all – he was not in favour of opening up mission fields in foreign lands when there were not enough helpers to
serve the needs of the primary mission in his own country. Rather,
in this phrase he was providing a rationale for having broken one
of the limiting rules within the Anglican tradition – he preached
within the boundaries of another priest's parish. His argument
to the Bishop of Bristol, who called him on the carpet, was to
say that his ordination at Oxford was not limited by the usual
expectations of parish ministry – he was not restricted by the demarcation of parish lines. The basic principle here is that Wesley's
field preaching was a branching into innovative ministries, crossing parish lines, not limited by institutional boundaries. This idea

of creating new approaches to ministry under the primary impulse of spreading the gospel is a powerful call to think outside the box when it comes to applying Wesleyan traditions to contemporary situations.

This suggestive use of tradition does not have a set method or pattern in mind, much less a predictable content, but rather challenges the idea that 'one size fits all'. The tradition can, in fact, adapt to different contexts in different ways and still be faithful to the heritage. Faithfulness as such is not just a matter of careful passing on, in keeping with the best of the past. Faithfulness also entails appropriate reception, in keeping with the needs of the present and future. Hearing our story again with new ears, receiving the tradition with new problems in mind, finding the overlooked messages in our heritage, can be an exhilarating moment of discovery that might have significant consequences for our present self-understanding as a Church in the Wesleyan tradition.

The suggestion that social holiness, in terms of programmes of social outreach, should be viewed as a logical (or theological) outgrowth of Christian perfection, in terms of loving God and neighbour, is a constructive connection of two Wesleyan ideas that are never quite put together that way by Wesley himself. The reference in Chapter 7 to 'Wesley's emphasis on Christian perfection as social holiness' might seem like historical reconstruction, but the connection between the two concepts can easily be developed today in ways that Wesley himself might never have conceived but with which Wesley himself might be in total agreement, especially in terms of the outcome or fruits of that approach. The community acting in love to their neighbours in programmes of social concern that are motivated by pure love could certainly be understood as a manifestation of Christian perfection by the congregation of the faithful. In Methodist terms, this sort of action would not just be a group of people doing something in society, but rather a society of people that is doing something very Christian.

A similar comment might be made about another common concept that is used today as though it were a basic part of Wesley's method, namely 'holy conferencing'. The idea comes from the reference in the Minutes to the importance of the means of grace, and the naming of the five 'instituted' means that are grounded in the ministry of Christ: prayer, searching the Scripture, the Lord's Supper, fasting, and Christian conference.[15] The phrasing in that context is further illuminated, however, by Wesley's subsequent comments about 'ordering our conversation right', planning our conversation beforehand, and limiting our conversation to an hour. He was apparently talking about private conversations between individuals, which could be seen as an occasion for the experience of God's presence and power. But that concept could certainly be broadened into group conversations such as occur at Methodist annual conferences, without doing damage to the basic Wesleyan concept that such holy conferencing could be seen as a means of grace. And certainly the prospect of an hour's limitation at a time could be understood as a useful suggestion in that context as well!

This suggestive use of the tradition by constructing new approaches based on timely principles represents one of the most exciting prospects for the ongoing vitality of the Wesleyan tradition. And fortunately, many of the positive suggestions in the foregoing chapters are based on just such an approach. It seems that Wesley would be confident that with such an approach to the future, Methodism would certainly not become a dead sect, but would be filled with the power as well as the form of religion, as he understood it.

Methodism in the Future

These observations, as well as those drawn out more extensively in the previous chapters, contain several reasons for being optimistic about the future of the Wesleyan heritage. Wesley himself probably did not anticipate that Methodism would become such a thriving presence around the globe. His view was much narrower and, quite honestly, much more focussed. He accepted the traditional view that the Church was 'the congregation of faithful men in which the Word was proclaimed and the Sacrament duly administered', but Methodism was much more than that. His little treatise on *The Marks of a Methodist* suggests what 'faithful' means when he says that the true Christian (with whom he equates the true Methodist) is one who loves God and loves neighbour. I would suggest that while this is the heart of the distinctive Wesleyan expression of Christian perfection and a central mark of a Methodist (and a Christian), several other characteristics distinguish the Wesleyan heritage in our own day and provide a realistic hope for its vital future.

Many people choose a church to attend based on what seem to be quite superficial criteria, such as geographical location and attractive facilities – pleasing sanctuaries, beautiful organs, and special features such as nurseries, kitchens, and gyms. But these features, important as they might be, are not denominationally specific and not distinctive to any particular heritage. Over the years, historians of Methodism have suggested several reasons for its particular attractiveness to society. The common reasons given have been good biblical preaching ('plain truth' *ad populum*), powerful spiritual singing, good religious education, concerned pastoral care, and widespread social outreach.[16] While these five (or six, including the final paragraph) elements are significant elements of Methodism's identity and success over the years, I would suggest five other features that have strong roots in the Wesleyan tradition and will help determine the ongoing vitality of our heritage.

Focus

Methodism will continue to exhibit the 'power' of religion so long as it stays focussed on its primary mission to spread scriptural holiness. Those particular words need not be used to specify the purpose of the organization's single intention. Wesley said that his preachers had nothing to do but to 'save souls'. That terminology can be expanded and updated to include a wide range of ways by which the company of faithful might nurture the love of God and of neighbour, might help people overcome their sinful tendencies, might encourage the imitation of Christ, 'who went about doing good'. There may be many means to this end, but the Church will be most relevant to society if it stays focussed on this mission rather than becoming fascinated by the various methods of achieving that goal.

Discipline

Methodism has never been a movement that simply promoted 'having faith'. Such solafidianism often results from apathy toward the holy habits that energize the Christian life of love. As any athlete, student, artist, or teacher knows, discipline is the secret to success in reaching goals in many fields. A life marked by careful patterns of thought and action in concert with others committed to the same goals can become a powerful agent for change in society. And within that approach, accountability to each other and to God has always been a notable feature of Wesleyan communities of 'faith working through love'. Combined effort, concerted teamwork – people helping each other become more Christ-like – provides a most effective approach to making a difference in the world today.

Flexibility

Methodism has always been able to adjust to the needs of its context. Whether that meant Wesley adapting his theology to meet the perceived needs of the people, or Coke widening the Wesleyan mission to include overseas ventures, or Asbury crafting the itinerant system to meet the challenges of the American frontier, our tradition has characteristically been flexible enough to make adjustments in the light of changing circumstances. Just as Wesley had a firm framework within which to revise his thinking (his critics needed to demonstrate their point by Scripture and reason), so the revisions within the tradition should be constrained by the principles of the primary mission of the movement. But as we have said, the movement can remain relevant and become most vital if it is able to confront the distress of people in the present day and anticipate the needs of God's children in the future. This approach may mean using time-tested methods of action; it may mean revising older systems that no longer function well; it may mean coming up with innovative approaches to challenges, old and new. The use of new technologies, appropriate art forms, creative methods of communication, and other advances in our own day can certainly enhance the long-range implementation of our mission.

Connexion

Methodism has always been a connexional organization. The strength of that organizational arrangement rests not so much in its pattern of itinerancy or programme of combined finances as in the commitment of leaders and members to a common mission. Every local situation has a unique combination of needs within that common vision, which is why the itinerant system has the potential of being effective in such situations. Pastors can be assigned according to the particular needs of the parish, and a continuing succession of pastors can meet the constantly changing needs of any given situation. The Wesleyan Connexion has always thrived on a shallow organizational chart with a very large percentage of the members participating in leadership positions. This approach, of course, depends upon careful mentoring of those in positions of responsibility. But when more people have a stake in the implementation of the goals, progress to the achievement of the mission is more likely.

Practicality

Methodism has always been concerned with the practice of Christian living. Certainly, our heritage is firmly grounded in scriptural doctrines and carefully nurtured through theological reflection. We try to provide leadership that has appropriate gifts; we look toward having a sound rationale for our organization. But as with Wesley, we are most concerned with the 'fruits' of our endeavours; we measure success by how well God's mission has been implemented in the lives of individuals and communities within our sphere of influence. Being a Methodist means that being a Christian makes a difference in the way you live. *Praxis* has become a watchword for many Methodist theologians who try to translate Wesley's pragmatic approach into the contemporary scene – 'practical divinity' has become a favourite, if not carefully defined, way of describing the Methodist way of understanding and implementing Christianity. As long as the followers of Wesley continue to see themselves as agents of change and hope within God's transforming mission in the world, Methodism will thrive as a dynamic part of the Body of Christ.

In order to 'exercise the presence of God', as Wesley suggested, we must be open to the work of the Spirit in our midst. We must also see ourselves as channels of God's grace (divine presence and power) active in the world. As a Church as well as a movement, Methodism has always been most effective, and will continue to be most effective, when it realizes that its goal is to help realize the Great Commandment in human existence: to love God and love neighbour.

Methodism can perhaps be best understood itself as a means of grace that presents opportunities for people (individually and corporately) to experience the power and presence of God in their lives, enlightening them, judging them, liberating them, empowering them, sustaining them, comforting them, and transforming them into disciples of Christ to help establish the Kingdom of God.

Notes

1 The one exception could easily have done so, but the author chose to make no references to any work prior to 1982, much less to Wesley or the Bible.

2 Different approaches to the authority of the tradition are not unlike the spectrum of hermeneutical approaches to the authority of Scripture, as outlined in Chapter 2, above.

3 This list was suggested by Prof. Rex Matthews at a session of the 2008 meeting of the Wesleyan Studies Working Group at the annual meeting of the American Academy of Religion in Chicago. The list as given here omits the non-positive approaches, which would see past tradition as either neutrally irrelevant or negatively destructive ('bad for your theological health'). Since the studies in this book do not display these negative approaches, we will not spend time discussing them here.

4 James Russell Lowell, 'Once to Every Man and Nation'. Many people

have forgotten that Lowell wrote this poem as an anti-slavery protest against the Mexican War of 1845, fearing that the annexation of Texas into the United States would increase the extent of slave-holding lands.

5 The High Court of New Zealand recently determined that a decision by the President of Conference that a position of the church did not contradict the *Sermons* or *Notes* was a satisfactory determination by the church, regardless of any historical or theological evidence to the contrary.

6 Such as in the United Methodist Church, which includes the former Evangelical United Brethren *Confession of Faith* as a constitutionally protected standard of doctrine as a result of the 1968 union.

7 See Ted Campbell, 'The Myth of the Wesleyan Quadrilateral' in Thomas A. Langford ed., *Doctrine and Theology in the United Methodist Church*, Nashville, TN: Kingswood, 1995.

8 AlthoughWesley strongly opposed indifference or latitudinarianism, he noted in 1783, 'It is the glory of the people called Methodists that they condemn none for their opinions or modes of worship. They think and let think' (letter to Mrs Howton, 3 Oct. 1783); see also his journal entry for Sunday, 18 May 1788 – so far as he knew, the Methodists were the only 'religious society under heaven' that did not require prospective members to subscribe to a set of beliefs.

9 From the early days of the movement and throughout his life, Wesley suggested that these three rules did not represent the best outline of spirituality or religion, but in the 1740s he codified them in the General Rules as the basic expectations for a person who was pressing on toward salvation.

10 Preface (¶5), *Sermons on Several Occasions*, 1746.

11 *Minutes of the Methodist Conferences*, London, 1862, pp. 518–19.

12 Under the general category of 'acquired talents'. Wesley listed a wide range of areas with which one should become conversant. In the Minutes, he listed both a programme of reading and a list of books that should be kept in the preaching houses at London, Bristol, and Newcastle.

13 See Preface, *Sermons on Several Occasions*, 1746, pp. 8–9.

14 Several recent titles from Epworth Press and in the Kingswood Books series from Abingdon Press exhibit the new and exciting possibilities of Stage Four.

15 'Large' *Minutes* (1780 and 1789), answer to Qu. 48 (numbered 44 in 1770 and 1772; unnumbered in 1763).

16 For example, see William B. McClain, 'The Appeal of Methodism to Black Americans', Ch. 4 in *Black People in the Methodist Church*, Nashville, TN: Abingdon Press, 1984, pp. 19–37, and Tik-Wah Wong, 'Why John Wesley in the 21st Century?', Ch. 1 of 'Eschatological Living in John Wesley's Theology' (PhD Dissertation, Melbourne College of Divinity, Victoria, Australia, 2008), pp. 1–4.

9

Growth in Grace and Holiness

ANGELA SHIER-JONES

In his 1786 treatise entitled *Thoughts on Methodism*, Wesley wrote:

> I am not afraid that the people called Methodists should ever cease to exist either in Europe or America. But I am afraid lest they should only exist as a dead sect, having the form of religion without the power. And this undoubtedly will be the case unless they hold fast both the doctrine, spirit, and discipline with which they first set out.

It is a text which challenges each generation of the Methodist family to reflect on its existence and ask, using the words of Charles Wesley's hymn, 'And are we yet alive?'

The contributors to Part One of this volume have, for the large part, presumed that the answer to this question is 'Yes'. It falls to the preceding generations however to examine the evidence that they provide in support of their confidence and ask – 'But in what form?' Statistical evidence suggests that all the main-line denominations, not just the British Methodist Church, are in a state of general decline. How accurate is this evaluation? Can Methodism be written off as a dead sect yet? Surely it would be ludicrous in this digital age, when accuracy ensures efficiency and vice versa, to claim that that an institution as large as the British Methodist Church has no accurate means of measuring either its growth or its effectiveness? Yet, as Curran has pointed out in his chapter, this is undoubtedly the case. There must, of course, be some cor-

relation between the figures recorded in the 'statistics for mission'[1]
and the 'growth' or decline of the denomination, but it would
be far too simplistic to state that falling numbers can be directly
equated to a failure to grow in any way which makes sense to
a Methodist. In spite of the increasing commodification of the
Church and the consequent intrusion of all things managerial and
professional into the sacred spaces of worship, fellowship, and
ministry, there is, I believe, real evidence in Part One of this book
of a desire for present and potential growth in Methodism to be
measured differently, perhaps even in what might be considered
a godly fashion. That the contributors in Part One are convinced
of the potential in Methodism for 'growth' is evident. In spite of
their critique of present structures, systems, and attitudes, there is
an undeniable note of optimism running throughout the first part
of this book. The challenges which are named as necessary to release the potential identified in Methodism also make it clear that
Wesley's fear is shared. It is echoed in the stories, challenges, and
reflections which the contributors offer. This is, it would seem, a
generation determined to resist the secular demand that their faith
and their work be measured through precision in their account-
ing. Instead there has been a conscious effort to focus on how
much attention is paid to holiness of life and how much emphasis
is placed on growth in grace.

Is this just a refusal to face facts? Ten years after *Methodism and
the Future* is there evidence of a real decline in Methodism which
the contributors are just unwilling or unable to recognize and address? To phrase the question theologically, in their celebration
of the optimism of grace, have the contributors neglected to take
into account the fullness of God's judgement? John Wesley called
Methodism a work of God; could it still be called that today?

Ten years ago, Marsh and Craske suggested that there were
only four possible options open to Methodism.

1 Methodism continues as it is and fizzles out sometime in the
next century.
2 Methodism continues independent of other Christian traditions
with a clearer focus on what justifies it being separate.

3 Methodism disbands and becomes reincorporated into the Church of England.
4 Methodism prepares to disband itself, whilst working towards a new, more fully ecumenical church in England.[2]

The small group of under-40s who have contributed to this book could never be considered representative of the whole of Methodism, but if their evaluations, judgements, and opinions are sound, then there would seem to be little evidence to suggest that Option 3 is a serious possibility. What then of the remaining three options? Have the contributors provided sufficient evidence of change to rule out Option 1? Likewise, have they uncovered sufficient progress ecumenically to justify a confidence in the direction proposed by Option 4? If, as seems most likely, Option 2 is the preferred direction of the contributors, then it is pertinent to ask whether collectively they have provided enough evidence of a clearer focus which can justify confidence in Methodism's continued existence as a separate denomination? If so, what is that focus?

In her chapter in *Methodism and the Future*, Jane Craske asked whether a vision of 'holiness' could inspire the Methodist Church afresh.[3] She insisted on the need for Methodism to be shaped into the sort of Church that holiness demanded, and for the Methodist people to be a 'holy' people. As she pointed out, however, 'Holiness is not a state to be achieved; it is activity and direction, and process.' Her definition is a succinct summary of Wesley's insistence that

> The gospel of Christ knows of no religion, but social; no holiness but social holiness. 'Faith working by love' is the length and breadth and depth and height of Christian perfection. 'This commandment have we from Christ, that he who loves God, love his brother also;' and that we manifest our love 'by doing good unto all men'.[4]

In what follows, therefore, I will use Craske's definition followed by Wesley's descriptions of the essentials, namely doctrine, spirit, and discipline, and attempt to discern whether or not the British

Methodist Church has had, and more importantly, still has, the potential to grow in grace and holiness. I will ask what evidence has been provided that Methodism has sufficiently refocussed on its calling to recognize itself and be inspired by its vocation to be a holy people, a work of God.

Holiness as Activity

Wesley's emphasis on social holiness meant that Methodists once had a reputation for being great activists. Throughout its history Methodism worldwide has been able to name among its members those who have campaigned for justice, challenged corruption, stood with and for the oppressed, and worked tirelessly for social change at every level. Concern for the Kingdom encouraged Methodists to participate in founding, sponsoring, supporting, and maintaining schools, hospitals, charities, and political movements. Roy Hattersley, for example, once wrote:

> The Independent Labour party was founded in what had been a Reform Methodist Chapel. We carried on the same tradition in the local co-op's 'old cobblers shop'. I knew in my teens that Labour owed more to Methodism than Marxism.[5]

The conviction of social holiness was translated by Methodists into incarnational theology. Christ's presence in the world called for the world to be made fit for a King. Christ's love for all meant that all people were worthy of dignity and respect; all people could be saved. Methodism walked a tight line between grace and law. They recognized the sin and the worth of each individual and were convinced that God, and God alone, could save and transform. They nonetheless insisted that salvation would be evident in the activity and the life of the convert. Being saved meant being willing to work, not just wait, for God's Kingdom.

For the last decade, here in the UK, the social gospel of the Church has been openly courted by the longest ever serving Labour government. Under Tony Blair the government invited and encouraged faith participation in shaping its policies and implementing its programmes of social cohesion. At the same time, the fabric of both Church and society has been stretched and at times noticeably torn by circumstances outside of their direct and immediate control. Global warming, GM foods, stem cell research, human trafficking, tsunamis, to say nothing of the threat posed by SARS and bird flu have all challenged the idea of local immunity from worldwide concerns. Air-borne viruses, international finances and the consequences of global warming are no respecters of national boundaries. Neither, it would seem, are terrorists. Globalization has profoundly altered the context in which the Church is called to serve God. It has, in many respects, brought what were once the primary concerns of the world mission field back home through the increased numbers of asylum seekers and refugees and the growth in international travel and migration. Both Church and society are more diverse than they once were, and, in spite of concerted attempts by both, are arguably considerably less united by any identifiably common thread or calling.

The British Methodist Church had already begun its own process of change and adaptation before the start of the century. The 'Our Calling' process which led ultimately to the adoption of 'The Priorities of the Methodist Church' began the process of tightening the Church's focus in the face of the increasing diversification which was threatening to overwhelm it. There were simply too many projects to be involved in, too many causes to campaign for, too many issues to evaluate and areas to address, and all too few people skilled and equipped to do the work. The threatened loss of identity was not one of denomination, but of purpose. What was the role of the Church in the twenty-first century? The report *Called to Love and Praise*, referred to by many of the contributors to this volume, provided the starting point for a collective connexional answer to the question.

What is particularly stimulating about the response being made in this volume to what is, after all, a perennial problem, is that it calls for the Church to discover a genuine compassion for all people, *but especially for those who are not yet Christian*. This sentiment is expressed in several of the papers, but most notably in Deigh's. Such a call would certainly meet with Wesley's approval, but it has long been noticeable by its absence from British Methodism and other major UK denominations. In the 1970s and 80s in particular, the social gospel lost much of its originating link with salvation and growth in grace. Good deeds were done for the sake of good deeds, out of common humanity, rather than for any specifically incarnational or soteriological reasons. Christians loved their neighbours, and were content to demonstrate it by doing good deeds, feeding the hungry, opening shelters for the homeless, raising funds for charities, etc. Compassion and charity were recognized as 'Christian' virtues, but there was little obvious interest in specifically building up the Kingdom of God. Thatcher's generation, on the whole, would have agreed with her statement:

There is much to be said for trying to improve some disadvantaged people's lot. There is nothing to be said for trying to create heaven on earth.[6]

As recently as 2002 a report warned the Church that it could no longer afford to act as though social action and the struggle for justice are the whole or even the predominant part of its mission agenda. In the opinion of its authors, the survival of the British Methodist Church was dependent upon the Church's ability 'to persuade people to become followers of Jesus Christ'.[7] The Church of England's Mission-Shaped Church programme and Fresh Expressions initiative illustrate the universal nature of the problem. The call was not just for a greater emphasis on evangelism or 'mission', however. The call was, and is, clearly linked to the need for a compassionate Church, a Church which can recognize the plight of those who live their lives without the Christian hope and without faith. It is a call for the Church to participate in the mission of God by responding to the needs of those who are lost with the same spirit of activism that the Church formerly invested in meeting the needs of the poor or the sick. It is a request for a shift away from an active generosity of spirit, towards a spirit of holy generosity which acts out of love for God rather than simply out of love for humanity. Having such compassion for those without faith replaces the call to promote a purely social gospel, one concerned only with the material and physical needs of the people, with Wesley's call to spread what he would term scriptural holiness. Wesley believed that it was impossible for anyone to be truly happy, satisfied, or even free in life if they were not holy, if they did not know God. It was therefore out of compassion that God raised up the people called Methodists to proclaim holiness and perfect love so that God's people could be happy. Methodists were called to share the good news of life before death, a holy life whose motivations, actions, and relationships could be entirely governed by love for God and neighbour.

Only scriptural holiness, with its emphasis on life now, on growth in grace and its openness to that which is truly 'other', is likely even to begin to address the challenges posed by Toppin and by Forster. Toppin's honest and frank appraisal of the difficulties presented by the diversity of the contemporary context of the Church illustrates the classic failure of the old-style 'social gospel'. It is not good enough to treat those who are different as somehow lacking or being in need. The challenge for the Church is to learn how to be open to discover the generosity of grace bestowed on the world through this amazing God-given diversity. Toppin's plea for improved education to enable people to begin to recognize their own worth and the worth of others finds an echo in the plea by Jobson for greater ecumenical engagement. Diversity is not confined to gender or ethnicity and it needs to be embraced and celebrated as God-given, not sectioned off.

When the doctrine of Christian perfection and the calling to be holy are held together, then (as Forster notes in his chapter) genuine respect and engagement with the other is not only possible but natural. The perfecting, holy love of God enables humanity to breach its own narcissism and recognize Christ in the stranger and the neighbour not as one coming in need, but as the Son of God, the King of Heaven and the bearer of *our* burdens. There are no easy solutions to problems of inclusivity and need. Practising holiness, however, and learning to love our neighbour out of a love of God rather than out of a love for humanity does at least have the potential to transform the calling to campaign for justice and freedom for all from a limited diversity issue into a universal divine imperative – 'You shall be holy for I the LORD your God am holy' (Lev. 19.2).

Holiness as Direction

Scriptural holiness presumes a knowledge of Scripture and a willingness to learn and engage with the text. The collapse of the metanarrative under postmodernity's incessant demand for relative truths and individual freedoms has undeniably affected the way in which Scripture is viewed both within the Church and in wider society. The role of Scripture as the primary source of religious authority has been repeatedly questioned over the last decade, most notably as a consequence of the debates in the Anglican Church on human sexuality and women in the episcopate. As Dean makes clear in his chapter, Methodists have not been immune from the general confusion surrounding the 'right' way to read Scripture, or the 'truth' that it contains. He does not underestimate the difficulty in being a people of 'one book' when the book is deemed largely irrelevant by a significant section of the population. Is there perhaps some correlation between the perceived decline in biblical literacy and love of hymnody and a decline in church attendance? Has the Church lost some of its power to awaken the sense of awe and wonder at the glory and majesty of God as a result of no longer knowing how to read and hear the powerful poetry and prose of Scripture? His suggestion of encouraging others to re-envisage Scripture, to allow its poetry to be heard rather than to always seek the 'right' interpretation of a text, reopens the possibility of using Scripture as a means of discerning a direction for living and for discovering the truth and value of Christian doctrine.

Ramsden's concern for the absence of any real understanding or appreciation of the sacraments and their relationship to discipleship highlights the need for the sort of re-visioning that Dean suggests. Like Dean, Ramsden is not seeking an alternative or contemporary reinterpretation of the story of Christ for this generation. Instead Ramsden calls for a greater awareness of the sacraments as a means of entering into, of participating and being immersed in, the story and hence into the life of Christ. Where he sees the sacraments as performances, Dean sees the Scriptures as the script. Together they allow the individual, regardless of academic ability or historical knowledge, to enter fully into the mystery of Christ and experience who they are in the presence of God. The postmodern challenges of 'whose way?', 'whose truth?' and 'whose life is it anyway?' are emptied of their power to silence the absolute when they are no longer responded to as either literalistic or pseudo-scientific enquiries. By inhabiting Christ in word and action through participation in the Sacraments and internalizing Scripture, the enquirer is able to locate the truth of their own being within the absolute which is God.

It is this incarnational knowledge, this participation in the presence of God, which resonates with Wesley's foundational understanding of scriptural holiness as being more than a way of reading a text, and so much more than a way of receiving bread and wine; it is a direction for living based on participation in Christ who is the way, the truth, and the life. When the believer is 'in Christ', they are as Scripture says a new creation, they are not outside of, nor are they separate from the truth which is God's truth. Yet their individuality is not lost, neither is their ability to discern the value or meaning of a specific truth.

Clearly imagination and language matter. Not only do they shape our self-perception, as Toppin notes, they also inform our reason. Reason is not separate from these gifts of grace but, as has been repeatedly shown, is dependent upon them. It is this which is so often ignored by those who find themselves at a loss to answer to the challenges made by Dawkins and his school of secular fanatics who pride themselves on their scientific rationality and decry what they consider to be the imaginative truths of faith.

To talk of participation in the story of faith through the sacraments, however, is dangerous in these days of religious extremism. The rise of fundamentalism in Christianity, Islam, and Hinduism is a source of real concern, when so many act out their religious convictions through acts of terror and abuse. The poetry and passion of the martyr, the language of sacrifice and of ritual, all need to be held in check by an acceptance of some form of orthodoxy and orthopraxy. What we cannot afford is a return to the sort of exclusive orthodoxy which takes no account of the diversity necessary to embrace the challenges posed by Toppin and Forster. The world is not, and the Church should not be, Eurocentric. Methodism is a member of a global denomination whose current centre of numerical growth is probably Asian, and whose primary centre of theological growth is arguably African. The doctrines of the Church are no longer as certain as they once seemed to be and the denominational boundaries are less exclusive than they once were. In some parts of the world Methodists are in full communion with Anglicans, in others they remain only in a covenant relationship. In some Methodist communities same-sex relationships are an acceptable expression of the love between two people, in others it is cause for discipline. Globally speaking Methodism is as fractured and divided on matters of doctrine as the Anglican Communion appears to be. Thus, poetry and performance notwithstanding, the question of religious authority is not diminished, but rather heightened by the direction proposed and seconded by Dean and Ramsden and advocated and sought after by Toppin, Forster, and Jobson.

Holiness as Process

Most British Methodists could be forgiven for thinking that the process of continually revising the structures of the Church is an integral part of what it means to be a Methodist. This is due to the thorough revision of the organizational and management structures of the British Methodist Church, a process which began in the late 1990s and which is still not completed at the time of writing. Leadership, oversight, and governance became the dominant words in the Methodist Conference Agenda for many years, while the ministry, work, and hierarchies of the Church were scrutinized, evaluated, revised, and reordered under the guidance of hired professional management consultants. Meanwhile the government, in response to changes in European legislation concerning human rights and pressure from civil rights groups, began exploring the nature of the relationship between the minister and the Church. Were Methodist ministers employees? If so, who employed them, God or the Church? What employment rights did they have? Could they be discriminatory in their selection procedures with regard to age, ability, sexual orientation? What disciplinary or grievance procedures are in place? How are ministers paid? The language of faith often seemed drowned out by the language of order as managers, bureaucrats, administrators, and lawyers in the Church struggled to balance the budget and create a structure for the Connexion which would enable it to survive into the future.

As part of the restructuring, the Methodist Conference, once the primary decision-making body of the Church, was downsized. This unfortunately led to lost opportunities to communicate the vision and strategy which lay behind certain aspects of the reorganization. In spite of the effort put in by the Connexional team to explain the new processes to Districts at synods there is little evidence in Part One of this book to suggest that it has either inspired or motivated people to work for mission or growth. Without a means of communicating the vision for the Church which may have intitally motivated the change, it has proved difficult to engage the hearts and minds of the Methodist people with it. If letters written to the *Methodist Recorder* and memorials sent to Conference are in any way indicative then a significant number of those who finally did engage in the process did so primarily to complain that the things that mattered to them – Women's Network, Racial Justice, the Methodist Youth Orchestra etc – were no longer going to be funded at connexional level.

One immediate consequence of the restructuring has been that the creeping congregationalism identified in *Methodism and the Future* can no longer be described as creeping. In part this is an inevitable result of the change in policy and the decision to make as many decisions as possible in the District rather than the Connexional Team. There is some evidence to suggest however that churches and ministers alike are increasingly choosing to become as disconnected as is possible from a Connexion that seems less and less relevant to the concerns and work of the local church. Methodism began life as a collection of societies loosely bound together by adherence to a common discipline and set of rules, so it is natural to expect it to continue as such.

The process of restructuring has understandably not been without pain or misunderstanding. But the essential question must be whether or not it has been and still is a holy process. The answer for many would seem to depend on what the envisaged end is, and whether or not the ongoing evolution of Methodist discipline in this manner will actually enable the Church to grow in grace and holiness. It is evident that *The Priorities of the British Methodist Church* has helped it to narrow the focus of its action and attention at national level, but it is not yet clear if it will play any part in inspiring and developing local church members' relationship with God. In what way will it help to ensure that the means of grace, prayer and fasting, the Lord's Supper, Christian conferring and searching the Scriptures are more accessible to those in need of them?

The Church insists that wherever possible it will work in partnership with others to achieve its priorities. It has already signed a covenant with the Church of England, and a joint implementation committee exists to explore ways in which that Covenant can be made to bear fruit. In spite of being less than a decade old, however, there is already clear evidence, as Jobson notes in her chapter, of a lack of engagement with the Covenant process and with ecumenism in general. There are many reasons why this might be happening; a failure to inspire much local church response perhaps, or an overemphasis on questions of ecclesial order (for example, discussing bishops rather than mission). Little comfort can be taken from the fact that the state of the Covenant may be nothing more than a reflection of the worldwide state of ecumenism as evidenced by the World Council of Churches, or even that of other similar international bodies such as the United Nations. Postmodernism places little value on metanarratives or overarching structures. The idea of one united Church therefore pushes at the contemporary liberal, individualistic mentality. This mentality favours networks or loose alliances to serve a present need, rather than fixed organic unions designed to serve for all time. This point is well made by both Jobson, and Curran.

Curran's exploration of the relationship between structure and belonging, in particular between statistics and growth, highlights both the positives and the negatives of the Methodist obsession with rules and structures. As someone who has been a part of the process for change his insights into belonging and Connexionalism are especially pertinent. His approval of the trend towards local decision-making may reflect something of the national tensions in British Methodism and the differences between Welsh and English structures. It is perhaps worth recognizing, however, that there are just as many dangers to this approach as there are benefits. In particular, any denomination which emphasizes a belief in the priesthood of all believers will have to take into account Wuthnow's appraisal:

> Another problem arises from the church's increasingly local identity: If laity care less and less about the denomination as a larger entity, then clergy will be the guardians of denominationalism. Perhaps this has always been so to a large degree. But clergy are the ones who will more and more care for the bureaucratic structures built up over the past century which are now in serious decline.[8]

Curran's challenge to the Church to own its own bureaucracy is startling, but so too is his belief that it could be re-imagined for contemporary mission rather than simply to cut the budget by 30 per cent and/or become more efficient. If this is true then it most certainly would qualify as a holy process.

That it is at least possible is evident from Forster's chapter. He claims that this was exactly what the Methodist Church of Southern Africa was able to do, and is looking to do again. The leadership of that Church was able to negotiate a path through the painful processes of apartheid and still enable the people of God to grow in grace. Forster attributes this to the MCSA's adherence to what Wesley called the Grand Depositum of Methodism, namely the doctrine of Christian perfection. His conviction of the role of theology in holding the Church to account for its policies resonates with Curran's challenge for the Church to recover and communicate its distinctive theological reason for being.

Methodist Doctrine, Spirit and Discipline

The above sections seem to suggest that the last ten years have seen something of a renewal of holiness in terms of activity, direction, and process in British Methodism. In spite of difficulties, there are hints of a return to an emphasis on social holiness, rather than just social action. Similarly there is clear evidence of a desire for a change in direction in Methodism's understanding and communion with the holiness of the 'other' as found and made known in God and neighbour. Although it is still too early to pass judgement on the process of change taking place in British Methodism, there is at least good reason to hope that it is a holy process, rooted in the desire to enable the Church to grow in grace and holiness. But what of Methodist doctrine, spirit, and discipline? Have the contributors shown that Methodism can be more than a 'dead' sect?

A significant number of the contributors believe Methodism's future lies in an understanding of Wesleyan doctrine. Yes, there are omissions, but the contributors were not asked to write a systematic theology. Their use of Wesley and of Church history emerged out of a desire to communicate a particular perspective on the area of Methodist life that they were invited to comment on. It would be foolish to suggest that the contributors are representative of Methodists under the age of 40, but it is refreshing to discover that at least some of Wesley's doctrines are being re-appropriated to serve a new generation. Can this be taken as evidence that Methodism is holding fast to its doctrine? Yes ... and no. Most of the chapters suggest a desire to recover more than history, to learn to own the tradition which emerges out of engagement with the Spirit of the doctrines which gave Methodism birth. But Toppin's work demonstrates how far the Church still has to go in translating those desires into reality. There can be no doubt that the failure of the Church to first practise the gospel it seeks to preach, actively inhibits the sense of belonging and purpose necessary to release the potential of the doctrinal tradition.

The spirit of Methodism has been variously described over the years in terms of its evangelistic zeal and its passion for social justice. Although there is significant evidence of a longing for and a commitment to meaningful evangelism in most of the chapters, there is much less evidence to suggest that it could be paired with an equal passion for social justice. Curran, Forster and Deigh offer the most hopeful signs that the Church is interested in more than numerical growth. The urgency of the mission of the Church must nonetheless be set alongside the very pressing demands for social justice today. How would the spirit of Methodism today compare with the spirit which made Wesley a firm abolitionist? After reading these chapters I am left with a niggling suspicion that the evils of our time are not taken as seriously or contended with as vehemently as in Wesley's day. Human trafficking and the sexual abuse of children, the rise in binge drinking and teenage pregnancies, children murdering children and the increase in knife crime – such things would surely have been challenged and denounced by Wesley in word and action.

Perhaps one of the reasons that issues of social justice feature less than might have been expected is the lack of Methodist discipline. It was obedience to the discipline which enabled Methodists to be in connexion with each other, to learn and to communicate that learning so that all could grow. The contributors make frequent mention of the need for education: education in the faith, in Church doctrine, in the value of diversity, in the meaning of the sacraments, in the content of Scripture. This was the task of the early Methodist class meetings. The discipline which Wesley would have recognized, however, went much deeper than regular attendance at class meetings. Methodist discipline was a commitment to a particular 'rule of life' which held each person accountable for the use of time and energy in the pursuit of holiness. The potential for class meetings is mentioned, but not our accountability before God. There is therefore little evidence at the moment to suggest that contemporary Methodism is holding fast to the discipline which gave it so much of its initial energy and life. Could it develop an alternative discipline which was just as effective? Only time will tell, but it would be difficult to assume on the basis of the work of the contributors that it is deemed an essential part of the Church's immediate agenda.

So is Methodism a dead sect? Not in the opinion of the contributors. The evidence suggests that it holds fast to some areas of doctrine, and that it still has some of the spirit but much less of the discipline which once gave it birth. It still seems to have sufficient knowledge of what it is, and what it can aspire to be, to believe in its own future. One clear difference between the contributions to this volume and those of the original book is the note of optimism and confidence which is sounded throughout. Although each contributor acknowledges the difficulties facing the Church in their respective area of engagement, they also, without exception, insist that these difficulties are not insurmountable; there is real present potential for a Methodist future. Is this optimism justified?

The easy answer is to say 'yes' – any denomination that can inspire a new generation to engage with its tradition, revise it, and at the same time work within it, is worthy of the optimism placed in it. The more realistic answer is to say 'not yet'. Yes, there has been growth over the decade. The Methodist Church has also taken radical, even unpopular, steps to address the problems which could prevent it from growing in the future. These steps are mentioned and by the contributors as both positive and negative. The impact of the 'Our Calling' process and the resulting tightened focus on the agreed Priorities of the Methodist Church seem to offer a means of responding to the changes identified by the contributors as necessary to release the present potential of the Church in the UK.

There is however an increasing danger of the Church being overtaken by global events. These may make its deliberately narrowed focus both petty and irrelevant. The rise of Islam and the necessity of discovering a better response to secularism than either entrenchment or fundamentalism has encouraged much greater cooperation between the major world faiths at all levels, locally, nationally, and especially internationally. The worldwide economic recession threatened by the international credit crunch is affecting both the assets of the Church and the ability and willingness of people to contribute to Church funds. It has likewise alerted the general populace to the fact that 'local' in the twenty-first century is more about spheres of influence than geography. High speed transport and communication media have made the world a much smaller place in every way. The fact that Methodism is part of a global diverse Christian community and that Wesley taught his followers to consider the whole world their parish may be the only real hope for releasing the present potential of Methodism to grow in grace and holiness to the glory of God.

Notes

1 The statistics are created by collating the numbers provided by each local church of, for example, those who attended worship in October, those who have been received into membership in the last 12 months or have 'ceased to meet', or have died.

2 Jane Craske and Clive Marsh, *Methodism and the Future: Facing the Challenge*, London: Cassell, 1999, p. 184.

3 Jane Craske, 'Towards a Holy Church' in Craske and Marsh *Methodism and the Future*, p. 178.

4 John Wesley, *Works*, ed. Jackson, vol XIV, 3rd edn, Albany, NY: Ages Christian Library, 1996, p. 437.

5 Roy Hattersley, 'The party faithful' in *The Guardian*, Saturday 14 June 2003.

6 Margaret Thatcher, *Statecraft*, London: HarperCollins, 2002, p. 432.

7 *Methodist Conference Agenda*, Peterborough: Methodist Publishing House, 2002, p. 126.

8 Robert Wuthnow, 'Church Realities and Christian Identity in the 21st Century' in *The Christian Century*, 12 May 1993, pp. 520–23.

Ten Years On: *From Methodism and the Future* to *Methodist Present Potential*

JANE CRASKE AND CLIVE MARSH

Contexts

Methodism and the Future offered a snapshot of where a number of us were up to in our love/hate relationship with an institution (the Methodist Church in Great Britain), and in our deep commitment to movements (Christianity, Methodism) in and through which we had each experienced something of the love of God and of meaning and purpose in human life. In taking the snapshot, we had to face up to the challenges of the moment. Though the contributors to *Methodism and the Future* were not even wholly representative of our age group in the Church, in the late 1990s we were quite unusual among our contemporaries. Like them, we were swept along with the cultural currents swirling all around us, which influenced our thoughts, values, and actions whether we were fully aware of it or not – changing family patterns, the ubiquity of travel, concerns about employment, a packed programme of leisure pursuits, the deep impact of popular culture. But we were still *in* Church. In looking at Methodism, and our place in relation to it, within that swirl of cultural influences, we noted the following as contexts in which we worked:

- the changing face of Christianity in Britain;
- ecumenism;

- the wider religious context;
- secularization;
- changing social patterns;
- particular characteristics of our age group;
- a willingness to be critical of individualism;
- political change.

All these facets of our society remain current and require exploration. Indeed, ten years on, we need to push some of them a little further. Christianity becomes increasingly diverse in the UK. The diversity is more to do with national and ethnic groupings than explicitly theological distinctions. There are many more Eastern European Roman Catholics, for example, and many more ethnically specific congregations springing up within and outside Methodism itself. This has sometimes led to a greater sense of Methodist identity. Immigrants entering Britain with a clearer sense of Methodist identity than many British-born Methodists have become a challenge to the whole British Methodist Church to clarify what it means to be Methodist at the turn of the millennium. When added to evidence of continuing numerical decline overall, the question of continuing and developing Methodist identity has to be sharply posed.

It might have been expected that the ecumenical context in the last decade would have been more clearly defined by *An Anglican–Methodist Covenant*, the hopeful agreement signed between the Methodist Church of Great Britain and the Church of England in 2003. In reality, while much thoughtful ecumenical work has continued at national level through a formal Joint Implementation Commission, developments regionally and locally are patchy to say the least. Recent developments in the Anglican Communion mean that talk of 'the Covenant' among Anglicans has come to signify the search for a form of covenantal unity among Anglicans worldwide. Anglican–Methodist concerns have slipped down the list of priorities. How *An Anglican–Methodist Covenant* sits alongside other ecumenical relationships is still a matter of uncertainty for many Methodists and in many local Churches Together groups.

Methodism and the Future appeared at the end of the Decade of Evangelism, and that 'Decade' offered a particular model of engagement with secularization and secularism. The major focus on mission of the last few years has been differently shaped, hugely influenced by the Church of England *Mission-Shaped Church* report. The language that report gave us of 'fresh expressions' is now widely used, though not always deeply explored. It is clear that even where there are churches – and certainly where there are not – what Christianity is, and how it works, have to be presented and offered to people in fresh ways. Questions remain, though, about resources to be put into the different forms and practices that result, and about how the 'fresh expressions' approach relates to debates that have existed since Pentecost about what church is and what it is for.

The 'multifaith' (or better, 'interreligious') society in which we all live and work has come yet more sharply into focus over the last ten years. The events of 9/11 caught secularists up short and one consequence was a new concern for the contemporary role of religion across the world. Journalists went scrabbling for their fact books, embarrassed about how little they knew about Islam, or about religions generally. Religion could not be ignored. Nor could the fact that religions have all too often been used for evil ends remove the fact that most people in the world follow a religion in one form or another, and that at their best they can be a profound source of, and force for, good. And what of the fierce challenge of the 'new atheists'? Would it be preferable to try to get rid of religion altogether and give a non-religious account of what it means to be human? Questions of respect for religion and for the adherents of many religions, as well as questions of the relative value of some elements of religion, deserve careful engagement on the part of today's Christians.

The changing social patterns we identified in *Methodism and the Future* – social mobility leading to extended families being stretched out geographically, increasing significance of friendship groupings, a desire on the part of many single people to live alone for longer – have continued to be significant. Perhaps the critique of individualism we thought we identified may need to be qualified. Even if there is an identifiable challenge to selfishness – rampant consumerism does have its limits, as the late 2008 credit crunch shows – the rise of Internet use and the impact of MP3 culture have also extended the attention to, and cultivation of, the primacy of the individual. This suggests that interest in social holiness – be that in the form of corporate spirituality or political concern – might be difficult to foster.

Has the political change we detected in the later 1990s continued? The decade since has been the Blair–Brown era, in which the extent to which socialist principles have been followed remains an open question. Reforms of public services and major institutions have been on the agenda. Greater compromises with private finance than would ever have been envisaged in most Labour governments of the past have led to new and often surprising partnerships. Complex funding arrangements have in turn led to fresh partnerships between churches and the state, especially at local government level. This is a new context in which the Church's mission must be reflected upon. At the same time, the rise in some places of extremist parties has caused churches to reflect anew on political engagement.

Methodism and the Future noted the beginnings of a process to clarify the British Methodist Church's focus. That process led to *Our Calling* and to *The Priorities of the Methodist Church*. Alongside this, major structural changes in the organization of the Methodist Church's life at national level (with respect to the Connexional Team, the officers who work representatively in specialist work on the Methodist Church's behalf) have been a feature of recent years. The extent to which the changes have been driven by that ongoing process of clarifying the Methodist Church's current purpose – i.e. driven by mission – or by financial considerations (a Church with a declining membership will have less money to allocate) is not easy to assess. Both factors are at work. But the effects of these changes on Methodist churches regionally (in Districts) and locally (in Circuits and congregations) has often been striking. Alongside the inevitable cynicism which exists in any human organization ('what do that lot up there think they are doing?'), there have also been bold local attempts made to ask fundamental

questions about what Methodism is for, now, in whichever particular place the question was being posed.

As a book recommended to stimulate reflection among those
considering their vocation in the Methodist Church, *Methodism
and the Future* played a small part in that process of thinking
about identity and purpose. The essays in it assessed Methodist
emphases and concerns within the contexts of the late 1990s. The
contexts towards the end of the first decade of the third millennium have similarities, but also some significantly changed features. So how do we see them shaping the analysis given by the
writers of this book?

Comments

What have we 'seen' within the chapters in this book? First, we
have seen a confident willingness to try to spell out what is British Methodism's specific task. Our own book had ended with
some uncertainty. This present one does not question whether
the British Methodist Church should bow out gracefully from
the Christian stage, having done its limited, time-bound task. On
the whole, it simply assumes the Methodist Church has a future,
and presses the question of what the Church should be focussing on or developing. There may be a number of reasons for
this confidence (or this assumption). Methodism continues as a
large, worldwide movement and, as Dion Forster shows, can do
great things. Karen Jobson's personal introduction to her chapter suggests how and why Methodism must not give up on its
specifics. So the potential derived from the present and the past
remains, even if it could be argued there is something of a lull
of energy and clarity of purpose in British Methodism just now,
while Methodists regroup.

Second, we have noted a realism about the Church, occasionally slipping into cynicism. In the midst of the desire to be hopeful,
there are also notes of caution. The Church is diverse, but does
not respect its own diversity. Shirlyn Toppin's chapter makes this
plain. And ecumenical engagement, though desirable, will not be
easy to maintain. Luke Curran's chapter raises serious questions

about the kind of faith that people are enabled to develop in the Church, or whether local churches are really sustaining the committed engagement of younger Methodists.

Third, we note an emphasis on mission. It is there in Martin Ramsden's testimony to a rediscovery in Methodism – partially realized, but always potential too – of the importance of sacraments. It is understandably explicit in Rachel Walton's chapter, which recognizes the enormity of the cultural changes in British Methodism which might be needed for appropriate forms of evangelism for the future.

Fourth, perhaps more implicit than the other three points, there is an assumption that we must learn from history. At many points (for Dean, Curran, Ramsden, Forster and Jobson, for example) it pays to look back, not in lazy nostalgia, but so that ways forward might be found. This is specific attentiveness to *Methodist* history too. Alongside an ever-present appropriate appeal to tradition, then, without which there could be no Christian belief structure, there are also particular Methodist stories to tell. In this way, we continue 'our' tradition and speak to other traditions of what we are about.

But what have we missed, or what do we disagree with? We must admit to feeling that the collection is still too 'churchy' (though must also acknowledge that this same criticism was made of *Methodism and the Future*). We have missed the strands that could lead to the development of a publicly engaged faith for the early years of the twenty-first century. Luke Curran's exploration of faith development and models of learning within British Methodism could have led into creative exchanges with forms of education *this side* of the general developments in literacy and schooling which have occurred since the late nineteenth century. Why is it, for example, that Christians look more to colleges and universities to be stretched in their learning about faith? This may not simply be a fault with churches. Perhaps churches should not even be trying to compete, but to be better partners of educational institutions, in which people of all faiths and none meet. Perhaps the challenge is to look at how churches (and synagogues, and mosques, and temples, and gurdwaras) enable believers who explore faiths critically elsewhere to make use of that learning in faith communities.

However, in the context of Methodism on a world stage, questions might also have been raised about British Methodism's immersion in a certain form of western mindset. Dean's and Forster's chapters show there is some major thinking to be done about the western European origins of Methodism as a movement. Wesley wrestled with rationalism from within, being both a child of the Enlightenment and one of its critics. But the very shape of Methodism results from that tension: form small groups, sing hymns, and be *moved* to the core of your being. At the same time recognize that there are Scriptures and other texts which have accompanied the living Church throughout its history, which need reading and interpreting with all the critical faculties we can muster. That's how Methodism began but is that tension appropriately retained, and does it need to be? Some ask if Methodism lost too much of its emotional element. Perhaps critical analysis of Methodism's origins might lead to new and diverse contemporary spiritualities and ways of doing theology which do justice to both heart and head and which are not simply forged in a western European Enlightenment mould.

There is vibrant concern for saving souls and for finding new understandings of salvation throughout the chapters. But what is this to mean? Without much more radical assessment of how traditional theological language is used, and how meanings of such terms as sin, redemption, penitence, and liberation are reached, alongside exploration of where such words now appear and of the forms in which the concepts materialize (in art, literature, and film), Christians are still going to be speaking largely to each other. Mission will make little headway. So we are back to 'churchiness', but also to the potential for much more imaginative engagement with the world around us.

Conclusions

The task we set ourselves was to read the chapters of this book through the lens of our experience in editing *Methodism and the*

Future nearly a decade ago. Assessing the potential of British Methodism today and looking towards the future from here, we have two things to propose.

First, we want to encourage the writers and their contemporaries (now our 'younger contemporaries' – we *are* starting to sound old) to be less assertive. We are not asking for boldness or enthusiasm to be tamed. The world can do with fewer sheepish Methodists. But we see in many of the contributions an assertiveness which is insufficiently supported or argued. At their best Methodists make good preachers. Preaching does not demand detailed argumentation (for arguments are for the seminar or lecture-room). But when a case is being presented, then we need to hear more of what the case is based on. So we mean: be more analytical; marshal more arguments; construct a better case. This will not mean simply gathering more information or describing more about Methodism's past or present. It will mean using what is contained in Methodism's life-story, digging behind it, thinking around it, sifting it, and reflecting upon it theologically to say what, and why, in God's name, Methodism is to do. This depth of engagement will equip all of us for mission in the public arena.

Second, we invite the writers (or if not they, then readers of this book) to venture an exercise in reappraisal. Finding faith, experiencing liberation, being transformed, being saved, encountering God, having a personal relationship with Christ, living by the Spirit – whatever basic expression one uses for what it means to be Christian – all of these formulations need connecting with a life structure of some kind. At its best this is what Methodism has been very good at providing. In British Methodism of recent memory, as can now be seen, this structuring of Christian faith too easily turned a local church into a total institution. Everything – with the possible exception of work – was done in or through the church: friendships, dating, leisure activities. British Methodism – indeed, much of British Christianity – has not recovered from the cultural shift to a more diverse set of social structures. Rather than equip Christians for life in a 'secular' society, in which religion is not necessarily absent, but appears, and sometimes needs to fight its corner in many different social settings, much Christianity (and much Methodism, therefore) has detached faith from life, and effectively privatized, or at least ghettoized it. So how is that process to be reversed?

The reappraisal exercise needed is this: to help twenty-first-century Christians work again at the private and public practices of their faith. In this task, a recovery of the word 'piety' might help. But other terms are possible: 'discipleship' or 'holy living'. What is needed is a reassessment of the practical structures needed for a living Christian faith. How can Methodism recover its responsibility to help ordinary people to structure their Christian spirituality in a manner appropriate for society as it is now, while shifting away from that over-used, ill-defined and currently over-individualized word 'spirituality'?

Methodists invite people to cultivate a social and public form of Christian practice. 'Social holiness' for Wesley meant the corporate context in which one discovers and explores a Christian faith which has to be put into practice. We need to explore again, for now and for the future, what kind of Christian practice is to be cultivated, which respects the facts that there is no such thing as a solitary Christian, that Christians live and work in many different communities and social settings, that Christian faith is not a private matter, and, perhaps above all, that to live such a faith in a complex, interreligious world is frequently difficult.

To define such a workable, social, and public discipleship is, we suggest, a struggle worth undertaking. The chapters in this book have given us some resources to work with. We have sought to look at them in a broader framework, precisely because we believe what these chapters are seeking to identify are resources still worth working with. There is more to be done with them, but that is a challenge readers will have to face.

Appendix 1[1]

34. Our Calling Conference Agenda
2000

INTRODUCTION

Conference 1999 received a report from the Methodist Council (Agenda pages 617–620) which summarised work done on this issue in the connexional year 1998/99. It agreed to the appointment of a Strategic Goals Planning Group to take the process forward. The Conference report noted that in the autumn of 1998 many individuals and churches, and some circuits, responded to an immediate invitation to participate in a process of identifying the Church's Strategic Goals. Every one of those responses has been carefully read.

1. The outcomes we dream about in the group which has prepared the material

The whole Church rediscovers a shared vision of what the Church is for.

In each local situation priorities come into focus, with imagination and energy released to achieve identified plans and targets.

Significant changes of culture take place – flexible and creative applications of the gospel to the Church's work in contemporary society; liberation from tired traditions and the Methodist obsession with procedures and rules ('CPD and all that').

A greater diversity of response to local situations is complemented by a strong sense of pulling together throughout the connexion in pursuit of our shared vision.

2. Use of language

This work started with talk of Strategic Goals. That was shorthand and not popular. We gladly leave it behind, in favour of more suggestive vocabulary: a vision of what the Church is for and where we are going.

3. What's new?

We have attempted only to crystallise what we all know about the Church in our heart of hearts. It would be nice to think we have expressed ourselves without too much jargon. We hope everyone can recognise the obvious links with people who have walked this path before us.

We put weight on the process we hope our material could trigger in every church. Local ownership of this process and its outcomes is everything. Courage to see what is important, to go for it and to leave behind what is secondary will make the difference. And it does not matter if another church nearby, inevitably in a different context, comes up with something different.

What we seek to facilitate is for every level of the Church – for the Conference, the Methodist Council, the connexional Team, districts and circuits as well as for the local churches. We are bound together by a single calling and a shared vision.

4. How shall we get things moving?

4.1 We want to make second nature among Methodists (and partners from other denominations who share our life at local level) the words which crystallise our vision of what the church is for.

The Church exists to
- Increase awareness of God's presence and to celebrate God's Love
- Help people to grow and learn as Christians, through mutual support and care
- Be a good neighbour to people in need and to question injustice
- Make more followers of Jesus Christ

To assist the memory, these words can be further condensed to read:

The Church is for
WORSHIP, LEARNING & CARING, SERVICE, EVANGELISM

4.2 We can help one another to absorb this shared vision in many ways. For example:
- Posters in churches and church halls.
- Everyone on our Community Roll and everyone who is interested in the Methodist Church can have a bookmark or a small card with the words of our shared vision printed on it.
- We can practise shaping the prayers of the Church within this framework week by week.

4.3 There will be a leaflet for every Methodist and for ecumenical friends. A provisional draft is included below. It has been drawn up to suggest a process, not to prescribe one. The questions under each main heading are indicative only. We do not pretend they are comprehensive, or perfectly worded. Our belief is that they are good enough to get the process underway. They can be adapted, edited or replaced by a church's own questions. The one exception, we suggest, is the final question in each section: 'What are our plans and targets for...over the next year?'

We believe a simple resource of this kind can trigger a serious review of priorities in each situation, an exploration of initiatives which might be taken locally and a better use of resources. Good ideas can be turned into specific plans and targets. Twelve months later each local church can see where it has got to, look again at its aims, its resources and its environment, and revise its plans. What happens is always in the hands of the local church. And so the process rolls on year by year.

The strength of the process lies in the confidence we may feel that throughout the connexion we share a vision of what the church is for, and we all judge ourselves as we see fit against that vision.

4.4 To assist the process we are preparing a Leader's Pack. This will contain guidelines on how to use the leaflet locally and at circuit, district and connexional levels. It may also contain supplementary materials for those who wish to read them: about possible outcomes of the process if it becomes an annual part of the Church's life; about the core principles we need to hold on to as the process develops; and about the changes in society which require fresh understandings of Christian witness and mission.

4.5 We intend to inaugurate a training programme operating on a 'cascade down' system.

4.6 We shall need a monitoring process to review outcomes and to develop processes over, say, a five year period.

4.7 Some churches will want to develop a much more wide-ranging, thorough and systematic understanding of their environment and their own skills and resources. The connexional Team has already prepared a significant resource, provisionally entitled 'Pilgrims Way', to meet such a need. It will be available from the Resourcing Mission Office in

Manchester, who will also advise about people who can work with churches to put it into practice. Some ecumenical resources covering similar ground are also available, e.g. 'Bridges of Hope' (CTE).

4.8 We anticipate that our own resources, all produced to show a family likeness to one another, will be available in January 2001.

THE METHODIST CHURCH

OUR CALLING
. . . TO FULFIL

What is the Church for and where are we going?

The calling of the Methodist Church is to respond to the gospel of God's love in Christ and to live out its discipleship in worship and mission

To fulfil our calling we need to develop plans of action at every level of the Church. We do this within a framework set by a shared vision.

The Church exists to:

- increase awareness of God's presence and to celebrate God's love

- help people to grow and learn as Christians, through mutual support and care

- be a good neighbour to people in need and to question injustice

- make more followers of Jesus Christ

OUR VISION

The Church exists to increase awareness of God's presence and to celebrate God's love

- What helps us to centre our worship on God?

- Where and when do we feel the presence of God? How can these experiences enrich services of worship?

- What motivates us to study the Bible?

- What helps us to express awe and wonder, thankfulness and praise, and love towards God? How can we use resources from the worldwide Church?

- What would help our worship to make sense to people who come only occasionally?

- Can we improve the comfort and décor of our surroundings and the welcome for people with disabilities?

- Is our worship much the same all the time? Should we explore styles and traditions of worship from other denominations and other parts of the world?

What are our plans and targets for improving our worship over the next year?

The Church exists to help people to grow and learn as Christians, through mutual support and care

- What church activities help us most to deepen our faith in God?

- How effective are our small groups, in linking faith to everyday life?

- How do we learn about the challenges of Christian life today from churches elsewhere in Britain and the wider world?

- Are there peripheral activities we should stop, to make time for our training and learning needs?

- What activities make it easy for others to join us? What links do we have with groups using our premises?

- What do we expect from our pastors? What do we expect from one another by way of support and care? Do we notice or care about those who drift away or leave?

What are our plans and targets for developing our life together over the next year?

OUR VISION

The Church exists to be a good neighbour to people in need and to question injustice

- How do we discover the needs in our community and respond to them?

- Who is involved in service to the community through charities or community groups? Are there opportunities for more of us to become involved? How do we give attention to the moral issues raised by daily work?

- Do we share with one another our concerns about things which do not seem right, or cause trouble in our community, or appear unjust?

- How do we relate to injustice in other parts of the world?

- Are we making the best use of our premises and our money for service to the community? Are we wasting resources? Are we spending our time and resources in ways which are consistent with our beliefs and values?

- How does the life of our community, and our involvement in it, feature in the prayers of the church?

What are our plans and targets for improving our community involvement over the next year?

The Church exists to make more followers of Jesus Christ

- How do we develop friendly attitudes towards everyone we meet?

- Do we have a clear message? Are the words we use straightforward and meaningful to those outside the Church?

- What attracts others to the Christian faith? Are there initiatives we could take to present our convictions? Can we do this with

Christians of other denominations? Where should the focus be – on church premises, or in the community?

- How can we learn about effective witness from Christians in other cultures?

- What can we do to make our premises more welcoming?

- Should we consider planting a new congregation in this locality?

What are our plans and targets for making more followers of Jesus Christ over the next year?

---

1 This document is available for download from http://www.methodist. org.uk/index.cfm?fuseaction=opentogod.content&cmid=138, December 2008

Appendix 2[1]

Priorities for the Methodist Church

METHODIST CONFERENCE 2004 REPORT

Priorities for the Methodist Church

(Report of the *'Where are we heading?'* consultation process)

1. <u>Summary of the key resources to which this report refers</u>

Our Calling:

The Church exists to:

- Increase awareness of God's presence and to celebrate God's love

- Help people to learn and grow as Christians, through mutual support and care

- Become a good neighbour to people in need and to challenge injustice

- Make more followers of Jesus Christ

———————

Priorities for the Methodist Church:

In partnership with others wherever possible, the Methodist Church will concentrate its prayers, resources, imagination and commitments on this priority:

To proclaim and affirm its conviction of God's love in Christ, for us and for all the world; and renew confidence in God's presence and action in the world and in the Church

As ways towards realising this priority, the Methodist Church will give particular attention to the following:

Underpinning everything we do with God-centred worship and prayer

Supporting community development and action for justice, especially among the most deprived and poor – in Britain and worldwide

Developing confidence in evangelism and in the capacity to speak of God and faith in ways that make sense to all involved

Encouraging fresh ways of being Church

Nurturing a culture in the Church which is people-centred and flexible

---

2. Introduction: the consultation process

In October 2003 the Methodist Council issued a consultation document which was widely circulated throughout the Connexion. It was entitled *"Where are we heading?"* The consultation document had emerged from initial conversations during the connexional year 2002–03 in the Council, in many other groups and in an open session of the 2003 Conference. A large number and wide range of responses to the consultation document were returned by the 10th March 2004, for which the Conference expresses its gratitude. They showed widespread support for the Methodist Council's proposals. The responses are summarised in Appendix 1 [see p. 239].

3. <u>Setting the scene</u>

3.1 The Methodist Church has stated its purpose in these words: "The calling of the Methodist Church is to respond to the Gospel of God's love in Christ and to live out its discipleship in worship and mission" (1996).

(This builds on the foundational statement of the Deed of Union, that 'in the providence of God Methodism was raised up to spread scriptural holiness through the land by the proclamation of the evangelical faith'.)

3.2 The Church has committed itself to a wide-ranging understanding of "mission"; it includes (1996):

- telling the good news of Jesus;
- calling people to faith in Jesus Christ and to Christian discipleship;
- caring for individual people and communities;
- sharing in the task of education and social and spiritual development;
- struggling for a just world;
- being alongside the poor;
- becoming friends with people of different cultures and faiths;
- caring for the earth;
- building partnerships with other Churches and other groups who share some of our mission aims.

3.3 The Church will always honour initiatives relating to any of the many aspects of its mission, encourage commitment to them and pray for their success. Who can tell how God will draw particular individuals or groups, with their distinctive gifts and working in particular contexts, to bear their witness and pursue their discipleship? The Church is a fascinating mosaic of diverse mission tasks, the sum of which can never be fully counted.

3.4 The majority of mission activities are linked to local church-es, where people gather to worship and pray, to grow in faith and to develop mutual care. In 2000 the Conference adopted the *Our Calling* process: a basic framework of inter-related, fundamental concerns and a pattern of annual review which is consonant with the purpose of the Methodist Church. It is designed primarily to help local churches. Thus, the Church exists to:

- Increase awareness of God's presence and to celebrate God's love
- Help people to learn and grow as Christians, through mutual support and care
- Become a good neighbour to people in need and to challenge injustice
- Make more followers of Jesus Christ

The consultation process (Appendix 1 [see p. 239]) illustrates the degree to which the *Our Calling* process has penetrated into the self-understanding and practice of local churches over the last four years. Where the *Our Calling* process, or something akin to it, has become a regular part of a church's life, church members have become much more aware of a number of important perspectives:

Local churches do not have to perpetuate what they have always done or continue to do things in the way they have always done them.

Local churches have become clearer in distinguishing activities which are central to the church's worship and mission from those which are peripheral.

Local churches have become more aware of where their strengths and weaknesses lie, as their life is assessed against the *Our Calling* themes.

Congregations have increasingly recognised that they may be authentic churches but that they cannot do everything that may be implied by the *Our Calling* themes.

Local churches have therefore become much more confident in agreeing together priorities in developing their worship and mission. Local churches know better than a Circuit or District ever can the details of their social context; and they know well the people who are available to do the work of God in that situation, utilising their experience and gifts. They have therefore brought together resources, commitment and imagination to take agreed initiatives, or to attempt core Christian responsibilities in new ways. *"The Buzz"* (circulated monthly by e-mail) provides stories which celebrate both small changes in local churches and large and risky projects, in response to each of the *Our Calling* themes

Local churches, bolder in reviewing what they have always done, adapting it, doing it differently or initiating new ventures, have increasingly taken a longer view of the changes they would love to see in their worship and mission. So the challenge has become one of vision: where do we want to be as a Church in five years' time? What steps have we to take to get from where we are to what we believe God is calling us to become? Once these questions are entertained, the challenge of good leadership is never far away.

The sort of review and vision-setting processes sketched above have rekindled an interest in connexionalism and partnership. If a local church cannot be entire and complete in itself – though it can certainly be authentic and valid, a true focus of worship, learning and caring, service and evangelism – it can develop partnerships with other Methodist churches in the Circuit and with ecumenical partners. If its stimulating ideas for mission need resources, it can call upon Circuit, District and connexional help. If it has a good story to tell, it can encourage other churches.

3.5 Not all local churches have yet entered into the transforming culture sketched above. They may be living off the "spiritual capital" of earlier generations and doing their traditional things very well indeed. Some have closed themselves off from the possibilities of change, or from creative engagement with their local communities. So we hear of churches in "maintenance mode" or enveloped in what is sometimes called "chapel culture".

3.6 In 2000 the Conference provided the *Our Calling* process as a tool for review, for focusing on priorities and for the release of creativity, not just for local churches but for the Connexion as a whole. In differing degrees it has begun to re-shape the self-understanding of Circuits as the principal units of mission within the Connexion. Consequently Circuits have started to take a more strategic approach to their resource needs and their resource deployment. This in turn is encouraging Circuits in many places to look towards co-operation across Circuit boundaries. The *Our Calling* process has also influenced the role of Districts. It has become a key component of the self-understanding of the Connexional Team, whose principal strategic goal in the period 2000-04 (now 2005) has been:

To promote and support the Our Calling process throughout the Methodist Church and liaise with the Districts about its progress.

3.7 The Our Calling process remains the basic framework and process through which the Methodist Church in Britain, in all its aspects (local churches, Circuits, Districts and connexional bodies) will express its purpose in obedience to the challenges and guiding of the Holy Spirit.

3.8 The Conference now listens to the insistent demands that are emerging from beacons of hope and creativity in the Connexion and from the thoughtful prayers of God's people – to "do things differently", to try new initiatives, to confront profound questions and challenges in contemporary society in the name of the gospel and to clarify our vision as a Connexion of where we are heading – and affirms Priorities for the Methodist Church for the next few years.

4. <u>Priorities for the Methodist Church</u>

The Conference is invited to take one step back from the release of energy and creativity inspired by the Our Calling process.

Are there challenges and imperatives of great importance which are shared issues right across the Connexion?

The outcome of the consultation process makes it clear that there are. In whatever context local churches and Circuits are set, in and through the attempts to apply Our Calling locally, some common concerns have been identified . We need to help one another throughout the Church to address these concerns.

If we do not together give concentrated attention to these shared challenges and imperatives, we shall fail as a connexional Church to support the rich and diverse local expressions of worship and mission which are the throbbing heart of the Church in congregations and Circuits.

Conversely, if we pull together in addressing these shared concerns – Circuits and Districts, local churches and the Connexional Team – we shall discover a strong sense of journeying together, and confidently, into the early decades of the twenty-first century. We shall know where we are heading. (See Appendix 2 for more detail on this theme.)

These shared challenges and imperatives thus become Priorities for the Methodist Church. In summary they may be expressed like this:

In partnership with others wherever possible, the Methodist Church will concentrate its prayers, resources, imagination and commitments on this priority:

To proclaim and affirm its conviction of God's love in Christ, for us and for all the world; and renew confidence in God's presence and action in the world and in the Church

As ways towards realising this priority, the Methodist Church will give particular attention to the following:

Underpinning everything we do with God-centred worship and prayer

Supporting community development and action for justice, especially among the most deprived and poor – in Britain and worldwide

Developing confidence in evangelism and in the capacity to speak of God and faith in ways that make sense to all involved

Encouraging fresh ways of being Church

Nurturing a culture in the Church which is people-centred and flexible

5. <u>How do we understand the Priorities for the Methodist Church?</u>

5.1 Adopting the Priorities for the Methodist Church is a commitment to a journey rather than subscription to settled ideas or particular programmes. We have to help one another over the coming years to explore ever more deeply, in all sorts of settings, the meanings and implications of each of the Priorities for the Methodist Church. Certainly there are challenges here to theological study as well as to the development of practical projects. We will pray for and expect a 'thousand flowers to bloom' from these short seminal sentences. But we know enough to make a difference straight away! And we can start dreaming dreams of what might become possible.

5.2 The richest understandings of the Priorities for the Methodist Church and the deepest challenges to the way we communicate our faith in word and action will come from taking seriously the context in which we are set in twenty-first century Britain. It is impossible to grasp fully the diversity of cultures that make up contemporary society or the rapid changes in culture that are taking place. It is not necessary to wait for the elusive goal of a comprehensive understanding of the world in which we are called to be disciples and witnesses. But helping one another to understand more deeply what is happening in us and around us is integral to the development of the Priorities for the Methodist Church in the coming years. Ours is a contextualised mission. Our faith is that God – the God and Father of our Lord Jesus Christ – is present and active in every facet of society and is calling us to follow where the Spirit leads. Whatever may be the details of the social, political and economic situations in which we live, in particular places and organizations, some general themes are likely always to demand our attention. Such as:

The scandalous disparity between rich and poor in the world

Deep-seated prejudices – racism, sexism, ageism, and the like

The ephemeral and unpredictable nature of human commitments

The widespread sense of meaninglessness

The challenges of a multi-faith society

The confusions in personal identity

Distrust of all authority

The threats of violence and terrorism

Rapid changes in technology and the media of communication

The adulation of celebrity personalities and consumerism

The dangers of environmental pollution

5.3 In the midst of all this change and confusion our central and overriding concern is the reality of God . How is 'the Gospel of God's love in Christ' to be heard in contemporary society in a way that is both true to the revelation in the scriptures and persuasive, attractive and life-changing to modern women and men? What words and metaphors shall we use to elicit awareness of God's grace? How do we recover confidence in God's love for all when the circumstances of so many of our contemporaries are so hard to understand or empathise with? How do we deepen our own trust in God when difficult questions have to be faced day by day, when relationships break down, or when disappointments break our hearts? Can we really find joy and confidence and creativity through God's Spirit in our hearts when so much about God's Church feels like a burden or trivialises life's challenges, or dismisses our day-to-day concerns as of little account? How indeed do we find God afresh and give our hearts to God in daily life – at work, in the family and local community, in the political debates provoked by everyday events? Are we willing (shaped as we are by the values of our society) to stand alongside the poorest and most vulnerable members of our community and work with them for their betterment and for social justice? Are we able to break out of inward-looking church life to make friendships and to speak of God and of faith with people we meet in secular and multi-faith settings?

5.4 To stimulate further reflection on the Priorities for the Methodist Church , some notes are included here, both from the Methodist Council consultation document 'Where are we heading?' and from the responses received.

(i) **In partnership with others wherever possible.** Partners will include: Methodist Churches throughout the world; ecumenical partners; Christian agencies; and secular organizations. In respect of 'ecumenical partners', much reference is made to developing rapidly and consistently the implications of the Anglican–Methodist Covenant signed with the Church of England on the 1st November 2003. The joint pastoral strategy with the United Reformed Church is also important. Many Methodist churches who are in local ecumenical partnerships with the URC looked simultaneously at 'Where are we heading?' and the URC equivalent consultation document "Catching the Vision", noted their similarity, regretted that there was not already one document being consulted on for both Churches and urged us to implement our shared vision together.

(ii) **To proclaim and affirm its conviction of God's love in Christ, for us and for all the world; and renew confidence in God's presence and action in the world and in the Church.** There was overwhelming support for this as the key priority for the Church. At the same time, in the wording which was circulated for consultation (which included 'recapture' and 're-build' – see Appendix 1), it was controversial. Some were offended by the suggestion that all Methodist churches have lost their core convictions about God and confidence in God; or no longer share a universal vision. So it needs to be made clear that the Methodist Council was intending no such offence, nor was it in any way belittling the faith and commitment of Methodist people. Indeed, the Council and the Conference comprise people of deep faith and broad vision. The wording has been amended in the light of these helpful comments.

However, the force and significance of this key priority must not be blunted. The depth of the challenge the Church faces is illuminated by reflection on some stark realities:

The institutional Churches in Europe, including the Methodist Church in Britain, have been in numerical decline for a long while, and have reached a critical point where large changes are necessary if we are to recover confidence as a movement for transformation in society.

The National Church Life Survey (2001) sharply described the Methodist Church as it is and illuminated the mismatch between what we aspire to be and what we achieve. For instance, we long to communicate the gospel to all, but in fact our age profile is heavily weighted to the higher end of the age spectrum, raising questions about our capacity to engage children, young people and people in their 20s and 30s.

People with energy, enthusiasm and vision, who want to experiment and take risks in developing new forms of worship and mission, regularly report that the traditional church structures are fearful of change or discouraging, curled in on themselves and able to consider only the faithful maintenance of the way things have always been.

The changes in society and the insistent questions put to Christian faith by thinking people have proved to be profoundly unsettling, so that churches have become refuges from the world instead of places where energy and confidence are rediscovered for creative engagement with everyday life in the name of Jesus Christ.

The Methodist Council suggested a small number of implications latent in this first priority: "We therefore need to work creatively to:

Bring the Bible alive to ourselves and to our contemporary world;

Provide safe and loving places in which to share honestly the deepest concerns and questions of our lives, to become vulnerable to one another, supportive of one another and challenging of one another;

Develop renewed confidence in connecting faith with work and everyday life."

All these – and many more such themes – will need attention in the next few years, building on what is already available but concentrating much of our "learning and caring" on these challenges.

(iii) **Underpinning everything we do with God-centred worship and prayer.** The replies to the consultation confirm this to be the theme which requires deepest attention. It flows immediately out of the key priority referred to in the previous section, and sets the theme for all that follow. Thus the central question of God, and response to God, flow through the Priorities for the Methodist Church from start to finish. All that we say and do as disciples, dispersed in everyday life or gathered together in fellowship, must be open to God's grace and energised by God's Spirit. God's love casts out all fear and enables us to trust God whenever we seek God and seek to serve God.

Imagination, flexibility and varieties of style in worship services are now urgent concerns. So are the quality of worship and the care with which it is prepared – whatever the style. There is a need to look afresh at participation in worship, so that the breadth of human experience – joys and sorrows, successes and failures, conventional feelings and also troubling doubts and fears – are prayerfully placed within the mercy of God.

(iv) **Supporting community development and action for justice, especially among the most deprived and poor – in Britain and worldwide.** Few notes may be necessary here, but they are of great significance.

We cannot but continue and deepen our "mission alongside the poor": it sustains something fundamental to Methodist identity.

This is manifestly a global commitment and demonstrates the interdependence of British society and nations in distress in many parts of the world.

Theologically this dimension of our mission confronts us sharply with the challenge of the cross of Christ. Do we allow the gospel effectively to question the life-style choices, the pursuit of power and the "culture of contentment" that prosperity has brought us? Are we committed, to the point of self-sacrifice, to the ministry of reconciliation and peacemaking in situations where conflicts and violence are aggravated by disparities of wealth and opportunity?

(v) **Developing confidence in evangelism and in the capacity to speak of God and faith in ways that make sense to all involved.** Once again, if there are few notes here, it is not an indication of disinterest or complacency. On the contrary, it is recognised everywhere in the Church that if we need help with any of the Our Calling themes more than the others, it is with this one. And yet we know we are nothing as a Methodist movement without recovering our confidence and skill precisely here. As with "mission alongside the poor", commitment to evangelism is a distinctive mark of the Methodist way of being Christian. So strategies for evangelism, training for evangelism and sharing good stories of inventive presentations of the gospel story (using Creative Arts, developing a new vocabulary, and encouraging rigorous intellectual approaches to contemporary knowledge and secular philosophies) will be of paramount concern.

(vi) **Encouraging fresh expressions of Church.** For many correspondents the phrase "new ways of being Church" which was used in the "Where Are We Heading?" material caused confusion. What does it mean? Is it more than a piece of jargon? During the period of consultation on "Where are we heading?" , the Church of England produced a valuable resource which will help us to grasp the scope of what might be entailed in "new ways of being Church". It is A Mission Shaped Church (2004).

Some correspondents expressed concern about the relationship between "new ways of being Church" and the refreshment of traditional ways of being Church. Both are necessary: the innovative, provisional and exploratory attempts to express corporate Christian worship and mission ("new ways of being Church") and "traditional" forms of Christian fellowship, worship and mission (with the latter being renewed in hope through the Spirit's power). The phrase now used in the priorities – **fresh expressions of church** – better expresses the commitment both to new ways of being Church and to the refreshment and renewal of the traditional. Indeed one of the urgent challenges is the networking between the two, to mutual advantage – especially when the new way of being Church is routinely ecumenical and the traditional form of Church is typically denominational.

Other correspondents have expressed concern about the identity of some new ways of being Church. How can we be sure that they are genuinely an expression of what we mean theologically by 'Church', when they are so different from traditional churches in activity and aspiration, in leadership and spirituality? It may be useful to refer again at this point to the Methodist Church's Statement of Purpose and the themes of Our Calling (3.1–4 above): they set a simple template against which diverse interpretations of what "Church" means may be assessed. A comprehensive source to refer to on this matter is the Conference Report Called to Love and Praise.

But even if there is mutual recognition as churches between traditional and new ways of being Church, there is no doubt that in the coming years a great deal of work will be required to look afresh at what in traditional church we call 'faith and order' questions, to enable the Conference both to affirm and to learn from "new ways of being Church", within an ever-broadening understanding of "Connexion".

(vii) **Nurturing a culture in the Church which is people-centred and flexible.** The consultation document hinted at what may be involved here: we want "to become the sort of community where:

We concentrate on people and relationships and value everyone

We strive to release the gifts and talents of individuals and encourage their use

We help one another to deepen commitment, expect lives to be transformed and empower faith sharing (including, however, the expression of doubts)

We are tolerant of different views within the Christian family

We *cope with change* confidently and support people who take risks for the sake of the Church's mission".

Maybe unhelpfully the consultation document referred here to a "new" culture in the Church. Many correspondents reminded us that this has always been the sort of culture we have aspired to and which God in Christ both requires and empowers.

On the other hand, it is a moot point whether we have ever achieved our ambition here. In the present consultation it has been frequently reported that our systems and procedures, our institutional frame of mind, readily deflect us from our aims. So instead of local churches flourishing by discerning and using the multitude of gifts among their members, they become somewhat atrophied by 'shoehorning' people into fixed roles where they cannot easily play to their strengths.

In addition, there is throughout the Connexion an anxiety about the impact of an "over-managerial" approach to church administration – as opposed to a "pastoral" approach. Of course, in practice situations are much more complex than these analyses suggest. But this Connexional Priority indicates commitment to a vision of how in every Christian community, and in all aspects of connexional life, we help one another to grow and learn as Christians, honouring the amazing potential of every individual as a channel of God's grace and wisdom.

The phrase "tolerant of different views within the Christian family" is a focus for many issues.

Some correspondents wrote about the need for limits to toleration in the Church. Everything must be tested against the truth of the gospel. In a diverse Church there are many interpretations of the gospel, as there are many understandings of the authority of the scriptures. So debates about the meaning of faith, tradition and experience are part of our ongoing 'Methodist way' of being Church.

Some correspondents expressed concern about the voices that are rarely heard or that are marginalized in the Church: the voices of ethnic minorities, for example. Racial justice within the Christian community, with empowerment of black and Asian voices in the Church, is an integral part of the wider struggle in British society to root out racist talk and behaviour, and institutional racism.

Participation in the Church by children, young people and adults under 40 has been mentioned frequently. It is an area of great concern, to be vigorously and consistently addressed. Without doubt children, young people and adults under 40 can make distinctive contributions to all aspects of the Priorities for the Methodist Church , and must be empowered to do so. And there are seamless links from the ministry of younger people in the Church to a radical re-think of the Church's mission and strategies for engaging effectively with students in schools, FE and HE, and with younger people at work.

6. Conclusion

The Methodist Church in Britain is ready for change. We sense in many places signals of hope, a willingness to take risks and creative actions inspired by the gospel. We can re-group our resources and make a difference, especially in partnership with others. We can glimpse a shared vision of God's action in the world and feel again the compulsion of sharing in God's mission. We are beginning to enjoy again the strength and encouragement that come from pulling together across the Connexion and rediscovering our connexionalism. Long-standing problems are no longer being avoided but are being tackled with energy and imagination. God's Spirit is re-building our confidence.

But we cannot do everything. Each local church must sharpen its missionary vocation, appropriate to its context, inspired by the

Our Calling process or an equivalent system of review. Circuits too and Districts, along with connexional bodies, are refocusing on their mission, grasping opportunities and confronting or working round obstacles. Structures and systems, including those which have served us well for generations, are now under scrutiny. Methodists are increasingly aware that if we simply continue as we are, our systems and structures will come under ever greater pressure and our sense of being a stretched, exhausted and marginal institution will increase. We need structures and systems which facilitate mission and do not thwart it. We are learning to be more courageous in setting priorities – and by implication, saying 'no' to other options.

In this environment we have identified through prayerful conversation and consultation our Priorities for the Methodist Church – shared and urgent claims on us in every part of the Church, as we take stock of Our Calling at the beginning of the twenty-first century. When the Conference has adopted the Priorities for the Methodist Church, churches, Districts, the Connexional Team and Circuits can exercise their decision-making powers to make their own contribution to the outworking of the Priorities for the Methodist Church. And in learning from one another, we shall journey purposefully together where God guides us.

***Resolutions

1. The Conference receives the Report.
2. The Conference adopts the Priorities for the Methodist Church in section 1 of the Report.
3. The Conference directs the Methodist Council to work with the Connexional Team to bring to the Conference of 2005 a Strategic Plan for the Team covering the period 2005–08 which is developed with Priorities for the Methodist Church as its principal focus.
4. The Conference invites Districts, Circuits and local churches to make their contribution to the outworking of Priorities for the Methodist Church as they shape their own mission.

APPENDIX 1

Analysis of the replies to the consultation document Where are We Heading ?

555 replies were received to the questionnaire. Of these, 106 were certainly from groups, of varying sizes. In the case of 121 responses to the questionnaire, it was uncertain whether they came from an individual or a group. In the remaining 328 cases the replies were certainly from individuals.

Is your church using the *Our Calling* process to help you move forward?

Yes 418
No 114

The heart of the challenge we face: 'We need to recapture a conviction of God's love for us and for all the world, and re-build confidence in God.' Does this statement ring bells with you?

Yes 473
No 45

Urgent needs: do you sympathise in general terms with the following priorities?

Develop confidence in evangelism and in the capacity to speak of God and faith in ways that make sense to all involved

Strongly 392   Moderately 134   Not really 17

Encourage new ways of being Church

Strongly 315   Moderately 187   Not really 27

Support community development and social action, especially among the most deprived and poor – in Britain and world-wide

Strongly 412   Moderately 138   Not really 5

Re-build confidence in worship and prayer

Strongly 483   Moderately 63   Not really 5

Nurture a new culture in the Church

Strongly 333   Moderately 116   Not really 53

In addition to the above questionnaire responses, 96 letters, extended reflections, mini-theses and a poem were received. There has not been opportunity to acknowledge all these or respond in depth to them.

This is a place to express our thanks to all who contributed to the consultation.

The Report is informed also by workshops, groups and conversations that have been held throughout the Connexion, on at least a weekly basis throughout this connexional year.

---

1 This document is available for download from: http://www. methodist.org.uk/index.cfm?fuseaction=opentogod.content&cmid =879, 26 December 2008.